D1604574

The Journeycake Saga

**The story of the first American Indian
Ordained a Catholic priest
in the United States**
and
**His Delaware Grandfather
War Chief Buckongahelas**

CHARLENE SCOTT-MYERS

*Charlene Scott-Myers
To patrons of this fine
library*

Other books by Charlene Scott-Myers

"Holy Shroud: Research Continues"

"Skreechy," a children's book

DEDICATION

"A people without a history is like wind on the buffalo grass."

-- Crazy Horse

I dedicate this book to my son, Christopher, my daughter, Anne, and my grandchildren, Rachel, Rebecca, William, and Cassie, in the hope that they will learn the history of their Delaware ancestors and relatives, and pass this history on to their children and their children's children.

TABLE OF CONTENTS

ILLUSTRATIONS

ILLUSTRATIONS CONTINUED

ACKNOWLEDGEMENTS

David Scott Myers

I wish to express my deep gratitude and love to my husband, David Scott Myers, editor of the *Southwest Kansas Register* in Dodge City, Kansas, for his years of support, humor, encouragement, and patient assistance, and especially for his fine layout of this book.

I also want to thank my brother, Dennis, and my daughter, Anne, for their help in proof-reading the book.

I want to acknowledge our friend Tim Wenzl, archivist of the Roman Catholic Diocese of Dodge City, who sent me the book *Come Blackrobe* and shared with me another of the many books he has written, *The Church in Kansas, 1850-1905*. That book contains information regarding Watomika, one of the grandsons of Chief Buckongahelas. Watomika grew up on the hilly lands of eastern Kansas on the Delaware reservation near Leavenworth and Lawrence, and to the surprise of everyone–including himself–became the first North American Indian ordained a Catholic priest in the United States, a member of the Society of Jesus (the Jesuit religious order).

Wenzl, a historian and former editor of the *Southwest Kansas Register,* also connected me to Dr. David P. Miros, archivist of the Midwest Jesuit Archives in St. Louis, Missouri. Dr. Miros granted permission to use photographs of Father Bouchard as a young man and as an older priest, and also graciously allowed the inclusion in this book of a sketch of the boy Watomika praying at the scaffold bearing the body of his slain Delaware father, Chief Kistalwa, son of Buckongahelas.

I also especially want to thank the artists who have contributed to this book. I owe a debt of gratitude to artist and muralist Boris Koodrin of San Francisco, California for permission to use a portion of his exquisite mural *Spiritus Magis* (Latin slang coined by St. Ignatius which means "the spirit of more or the greater good"). The left portion of the mural portrays Father James Bouchard (grandson of the Delaware Chief Buckongahelas) and his French mother, Marie, painted for the sesquicentennial (150th) anniversary of St. Ignatius College Prep School in San Francisco in 2005. I thank Paul Totah for permission to include his photo of the mural portion in this book.

I also want to thank sculptor Ross Straight of Buckhannon, West Virginia. My husband and I visited Straight's powerful statue of Buckongahelas and his murdered son Mahonegon in the city park of the West Virginia town of Buckhannon. We also met Ross and his wife, Molly. Ross created a bust of Buckongahelas for us from the statue. The bust rests on top of our piano and has been exhibited at the Carnegie Center for the Arts in Dodge City, Kansas. Hans Straight, son of Ross and Molly Straight, was the model for Mahonegon. (The Straights lost their other beloved son, Shane, to death when he was a young man, as did Buckongahelas, whom Ross had sculpted prior to Shane's death.)

I also thank my twin brothers, David and Dennis Scott, for the art they have contributed to this book.

My appreciation also goes to Tulsa's Gilcrease Museum of the Americas, which has the largest collection of American Indian art in the world, for permission to quote the transcript of *George Washington's Letter to the Delaware Indians on May 12, 1779*; to Tom Young of the Chapman Library of Philbrook Museum of Art in Tulsa for introducing me to the writings of Roberta Campbell Lawson (an Oklahoma Delaware born in 1878 and also a descendant of Buckongahelas); and to Joshua Peck of the *Tulsa Historical Society* for his assistance in locating books about the Delaware Tribe in Oklahoma for me.

Aaron O'Donovan, MLIS, Curator of Digital Collections at the Ohio Historical Society, was most kind in sending me a print of William D. Howell's sketch of the massacre of Delaware Indians at Gnadenhutten, Ohio

I am indebted to Sam Shipley of the Dodge City Public Library and his sister Cindy Shipley, head of that library's Interlibrary Loan Department, as well as to Leesa Shafer of the Spearville Library in Kansas. The assistance of these librarians in procuring in-house and out of state books and microfilm for me was invaluable.

I also thank Coordinator Jo Crabtree and Debbie Neece, collections manager, of the Bartlesville Area History Museum for their help in obtaining Ruby Cranor's re-issued book, *Kik Tha We Nund, the Delaware Chief William Anderson and His Descendant*, as well as photographs of Nellie Johnstone, for whom the first Oklahoma oil well was named, and the Delaware delegates, including Charles and Isaac Journeycake, who signed the Cherokee-Delaware Treaty of 1867 in Washington, D.C. I also thank my cousin Bob Korthase and his wife Carla of Bartlesville for sending me two other books by Ruby Cranor and a book about Charles Journeycake.

I appreciate Betsy Caldwell of the Indiana Historical Society, who forwarded me microfilm of an unpublished manuscript by Halford R. McNaughton, *Buckongahelas, Last of the Great Delaware War Chiefs*. I thank the Allen County Public Library Foundation for allowing me to use material from *A Biography of Buckongahelas* from the journal *Delaware County Genealogist and Historian*, and Judson Press for permission to use photos of the Journeycake family from *The Indian Chief, Journeycake (1895)*.

I am grateful to the Denver Public Library for allowing me to copy the writings of Helen York Rose, another descendant of Buckongahelas and relative of Father Bouchard. Rose wrote *I Walked the Footsteps of My Fathers*. And I thank Woody Max Crumbo, (whom we met in 2006 at a Kinsley, Kansas dinner in honor of his famous father) for permission to repeat excerpts from his touching story about the childhood of the great American Indian artist Woody Crumbo.

I also want to mention the kindly staff of the Family History Center of the Genealogy Library of the Church of Jesus Christ of Latter Day Saints (Mormon Church) in Dodge City, Kansas, where I spent many Thursdays with staff members researching my family tree. I also appreciate the Kansas Genealogical Society, Inc. for introducing me to Genealogist Dr. Arlene Eakle of Utah, who spoke twice in Dodge City, and enlightened us regarding the Scots-Irish immigration to this country.

I also thank my Delaware friend Annette M. Ketchum, not only for critiquing the book and offering helpful suggestions, but also for her gracious hospitality to my daughter and to me when we attended a Delaware powwow in Copan, Oklahoma.

I appreciate another Delaware, Jane Johnstone, a descendant of the oldest daughter of Chief Charles Journeycake, Mary Elizabeth Journeycake Armstrong. (Jane was named for Jane Journeycake, the wife of Charles.) Jane assisted me by reading the book, sending photos, and offering encouragement.

And finally, I want to thank my faithful Labrador dog, Sarah, for resting beside me these past eight years as I pounded away on the computer to compile this book. She sensed when I grew weary, and would plop her head in my lap, tilting her face up to me as if to say: "Good job, Mom. Time to take a break!"

Charlene Scott-Myers
Dodge City, Kansas, 2014

INTRODUCTION

Kathleen Scott, the author's mother

"Within the span of 20 generations, an individual has on his [or her] family tree more than a million grandfathers and grandmothers – to say nothing of other assorted kinfolk."
– N. C. Browder

Lorraine Walker, the author's aunt

This book is the history of a portion of the First Americans: the Journeycake Family, but in the telling, it also relates some of the history of the Delaware people, who were much like the fictional Forrest Gump of movie fame: always showing up in unexpected places with unlikely persons.

Who would have thought that Delaware men acted as guides for the notorious George Armstrong Custer and the controversial explorer Colonel John Charles Fremont, although the French priest Father Valentine Sommereisen, a missionary to Indians who learned the Sioux language, accompanied Custer and his Seventh Calvary as an interpreter on an expedition to Yellowstone in 1873.

Who knew that a Delaware Indian would shoot the only member of Quantrill's band of butchers to be killed during their horrible attack on Lawrence, Kansas? I also was surprised to learn that the Delaware fought with the United States against the Seminole Indian Nation in Florida. And after abhorring Catholics for centuries, even the Delaware were shocked to learn that one of their own became the first American Indian ordained a Catholic priest in the United States, a Jesuit.

One of those Delaware who didn't like Catholics--or any Christians for that matter--was the patriarch of the Journeycake family: the War Chief Buckongahelas (pronounced "Buck-onga-hee-las") Journeycake. This is his story and the tale of his four sons: Mahonegon, and Chiefs Kistawa, Whapakong, and Solomon, as well as his two daughters (one of them my family's ancestor, among our many great-grandmothers). This book also traces the lives of two of Buckongahelas' grandsons, Watomika, the Native who joined the Jesuits and became Father James Bouchard, S.J., a famous Catholic preacher in the great Northwest, and the Rev. Charles Journeycake, a beloved Baptist minister and chief in Kansas and Oklahoma. This also is the story of their famous grandfather Buckongahelas, the Delaware War Chief.

Europeans named the ancestors of Buckongahelas "the Delaware," but they thought of themselves as the Lenni-Lenape, meaning "original people." They were the grandfathers of all the other Eastern tribes, who originated from them.

Buckongahelas was described as "the George Washington of his people." He cordially met with President Washington twice and President Jefferson once. But following the murder of his son, Mahonegon, Buckongahelas would become a notorious Delaware war chief who fought as a rebel *with the British* against the colonists in the Revolutionary War. The Buck, as he was called, chose this perilous and ultimately disastrous path after a white Indian hater murdered his teenage son in the ancient forests of what now is the state of West Virginia.

Buckongahelas also figured prominently in the fate of nearly 100 Christian Delaware relatives and friends who were slaughtered during the Revolutionary War in 1782 by a Pennsylvania militia at Gnadenhutten (pronounced *Ga-naden-who-ten*), Ohio. These Delaware met their death after ignoring the pleas of Buckongahelas to flee with him to safety.

Leading nearly 500 warriors, Buckongahelas joined two other chiefs, Little Turtle and Blue Jacket, with their 700 warriors in battle against Gen. Arthur St. Clair in 1791. In that battle, the most devastating defeat of American troops ever by Indians--known as "the Shame of St. Clair"--the general lost 913 soldiers, 68 of them officers, from his army of 1,400 men. (The more famous 1876 defeat of Lt. Col. George A. Custer and the U.S. Army 7th Calvary at the Little Bighorn produced a death toll of 268 officers, troops and scouts.)

The march of whites into Indian lands forced the Delaware to migrate from the New York and New Jersey areas along the Atlantic coast into Pennsylvania, Virginia, Ohio, and Indiana. Eventually they would be pushed into Arkansas, Kansas, and the Indian Territory that became Oklahoma. Buckongahelas settled along the White River, and died in Henry County, Indiana between 1805 and 1818. My great-grandfather Thomas H. Greenstreet, a descendant of The Buck, was born in Henry County, where the Delaware lived and his ancestor

Joseph Tighe

Buckongahelas breathed his last. Three of Greenstreet's five children were born in Henry County, while my grandmother Edna and her brother Earl were born in Wayne County, Indiana.

Great-grandfather Greenstreet left Henry County, Indiana by covered wagon after the last of his five children, my Great-Uncle Earl, was born in 1895. With his wife, "Jennie" (Hannah Jane Burnett), the family settled in Cherryvale, Kansas, where Greenstreet was supervisor of the brick factory. He returned in his old age to Henry County where his ancestor The Buck had died, and breathed his last there on June 29, 1927. His son Earl, and his son, who died in a plane crash during World War II, and his sister, my Grandmother Edna, are buried at his old farm in Cherryvale, Kansas.

Mary Ollive Tighe

The oldest of the three Greenstreet daughters, Mary Ollive, later moved to Tulsa, Oklahoma, where her husband, Joseph A. Tighe, became the town's first Catholic printer. In the early 1920s, the Ku Klux Klan burned a cross on his lawn when he launched his print shop, the Standard Printing Company at 808 E. 3rd St. in Tulsa.

Our Great-Aunt Mary Ollive and our mother, Kathleen Jane Scott, repeated Chief Buckongahelas' surname *Journeycake* to me and my five brothers throughout our childhood. Family oral tradition also came to us from Mother's younger sister, Lorraine Walker, and from Mary Olive's younger sister, our other Great-Aunt Goldena Trimmel. All were descendants of Buckongahelas Journeycake, whose family tree dates back to the brother of the Chief Tammany who met with William Penn in 1682.

Like the great Irish storytellers from our father's side of the family, these strong and loving women of our mother's family were oral historians for us long before we read our family tree.

"The kings and queens of the [Irish] storytellers were called Shanachies (Shan-uh-keys)," author Sharon Moscinski has pointed out. "The Shanachies were not only the greatest storytellers, they were especially good at recounting the local tales, family sagas, and genealogies (histories) of their towns and villages. The Shanachies were the living history books of Ireland." [3]

My mother and three aunties were "the living history books" for my brothers and me, documenting the story of our relationship to Chief Journeycake. As the Moravian minister David Zeisberger observed during his many decades of living with the Delaware: "They are well versed in their genealogies and are able to describe every branch of the family with the greatest precision." [4]

The women in our immediate family received their information about The Buck directly from my Great-Grandfather Greenstreet, known affectionately as "Tom." He was descended from Buckongahelas through his mother, Mary Elliott Greenstreet, my great-great-grandmother (whose photograph is the oldest one we possess from that side of the family.) Mary's mother, Sarah Toms Elliott, was the great-granddaughter of Buckongahelas.

Mary E. Greenstreet

Another descendant of Buckongahelas through his son Solomon, the writer Helen York Rose, noted: "Indian genealogy: Unless one has the patience of Job and the tenacity of a bulldog, never start it. You have never known a difficult search until you try to find your Indian heritage.

"To quote a letter to me from my friend, Robert H. Richardson, Tiltonsville, Ohio, 'Indian genealogy is very difficult to investigate and confirm due to the lack of written records. And so, it is necessary to rely on tradition and the testimony of the 'old ones' and what few scraps of information can be found in the ancient records of the traders and missionaries and military men.'" [5]

The story of the origin of the name "Journeycake" is as intriguing as the name itself. I read in Helen York Rose's manuscript at the Denver Public Library a mention of the little boy Buckongahelas who was kidnapped and kept alive by a corn cake. It is an enchanting story, which I have embellished. The first chapter of my book contains the tale as I have told it to my grandchildren. After hearing the first chapter, my only grandson William said, "Ah, so that's how he got his name 'Journeycake!'"

The first chapter and second chapter of *The Journeycake Saga* have been awarded first and second place awards from the *Kansas Authors Club* district and state competitions.

My brothers and I are not members of the Delaware Nation–nor do we speak for any of its tribal members--but I consider myself and my siblings, my son and my daughter, and my four grandchildren to be members of the Delaware family. The blood and DNA of our Lenni-Lenape ancestors still enliven our bodies, and the story of the Delaware people is our story too.

During the eight years I've worked on this book, I've kept in mind the words of the great Delaware Chief Teedyuscung: "When you begin a great work, you can't expect to finish it all at once; therefore do you and your brothers press on, and let nothing discourage you till you have entirely finished what you have begun."

-- Charlene Scott-Myers

1. Sperber and Lax, *Bogart*, p. 153.
2. Ibid, p. 200.
3. Moscinski, *Tracing Our Irish Roots*, p. 9.
4. Zeisberger, *History of Northern American Indians*, p. 92.
5. Rose, *I Walked in the Footsteps of My Fathers*, p. 132.

Charlene's great-aunt, Mary Ollive Tighe, seated left, setting type at her husband Joseph Tighe's print shop in Tulsa, Oklahoma.

The Journeycake Saga

The first American Indian
Ordained a Catholic priest
in the United States
and
His Delaware Grandfather
War Chief Buckongahelas

CHARLENE SCOTT-MYERS

1

A Child in Danger

The night was warmish when the dance began. Round and round the leaping fire the dancers stepped in unison, chanting their praises to an unseen God, losing their thoughts in the rhythm of the water drum. The night was dark, the moon a faded blur behind the clouds.

A child of six winters left the row of dancers, shuffling silently into nearby trees to relieve himself. The boy Buckongahelas was a sturdy lad, stocky, but not fat, born around 1720. Small shells sewn on leather bands around his ankles made a swishing sound, like a rattler about to strike, as he strode into the darkness.

As the boy lifted the fringed buckskin skirt that covered his loin-cloth, a rough hand appeared before his face and clamped itself over his mouth. This happened so quickly that the boy could not scream.

Three Natives from another tribe, sticky and smelling of smoke and sweat, had entered and violated the western Ohio land of the great Lenape chief, Windaughala. The intruders kidnapped the chief's son, taking the little boy far away from his family and the forests that he loved so much.

The boy did not go easy into the night. He kicked his kidnappers with both legs as soon as he was hoisted from the ground. It took two tall men to subdue him. The boy bit one kidnapper's hand as hard as he could, but in his fear and anger, the little one wet himself and was ashamed.

All the way to the faraway camp, the boy frantically marked the route in his mind – already making plans for eventual escape. It was dark, but the moon had taken notice of his plight and rolled away from the clouds to offer him better light. With the moon's bright face beaming benevolently upon him, the boy could see and remember the shape of a broken tree, a bend in the river, a cliff that curved like the beak of a bird.

The new tribe adopted the kidnapped boy to replace a child who had died. No thought was given that this young boy could ever find his way back to his original home. The boy missed his real father, who was known as a strong and exceptional chief. The boy could not forget the tenderness of his real mother, who cuddled him at her breasts when he was a babe – and sang sweet songs to lull him to sleep.

He befriended the tribe with whom he lived, however, learning much from the men and endearing himself to the women, especially the elders. During his first week in the camp, he met a dear old Indian lady who told him she was 102 years old.

"I am 102 years old, too!" the boy exclaimed with enthusiasm, instantly earning a laughing new friend. Bowing slightly, he suggested, "Let us have some bee balm tea (a mint tea)." Although he was charming to his captors and truly cared about his new friends, the little lad began to plan his escape.

After a time, the tribe who had stolen him allowed the boy to run free in the nearby wilderness. He befriended and named the ancient forest animals and plants, so that when finally he made his escape, they would not whimper a warning or in any way indicate his passing. He sought out the Little People of the forest, friends of the Lenape, who assured him of their friendship.

One evening in early springtime, the boy stuffed his stomach with so much food that he thought that he would burst.

"Such a meal should last me a long time!" he told himself proudly, patting his full stomach. But in case of an emergency, he concealed a plump warm corn cake under his cloak, an act that went unnoticed.

As darkness descended upon the camp, the boy pretended to sleep, but he was praying fervently. Buckongahelas had been taught about *Kishelamukonk* (the Creator) at an early age, but when he prayed, he and other Delaware addressed the Almighty as *Kishelemienk*.

When the moon rose in the sky, he slowly rose from his mat on the floor and tiptoed out of the wigwam into the darkness.

His friends--the trees, plants, and flowers--nodded their greetings, turning their leafy fingers to point the way to him as he ran past. Wild animals took turns running in front of him, winking at him and bidding him to follow. The Little People who always helped the Delaware whispered in his ear, "Go that way! Quickly!"

By morning, the boy's stomach no longer felt full, so he nibbled on his corn cake. No matter how many bites he took, the tasty cake plumped back up to its original size.

As he wandered, the little boy found the broken tree, the bend in the river, and the cliff that curved like the beak of a bird. A linden tree (the boy's father made rope from its bark) waved a leafy hello; a smiling sturgeon leapt up in the river and swam away in the direction the boy should go; a Rose-breasted Grosbeak (sketched by Audubon in his fine book *The Birds of America from Original Drawings* [1]) signaled to the boy with its sweet, sustained warble and flew off toward the village of the boy's father.

When at last the weary child trudged up to his father's lodging, he was greeted with great joy. He had been missing for many months. He showed the tribe the tasty corn cake–still plump!--that had kept him alive. Then he popped the cake into his mouth and gobbled it down. His father, Windaughala, laughed heartily and called a council of his tribe's elders and warriors and wisest men.

It was the consensus of the council that this boy's family name and that of his descendants henceforth should be called "Journeycake." His kidnappers had nicknamed him "Fights Like a Panther," but his given name from his parents was Buckongahelas, "The Buck." He would become a mighty war chief of the Delaware Nation, and one of his grandsons, Watomika, would be the first American Indian ordained a Catholic priest in the United States, a member of the Jesuit religious order.

The Boy with the Journey Cake

I read another version of The Buck legend in the *History of Leavenworth County, Kansas.* This account varies from Helen York Rose's, because white men, not another Indian tribe, were blamed for the kidnapping of the Indian boy Journeycake, which was highly unlikely. Indians kidnapped white children to replace their youngsters who had died; white men did not kidnap Indian children to replace their deceased offspring.

"The city of Linwood, Leavenworth County, Kansas, which is situated at the junction of Big Stranger Creek and the Kansas River, was originally called Journey-Cake," wrote Jesse A. Hall and Leroy T. Hand. (There also was stage station named "Journeycake" in Linwood in Leavenworth County.)

Hall and Hand's account continued: "It [Linwood] was named after a Chief of the Delaware tribe around which the following legend was interwoven: 'At one time, a young brave of the

Delaware tribe was captured by white traders and carried to a far distance from his tribe. He eventually managed to escape and upon his long journey home, which was fraught with many dangers and hardships, he was forced to rely for subsistence upon a small cake of corn bread which he had concealed upon his person.

"Having arrived safely with his tribe and after telling them the story of his escape, he was immediately re-christened 'Journey-Cake.'" The name, which is purely of Indian origin, has been corrupted by the whites to that of Johnny-Cake." [2]

The boy who received the name "Journey-Cake" was not Charles Journeycake, another grandson of The Buck, who lived on the Kansas Delaware reserve and later in Oklahoma, but rather the name of his grandfather, Buckongahelas, whose last years were spent in Indiana. Many Indian Nations had the custom of kidnapping children–and adults–to replace their own offspring or tribal members who had died. Whites were puzzled by the fact that entire families would be attacked by Indians—with only certain children and women spared and taken. But it usually happened when an Indian family wished to replace a child or wife who had died.

Referring to the Delaware people, their Moravian missionary the Rev. David Zeisberger remarked: "They are very fond of white children. Hence Indian women run after white men and, when they have white children, make much of them, although they do not like the white people. Twins are regarded as particularly fortunate, being looked upon as favored people who have a great spirit." [3]

The boy with the corn cake, Buckongahelas, would grow up to become "one of the most proficient trackers" among the Eastern Woodland Indians, according to Judge J. C. McWhorter,[4] and the most feared of Delaware war chiefs of his day. Yet he was renowned as a just and merciful man. Soldiers and civilians taken prisoner under his command rejoiced because they would not be tortured or murdered.

"Nowhere can there be ascribed acts of cruelty in the welfare of this lofty-minded chieftain," historian Lucullus Virgil McWhorter (Judge McWhorter's brother) recorded.[5]

Buckonghelas would father four sons, among them Kistalwa (Runner of the Mountain Path) of Leavenworth, Kansas, the father of Watomika, the first American Indian to be ordained a Catholic priest in the United States. The grandson of The Buck, Watomika took the name Father

James Chrysostom Mary Bouchard. (His mother Marie's name was the French spelling of Mary, and "Bouchard" was an Anglicized version of his mother's maiden name "Beucheur." Thus he honored both his earthly and his heavenly mothers.

This lofty-minded chieftain—the little boy with his life-saving snack who grew up to be a powerful warrior--was my many greats-grandfather, Chief Buckongahelas Journeycake. His corn cake story reminds me of the Biblical account of Elijah and the starving widow whom he met in the town of Zarephath in Sidon. Only a handful of flour and a dab of oil remained in her cupboard.

To this woman, Elijah said, "Make me a little cake and bring it out to me. Then you can prepare something for yourself and your son." The widow shared the small amount she had, and for the next year, "The jar of flour did not go empty, nor the jug of oil run dry, as the Lord had foretold through Elijah."–1 Kings, 17:11-16. [6]

1. Audubon, *Birds of America from Original Drawings*, p. 127.

2. Hall and Hard, *History of Leavenworth, Kansas*, p.16.

3. Zeisberger, *History of Northern American Indians*, p. 89.

4. McWhorter, J. C., *Scout of the Buckongehanon*, p. 255.

5. McWhorter, Lucullus, *Border Settlers*, p. 164.

6. Catholic Biblical Association, *St. Joseph Edition of New American Bible*, pp. 343, 344.

Sketch by Phleat Boyd, 1976

23

2

A Midsummer Night's Dream

Buckongahelas bust by West Virginia sculptor Ross Straight.

"Within the span of 20 generations, an individual has on his [or her] family tree more than a million grandfathers and grandmothers – to say nothing of other assorted kinfolk." – Author N. C. Browder

I met the powerful Delaware Indian War Chief Buckongahelas Journeycake–the grandfather of Father Bouchard and my many greats grandfather--in a dream.

A leader of the Wolf ("Took-seat") Clan of the Lenni Lenape, The Buck, as he was known, was considered the "last of the great Delaware war chiefs." It was this dream that prompted me to begin research of my mother's family tree and of Chief Buckongahelas Journeycake and his religious grandsons Watomika and Charles.

Buckongahelas stood before me in the dream, an old man only slightly stooped, his bearing still magnificent--a majestic fellow, about 5'10" tall and powerfully built with piercing black eyes. He was wrinkled of face, born around 1720 and having lived some eighty-five winters.

He was clad in a simple leather robe over deerskin leggings. His raven black hair, barely tinted with gray at the temples, fell nearly to his waist and was pulled behind his ears. I later read that around The Buck's neck hung a necklace of bear claws and a pouch containing tobacco and certain charms. But in my dream he wore only the simple leather robe unadorned.

Although he uttered not a word, I sensed at once that the man in my dream was Chief Journeycake. I later learned that he also was known as Buckongahela, as Petchnanalas, "a fulfiller," as Pachantschihilas, "one who succeeds in all he undertakes," as The Buck, Petchenanalas, or as Buckongohanon, "Giver of Presents." The gift that Grandfather Buck, the giver of presents, brought to me was my dream of him.

It was not unusual for the Lenape Indians, especially warriors, to have many names. Buckongahelas was the "Head Heroe" [sic] of the Delaware, Mahican Chief Hendrick Aupaumut wrote in his journal in 1791, according to historian C. A. Weslager. [1]

Chief Buckongahelas stood stoically before me in the dream, staring at me unrelentingly with a great curiosity he could not seem to satisfy. His black eyes searched my soul, and finally seemingly satisfied, he left me longing to know more about him and my other Delaware ancestors.

Seven generations separate my brothers and me from Buckongahelas. However, fourteen generations separated Abraham and King David; another fourteen generations stood between King David and the deportation of the Israelites to Babylon; and an additional fourteen generations spanned the exile in Babylon to the time of Christ. The seven generations separating us from this mighty chief seem a minute number compared to the forty-two generations that bridged Abraham to Jesus.

The seed of this one man—like Abraham's seed—would produce many generations of fine men and women, including Watomika, the boy who became the man Father James Bouchard, S.J.

1. Weslager, "*The Delaware Indians, a History*," p. 335.

The bust of Buckongahelas by sculptor Ross Straight of Buckhannon, West Virginia, was exhibited at Dodge City's Carnegie Center. Former Executive Director Dona Lancaster (right) guides guests Craig and Stephanie Diell through the exhibits.

Photo by Charlene Scott-Myers

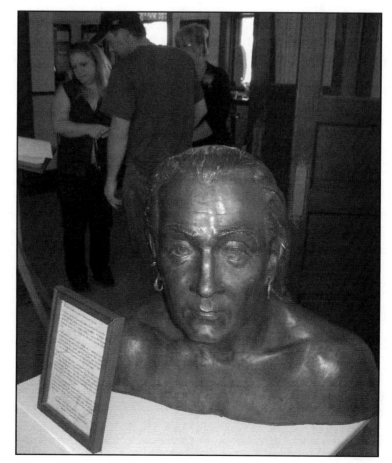

3

Burned at the Stake

This chapter tells the story of a horrible fire that changed the lives of every person connected with it, as well as those as yet unborn.

The family history of Watomika (Father Bouchard's Delaware Indian name), son of Chief Kistalwa Journeycake, is a fearful and fascinating one. It begins with his French grandparents who died in that horrible fire when the Comanches burned them at the stake in Texas. Their daughter Marie, who would become the mother of Father Bouchard, and her older brother Charles witnessed the fire as children.

"The first Indian of the Great Plains to become a Jesuit was a Delaware, Watomika (Swift-footed One) born in 1823, who in 1848 became James Bouchard, S. J.," Father John J. Killoren, S.J. wrote in the book *Come, Blackrobe.*[1]

Watomika was not only the first Indian of the Great Plains to become a Jesuit, "His is the distinction of being the first American Indian ordained to the Roman Catholic priesthood in the United States of America," Father John Bernard McGloin, S.J. explained in his book *Eloquent Indian.*[2] Father McGloin was an assistant professor of history at the University of San Francisco, the city where Father James Bouchard (Watomika) would minister for 30 years until his death in 1889.

At the Catholic seminary in Florissant, Missouri, Watomika wrote an account of his early life at the request of famed Jesuit evangelist to the Indians Father Pierre-Jean De Smet, who became a life-long friend. The young Indian seminarian strangely titled his autobiographical account *Biographical Sketch of Watomika,* as if Watomika was a different person than the one he was becoming, which indeed was true.

Watomika related how his father Kistalwa had married Marie-Elizabeth Bucheur (known simply as "Marie,") daughter of a Catholic Frenchman who fled the department of Auvergne, France with his wife and three-year-old son, Louis, to escape the bloody and atheistic French Revolution that began to rip the soul of France in 1789. More than 18,000 people–including King Louis XVI and his wife, Marie Antoinette–were killed during the revolution. Thousands were beheaded during the Reign of Terror from 1793 to 1794.

Perhaps Marie was named for the ill-fated wife of the French monarch who lost her head in the revolution, and Marie's brother named for King Louis XVI. (The horror of the French Revolution was brought home to me during my visits years ago to Mont-St-Michel, the 11ᵗʰ century Romanesque and Gothic abbey in Brittany, France and to another less grand monastery near Paris where the statues of Jesus, even the stone *Pieta*, as well as saints were headless, also victims of the fury against the Catholic Church during the French Revolution.)

The Bucheur family settled in a lush valley on the shores of the Rio Frio, a tributary of the Nueces River in Texas, at a time when the territory still was a part of Mexico. Little Marie was born after their arrival in the New World. Their neighbors were the Comanche, who were friendly at first and traded hides and meat for bright ribbons and other goods with the family. (An embarrassment of silk ribbons flowed into North America from France following its bloody revolution. The French frowned upon ribbons for years because of their association with the bourgeoisie, but the Indians loved the colorful streamers, and decorated their horses, hair, clothing, and even their trade blankets with them.)

Unfortunately, the Comanches' initial friendliness with the Bucheur family would turn to brutal murder in later years.

"Bucheur had spent about eight years on the banks of the Rio Frio in present-day Texas, then still Mexican territory, when stark tragedy brought bitter death to himself and his wife and unmitigated grief to his two children," Father McGloin wrote.[3]

Around the year 1815, when Marie was about seven and her brother eleven-years-old, the Spaniards massacred a party of Comanche hunters along the Rio Grande River. Unable to track down the killers, the Comanche sought blood revenge by burning the home of the Bucheurs along the Rio Frio and taking the French family captive.

What followed would be another tragedy that eventually would bring a Catholic priest--a "Blackrobe" as the Indians named the Jesuits--into the Journeycake family. According to Father McGloin, after the Bucheurs' capture, "The little family was hurried away in a northwestern direction to the village of the Great Chief of the Comanches, where the four were received 'amid the deafening yells of the savages who were eager to satiate their cruelty in the blood of their helpless victims.'"

The Comanche marched them for days to the village of their chief, a relative of the hunters the Spaniards killed. The chief called a council of elders and warriors of the tribe, who decided the fate of the frightened family. In revenge for the murder of the Comanches, the innocent Frenchman and his wife were condemned to death by fire.

The angry Indians led the parents of Louis and Marie to a tall wooden pole and tied them to it together. The logs around the stake were set afire, and the Bucheurs cried out, not for themselves, but for their children to be spared. Louis and Marie were forced to witness this horrid spectacle. Perhaps their parents should have remained in France, for to be guillotined would have been a less painful and swifter death.

Marie's mother burned at the stake.
Art by David and Dennis Scott, the author's twin brothers.

The famed missionary Father Pierre Jean De Smet, the "Apostle to the Indians" who came from Belgium in 1820 to White Marsh, the Jesuit Provincial House on a hill in Maryland, reported this incident to his superiors on January 30, 1857.

"The father and mother never ceased, until their latest breath, conjuring their cruel executioners to take pity on their poor innocent children," wrote Father De Smet, who befriended Father Bouchard during his years as a seminarian and priest.

"Little Louis and Marie were spared, on account of their infant years," Father De Smet said. "They were, however, forced to witness the sacrifice of their beloved parents, whom they could neither deliver nor comfort... The moaning of the father, amid his cruel tortures, and the agonizing shrieks of the dying mother, rent the hearts of these tender children."

The Jesuit priest, Father McGloin, gives a similar account:

"Bucheur and his spouse were handed over to a furious multitude and together they were roasted to death over a slow fire at the same stake.... They [the children] wept when they heard the groans of their tortured father and heart-rending shrieks of their agonized mother. So perished in tragic manner the grandparents of James Bouchard, Indian Jesuit.[4]

Mark Twain describes the horror of a burning at the stake in his book, *The Prince and the Pauper:* "Fagots had been piled about the two women, and a kneeling man was lighting them. The women bowed their heads, and covered their faces with their hands; the yellow flames began to climb upward among the snapping and crackling fagots, and wreaths of blue smoke to stream away on the wind; the clergyman lifted his hands and began a prayer. Just then two young girls came flying through the great gate, uttering piercing screams, and threw themselves upon the women at the stake.... Both the girls screamed continually ... but suddenly this tumult was drowned under a volley of heart-piercing shrieks of mortal agony." [5]

Having witnessed the mortal agony of their parents, Marie and her brother Louis received another tragic blow. Following the murder of their parents, the children were separated for life. A chief who had lost his only son in war claimed Louis as his adopted son to replace his loved one, a common practice among American Indians in those days. Thus Marie and Louis "were pitilessly separated, never to see each other again on earth," Father De Smet recorded.

"The chief claimed Louis to take the place of his son, put him on a beautiful horse, and conducted him to his country. From that time, they have never heard of him."

Father Bouchard later wrote that his Uncle Louis: "Probably still wanders with his red brethren in the boundless prairies of Texas, New Mexico, and the Great Desert, still replacing his adopted father as Comanche chief. The seven-year old Marie Elizabeth was borne off toward the northern limits of Texas by a Comanche brave who similarly adopted her into his wigwam and treated her as his daughter."

Thirty-two years after the murders of Marie's parents, the Comanche, "the Lords of the Plains," still were considered dangerous. Acaquash, chief of the Waco Indians, cautioned the Council of Texas Indians at Tehuacana Creek on May 15, 1844: "I am like the Indians of this country who are mixed in with the Delaware. My heart is half Waco; half Comanche. One thing I know, I don't want traders to take ammunition among the Comanche until after peace is made. They are a wild people...." [6]

Her new Comanche relatives treated Marie well, however. When she was thirteen, she accompanied her Comanche parents to a French trading post on the upper Red River of the North.

"Here contact was made with a group of Delaware Indians, among whom was the youthful and brave Kistalwa (He Who Walks the Mountain Path), son of Buckongehela [sic], the chief of the Delaware nation," Father McGloin wrote. "The Comanches and Delawares were friendly tribes; consequently, the two groups exchanged the compliments prescribed by intertribal protocol." [7]

Kitstalwa was instantly attracted to Marie. Even as a young girl of 13, she was said to be "a bewitching beauty," Watomika recalled years later in his biography.

"Kistalwa became so enamoured of Marie-Elizabeth that he could not rest until he had secured an interview with her and obtained her consent to accompany him to his father's lodge," Father McGloin quoted Father Bouchard's words from his "biography." [8]

Kistalwa asked the old Comanche chief, Marie's adopted father, for permission to accompany Marie to the lodge of his father, Buckongahelas, but the chief stubbornly refused. Kistalwa was strong-willed too, and he soon returned to the Comanche leader, placing a calumet (a pipe) and tobacco at his feet. The chief knew that if he refused to smoke the pipe, he would be refusing Kistalwa's request. The old man was worried by what this might mean. He knew that Kistalwa was a son of the mighty War Chief Buckongahelas. It would not bode well for the old chief to rudely refuse Kistalwa a second time.

The Comanche chief reversed his earlier decision and retrieved the peace pipe, the calumet, from the ground to light it. The pipe was passed from mouth to mouth to all those present, and the chief promised his adopted daughter to Kistalwa. In return, the young man gave the old chief two horses, several pounds of tobacco, and munitions.

Kistalwa brought the beautiful young Marie to the Indiana lodge of his father, Buckongahelas, and the chief received her with tenderness and affection. She remained with the Buck and his family for two years until her marriage.

1. Killoren, *Come Blackrobe,* p. 35.

2. Ibid, p. 182.

3. McGloin, *Eloquent Indian,* p. 37.

4. Twain, Prince and the Pauper, pp. 207, 208.

5. Ibid, p. 38.

6 Winfrey, *Texas Indian Papers 1844-1845*, pp. 51, 52.

7. McGloin, *Eloquent Indian*, p. 40.

8. Ibid, p. 39.

Muralist Boris Koodrin of San Francisco is the artist of Spiritus Magis, which portrays Father James Bouchard (Watomika, grandson of the Delaware Chief Buckongahelas) and his French mother, Marie, painted for the sesquicentennial (150th) anniversary of St. Ignatius Preparatory School in San Francisco in 2005.
Photo by Paul Totah

4

The Buck Gives Marie a Name

Marie-Elizabeth was given the name of Monotawan, sometimes spelled "Monotowa," meaning "White Fawn." "This compliment was paid to her as much for her delicate charm as for her white complexion," wrote Father McGloin.

Marie Bucheur, mother of Father Bouchard.

From the Spiritus Magis mural by artist Boris Koodrin

"It was Buckongahelas himself, Great Chief and father of the betrothed, who thus conferred her Delaware tribal name upon Marie-Elizabeth Burcheur." [1]

Monotawan gave birth to two sons, Chiwendota (Black Wolf) and his younger brother Watomika (Swift Foot). Watomika was born in a wigwam in 1823 in Kansas, where the Delaware had migrated from Missouri in the early 1820s. The Delaware reservation was located southeast of the present city of Leavenworth on the banks of the Missouri River. By 1838 when Watokia was 15, more than 1,000 Indians were living on the reservation. Watomika lived his early years learning to ride bareback, hunt wild animals with a bow and arrow, and prepare for manhood as a Lenape warrior.

"Watomika was the idol of his parents…," Father Bouchard admitted with a bit of vanity in his *Biographical Sketch of Watomika*. Watomika's father, Kistalwa, was born about 1775, and became a Delaware chief in about 1817, a post he held for fifteen years.

"His father, Kistalwa, belonged to the Delaware tribe, at one time one of the more powerful tribes in America," Catholic Archbishop I. J. Strecker years later revealed to his readers in his book *The Church in Kansas*.

"For his integrity and courage his father [Kistalwa] was chosen a chief of the tribe. His father long resented the taking of Indian lands by the government. He often quoted Thomas Jefferson's statement on justice to the Indians: 'Not a foot of land will be taken without the Indian's consent.'" [2]

In his biographical sketch, Watomika recalled that when he was only nine-years-old, he asked to join his father, Kistalwa on a war party pursuit of the Sioux to avenge a Delaware friend's torture and murder at the hands of a band of that tribe. When his father asked if he was not afraid of being scalped, Watomika took his father's hand and replied: "If my father be a coward, then am I also a coward!"

It was unusual for a boy of his age to accompany a war party, but Watomika later recalled that he was well trained in using a bow, tomahawk, and scalping knife, and "became very fond of these instruments of warfare and expert in their exercise."

Archbishop Strecker embellished the story further: "He [Watomika] became a daring hunter at an early age." [3]

Still, his mother tearfully opposed the inclusion of her young son in the war party, but Watomika joined his father and the warriors in their traditional war dance that lasted late into the night. And the boy was with them when they took off on their expedition of revenge the next morning. The year was 1832, and the Delaware chased the Sioux and caught up with them at the mouth of the south branch of the Platte River in the Rocky Mountains.

Years later while at seminary, Watomika recalled in his "biography" the memorable chase and midnight attack that was recorded by Father McGloin in his book *Eloquent Indian*: "…. The half-full moon, moving in queenly splendor over the fleecy clouds, shed her mellow light over the grassy bosom of the prairie…. When the appointed time arrived, they set out. Their march was slow, their step soft, as, with eagle eye, they scrutinized every object that darkened the plain before them.

"Thus onward and still onward, they moved, the fearless Kistalwa and his son all the while at their head, till at length the camp of the Sioux was descried on a small peninsula formed by the dwindling course of the river. It was evidently thronged, for the shadow of figures standing erect, as if on guard, darkened the ample sweep about the camp."

Suddenly a voice was heard, "shrill and hoarse," the Jesuit seminarian recalled. "Cries and shouts of approval from the excited crowd rang fearfully into the still ear of night. There was a fascination about the place that made even the brave Delwares (sic) pause….

"In a few moments, however, the Delawares were again in motion; but scarcely had they secured their position for attack when they were thrilled by a piercing protracted shriek, which was immediately followed by another voice, loud, hoarse and awful. It had a certain rude and prolonged vehemence that indicated great physical strength, and seemed like the despairing cry of a wild beast rather than a human voice."

Kistalwa directed his braves toward the point of attack.

"Instantly, the vindictive war-cry of the Delawares, charged thick with death, broke like peals of thunder upon the ears of the excited foe. A strange confusion now ensued. The enemy was at first filled with consternation and seemed spellbound; but the fatal spell was soon broken." [4]

The Sioux made "a tumultuous rush" upon the Delaware, the young seminarian remembered. "Now began a conflict which, though short, defies the power of language to describe." [5]

Watomika was slightly injured in one leg, but the nine-year-old boy rescued his father who was mortally wounded, pulling him into a thicket of brushwood. The loss of their chief infuriated the Delaware, and they inflicted death upon thirty Sioux before the enemy hastily retreated. The dying Kistalwa was placed on the horse of his brother, Whapakong, and returned to Monotawan. The lovely Frenchwoman, Marie (Monotawan) lost not a son, but a beloved husband that day.

Watomika's uncle, Whapakong, became a surrogate father to the boy, but the uncle also would be murdered by a Sioux a few months later in the spring of 1833 when Watomika accompanied him to a trading post on the upper Missouri River. A Sioux warrior attacked Whapakong for no apparent reason, and the Lenape died defending himself. With a frightened and sickened heart, the boy Watomika witnessed the latest senseless killing of a family member.

"Once more, tribal lamentation was continued until one of the tribe announced that he had seen in a dream the spirit of Whapakong entering, as had his brother Kistalwa, into the Land of Life," Father McGloin wrote.[6]

Watomika and his brother, Chiwendota, were too young to lead the tribe after their father's death, and Ketchum, their cousin, was named chief of the Delaware tribe instead. At first called "Catch Him" by whites, Ketchum became a leader of renown in his own right.

Kistalwa's mother left the Catholic Church at the time of his parents' marriage when she was 15, wrote Archbishop I. J. Strecker in his book *The Church in Kansas, 1850-1905, a Family Story.*

"He (Father Bouchard) knew his mother to fear and love God even though she did not go to church. At times she would put her hands on his head and ask the Great Spirit to bless him." [7]

After her husband's death, Monotawan (the French woman Marie) returned to her adoptive parents, the Comanches, accompanied by her oldest son, Chiwendota. The French woman's other son, Watomika, had no desire to be exiled from the Delaware, although he loved his mother deeply. Monotawan later remarried and bore two more children. When her Lenape son, Chiwendota, was grown, he married and fathered a son and daughter, but that son was stolen by another tribe and never seen again. The daughter married a Comanche and lived at Walters, Oklahoma.

Witnessing the murders of his father and uncle at the hands of the Sioux–and hearing about the deaths of his French grandparents at the fiery stake of the Comanches–deeply affected the sensitive child Watomika. But in his strangest dreams, the 11-year-old boy could not imagine that someday he would be ordained a Catholic priest and spend the last forty-one years of his life as a Jesuit.

1. McGloin, *Eloquent Indian,* p. 40.

2. Ibid, pp. 50, 74.

3. Strecker, *Church in Kansas*, p. 53.

4. McGloin, *Eloquent Indian,* p. 45.

5. Strecker, *Church in Kansas*, p. 53.

6. McGloin, *Eloquent Indian,* p. 47.

7. Strecker, *Church in Kansas*, p. 53.

5

A Black Robe in the Family

The boy Watomika brought food and prayed beneath his father's bier every day for a month.

The Delaware believe that souls are material, "although invisible and immortal," Watomika wrote in his autobiography after he became a seminarian. He explained the Delaware belief that the soul does not leave the body immediately, but descends with the body into the grave and remains for several days, sometime weeks or even months.

After the soul has left the tomb, its departure to the Land of Life is slowed by the bonds which held it so tightly, bonds which the soul must break. This is the reason the Delaware paint and carefully array the body before it is placed in the grave, and why they place tools, utensils and provisions in the grave, "which are indispensable to the soul in traversing the long and dangerous bridge which leads to the 'island of happiness,' " Watomika related to his superiors.

Watomika did his part to ensure that the soul of his father, Kistalwa, reached the "island of happiness." The boy prayed and placed a favorite dish at the bier of his father daily for an entire month. When the food disappeared, he was certain that the soul of his departed dad had accepted the offering on his behalf. Watomika never ceased repeating "this last testimony of filial love, fidelity to the manes [remains] of my father, whom I loved dearly," until he had a dream about Kistalwa. It was a Delaware custom for mourners and family members to mourn their lost loved one until a family member should see the deceased person in a dream. Watomika was the first to dream about Kistalwa.

"The dream assured me that the dear soul had entered into the 'regions of life,' and was in the enjoyments of all the favors and the advantages that the Great Spirit grants so liberally to those who have faithfully accomplished their obligations on earth," he wrote. [1]

Watomika was an intelligent, sensitive, and religious lad. His grandmother who was burned at the stake had grown up a French Catholic and taught her daughter Marie many of the church's beliefs. Marie was not able to practice her faith following her capture by the Comanches, but she must have passed her limited knowledge of her parents' beliefs on to her son, Watomika.

The Rev. Thomas Smith Williamson, a Presbyterian missionary to the Sioux and the Dakota Indians, visited the Delaware on a missionary tour in 1833, long before Kansas was declared a U.S. territory. During his visit, he chose Watomika and two other boys from among the tribe to be enrolled at the Christian non-denominational Marietta College in Ohio in the fall of 1834. When he entered Marietta to study to become a Presbyterian minister, Watomika anglicized his name to "Jacob Beshor," a variation of his mother's maiden name "Bucheur."

In his autobiography, Watomika confided to his Jesuit friends about his experience when torn from his native land and family and thrust into the strange and unfamiliar world of white people.

"You can easily imagine what were the thoughts and feelings of Watomika in finding himself so far from his native wilds, from his friends, and especially his mother, to whom he was devotedly attached, left among strangers whom he had ever been taught to suspect and hate and, above all, in entering upon a career so new, so different, from what he had been accustomed to."

When his two Indian companions returned home, Watomika refused to accompany them, saying that he would "first learn the Great Medicine of the White Man" (the white man's religion).

A few months away weaned Watomika from his clan he left behind in his forest home at Muskagola. He soon learned to read and write English, and became a model of piety and "contemplation of heavenly things." His companions ridiculed him for fasting rigorously once a week. He was studying to become a Presbyterian minister, but that would not happen.

Watomika was destined to become the first North American Indian to be ordained a Roman Catholic priest in the United States. (The first North American Indian ordained a priest was an Iroquois who was kidnapped as a boy in 1623 and taken to Spain, where he was received into the Augustinian Order and ordained in 1650. He spent his entire priesthood in Europe.)

The year that Watomika was born, 1823, was the same year that a Jesuit priest, Father Charles F. Van Quickenborne, led his company of eleven Jesuits (aka Black Robes or Black-Gowns) westward to Missouri. Watomika, grandson of Buckongahelas, would join the Jesuits in Missouri after his conversion at age twenty-four. St. Ignatius of Loyola, a Spanish knight, had founded the Jesuit Order, the Society of Jesus, in 1540. His society grew by 1,000 members by his death in 1556, and expanded during the next two centuries to almost 23,000 (today's membership is approximately 25,000).

It is doubtful that the young Watomika had ever heard of either Ignatius or the Jesuits when he made his trip to St. Louis. The Presbyterians found the Indian youth on the Kansas Delaware reservation and sent him to St. Louis for religious training. The seeds of his conversion to Catholicism and later religious vocation were planted during his stay in St. Louis, however. While exploring the mushrooming city–so different from the Great Plains where he grew up--Watomika strolled by a downtown Catholic church, St. Francis Xavier, on a Sunday afternoon.

"It was the moment of the children's catechism class," he later explained in a note to his lifelong friend, the Indian missionary Father De Smet.

"The altar, the crucifix, the image of the Blessed Virgin made a great impression upon me which I could not explain," he wrote. "With prayerful attention, I followed the priest's instruction. I returned home that evening with a more tranquil frame of mind, which now only the true light of faith could satisfy me," Archbishop I. J. Strecker later recorded Watomika's words in his book *The Church in Kansas, 1850-1905*. [2]

The priest at the St. Louis Church was a Jesuit, Father Arnold Damen, assistant pastor of the College Church. A native of Holland, he was brought to America by Father De Smet. Watomika's mind and heart were open to the Catholic Church and to this priest because his French mother, Marie, had been reared in the Catholic faith until her parents were murdered by the Comanches in Texas.

Father Damen, ordained after only seven years of study, offered to instruct the young Indian in the tenets of the church. The young priest became well known as an eloquent preacher who had "the unction that converted hearts." Father Damen certainly converted Watomika's heart, and the Delaware Native was baptized a Roman Catholic on May 23, 1847 at the age of 24 in the church in which he had "dropped by."

As a Jesuit priest, Father Bouchard later would be named an assistant to Father Damen at Holy Family Parish in Chicago, and the two would die within a week of each other many years later. When Father Bouchard died, a New York newspaper called him "the Father Damen of the West."

It was a Jesuit joke that Watomika went into the St. Louis church a Presbyterian–and came out of the church a Catholic. Less than a year following his baptism, he entered the Catholic seminary at the age of 24 at Florissant, Missouri near St. Louis. The seminary was founded in 1823 for Jesuit work among the Indians.

While preparing for his ordination, he received a request from Father De Smet at St. Louis University to write the story of his Delaware childhood and family history. Father De Smet was one of the founders of the Missouri Province of the Society of Jesus, and became a renowned missionary to American Indians.

Father Bouchard presented his autobiography, now in the Belgian Jesuit archives in Brussels, to Father De Smet as his 1854 Christmas gift. After reading the autobiography, Father De Smet wrote, "Watomika, a child of the forest, a worthy descendant of a powerful American race, adjured his errors, embraced our holy religion, and, some time after, enrolled himself among the followers of St. Ignatius."

Watomika adopted another more modified form of his mother's maiden name "Bucheur" at the time of his profession. He was ordained Aug. 5, 1855 by the Belgium Jesuit Bishop James Oliver Van Develde at the Church of St. Francis Xavier in St. Louis.

Father Bouchard later changed his name to "James Buchard," which evolved into "Father James Chrysostom Bouchard, S.J. (Society of Jesus)." Father Bouchard celebrated his first Mass at Florissant on August 15, 1855, the day that his friend Father De Smet pronounced his final vows in the same chapel.

"Father De Smet, the Apostle to the Indians, found a certain pride in the ordination of Watomika. All his prayers and efforts were answered in the conversion and ordination of this Indian of the prairie," Archbishop Strecker wrote. [3]

Inspired by Father De Smet, Father Bouchard responded to the missionary: "My one desire, and the object for which I pray daily, is to live and die a true son of the Society of Jesus, in whatever function or place God assigns me through the voice of my superiors." [4]

De Smet and Father Bouchard "shared the wish in their correspondence through the 1850s that they would be able to work together among the Indians, but Catholic missionary activities then did not point to the development of a native clergy," Father John J. Killoren, S.J., explained in his book *Come Blackrobe*. [5]

1. Bouchard, *Biographical Sketch of Watomika*.
2. Strecker, *Church in Kansas*, p. 53.
3. Ibid, p. 54.
4. Ibid.
5. Killoren, *Come Blackrobe*, p. 182.

6

Father Bouchard to Kansas

Father Bouchard was blessed to be sent for a year (1856-1857) back to Kansas Territory to minister in Leavenworth near the Delaware reserve, where his relatives still lived.

Father Bouchard, S.J.

Courtesy of the Midwest Jesuit Archives, St. Louis, Mo.

During the second year of his priesthood while still in Kansas, he befriended a secular priest, Father James H. Defouri, who described their relationship: "… often we rambled together, and in those solitary walks to and from the couch of the sick, Watomika gave me many details about the Delaware Indians, which undoubtedly will please my readers, coming from such a truthful mouth."

Father Defouri went on to write of Father Bouchard: "There I found him on November 1, 1856, an efficient priest, a good preacher, an excellent friend, and much loved by the Catholics of Leavenworth."

Defouri also mentioned that Father Bouchard's father, Kistalwa, had been deeply touched by the sad story of the French girl Marie's past when he first met her. "Kistalwa determined to tear her [Marie-Elizabeth], if necessary, from the [Comanche] tormentors of her unfortunate mother and father, and he therefore returned to the charge with such determination." [1]

Father Bouchard worked in Kansas as an assistant to Bishop John Miege, the Jesuit Vicar Apostolic of Indian Territory.

"The two were still young men in 1856, for Miege was but forty-one while Bouchard was thirty-three years of age. A picture of the Kansas Jesuit prelate is furnished by Father Coppens: 'He was a man of majestic appearance, but as unassuming as if he had been a simple priest. He had been raised to the Episcopal dignity much against his will,'" Father McGloin wrote. [2]

Tim Wenzl, archivist of the Diocese of Dodge City, recorded in his book *A Legacy of Faith*: "Father John Baptiste Miege was appointed vicar apostolic of this Indian territory in a document dated July 23, 1850. Father Miege had been recruited for the apostolates of the Missouri Jesuits by

Father Pierre De Smet in Europe only two years before."

Wenzl explained that at the age of 35 and only three years ordained, Father Miege felt unworthy and unqualified to be a bishop.

"Father Miege sent the papers back to Rome calling the appointment 'a mistake.' The documents were returned to him, however, with a formal command to accept the office. Father Miege was consecrated [bishop] by Archbishop Peter Richard Kenrick in St. Francis Xavier Church on March 25, 1851, in St. Louis." [3]

The Jesuits invited Bishop Miege to establish his See at St. Mary's Mission in Kansas. He arrived there after seven days on the Missouri River and five days by mule-drawn wagon. Any friend of Father De Smet was a friend of Father Bouchard, who found himself working with one of the finest missionary bishops in the country. The young Indian priest was assigned to pastoral duties at the humble church that served as the pro-cathedral of the vicariate.

Father Bouchard wrote a letter to Father De Smet during his year of priestly service in Kansas, mentioning his own ill health that had brought him back to Leavenworth for recuperation with his Delaware relatives and friends.

"My health has been very poor for the last few days--pain in the breast and debility--owing probably to the extreme heat which we have to endure …. I am not too pleased with my present situation, that is to say, I would prefer to live in community with our own brethren, to that of living with secular clergymen….

"I have paid two visits to my Delaware friends since my arrival in this city – the second visit only a short time ago. This time, I spent some days with them which I passed very agreeably in visiting my relations. My old uncle, Capt. Ket-chum [sic], received me with open arms. He was quite sick when I arrived at his house, but he was so overjoyed at seeing me as to quite forget his illness. He had a world of news to tell me–some good, some bad. And a world of business to be attended to for the tribe, which he was anxious to entrust to me as if he expected me to succeed him in the chieftainship.

"But owing to my Rule [Jesuit], I declined undertaking any secular business, even for my dearest friends--though, I must say, that I did it with regret; for I would gladly be the first to call

U.S. [United States] to an account for his connivance at the violation of the late treaty with the Delawares, for the unpaid-for reservation ceded to the government some fifty years ago (in Ohio), and for the unjust appropriation of Delaware funds by wicked and selfish agents, and a host of other things.

"My friends are all anxious to have me reside permanently among them. They have even expressed a desire to have me preach to them–but in this, I should, no doubt, be much opposed by the heretical missionaries, of whom there are no less than four different sects, viz: Moravians, Baptists, Methodist--South and North, and their particular adherents.

"I can but weep and mourn over the ruin of a beloved people [the Delaware], a people who deserved a better fate; but what better fate could be expected from an infidal [sic] government, an avaricious nation, whose only God is the almighty dollar, whose only shrine of devotion the territories of the weak and defenceless [sic]. Oh! My heart saddens, sickens, when I look at the future of my people, wronged, perverted and crushed by the bloody hand of a so-called *Liberal Government*." [4]

In 1857, the young priest learned that "his Delaware tribe was being despoiled terribly of their land in defiance of treaties. He wrote Father DeSmet: "I can but weep over the ruin of my tribe. They deserve a better fate—my heart bleeds at the thought of their future." [5]

In his book, *Eloquent Indian*, Father McGloin mentions Chief Ketchum as the "cousin" of Watomika (Father Bouchard) and his brother Chiwendotah. But in Father Bouchard's letter to Father De Smet, written July 1, 1857, he calls the chief "my old uncle, Capt. Ket-chum." [6]

Ketchum, whose Delaware name was Qui-sha-to-wha, died at the age of 77 on July 11, 1857, only ten days after Father Bouchard wrote his letter. Perhaps the young priest officiated at his funeral. Ketchum was buried at White Church, Kansas in a cemetery adjacent to the Christian Church. We visited his gravestone, which displays a lamb reclining under rays of the sun. Ketchum was born in Tuscarawas County, Ohio in 1780. (Father Bouchard's Uncle Solomon, son of Chief Buckongahelas, also is said to be buried in the White Church Cemetery.)

Rev. Pratt wrote that the old Chief Ketchum lived on Lawrence Road and that "his funeral was attended by a large number of Indians, who came in their colored blankets and painted faces, carrying their guns." Ketchum was succeeded as Delaware chief by "his sister's son, John Connor, although James Connor was the designated heir."

The son of the Delaware Indian Kistalwa and the French girl Marie, the young priest Father Bouchard, was appointed to the Jesuit mission in San Francisco in 1861, and when informed that he would serve in California, he sent Father De Smet a heartfelt poem, entitled *Remember Watomika*, that ended with these two lines:

Kind friend, 'tis thus I'll muse on thee,

And think that thou are always near. Farewell!"

Father Bouchard sailed via the steamer *Champion* from New York to the Isthmus of Panama on July 22, 1861. After his arrival in San Francisco, on August 16, 1861, he wrote to a friend, describing the steamer as "an old tub." His first ocean voyage on his 23-day journey to California was a rough ride he did not relish or wish to repeat.

"How gladly," he confessed to his journal, "would I go back to Kansas! I fear my going to California is too much like Jonas' fleeing from Nineveh!"

There was no turning back, however. Father Bouchard would serve throughout California for nearly 30 years, ministering to the residents of San Francisco and to gold miners at their camps, and conducting hundreds of missions not only in California, but also in cities and country churches of many other states.

The healing of his childhood traumas that the young Delaware Indian, Watomika, sought by serving God was reflected in his handwriting in a textbook he had used at Marietta: "*Joy, that twines about the heart, or beams with luster from the eye, now make thy first and fond pursuit, and thou shalt far from Sorrow's Sea...."*

In another letter, he charged that the United States observed its "sacred treaty" for the Kansas Reserve "by allowing a promiscuous throng of bold adventurers to squat all over those beautiful prairies, and by prohibiting free bidding on the day of sale! Oh Justice, how little are thou known in this proud, boasting nation! Such is the sentiment of a poor wandering Delaware."

Father Bouchard also wrote his opinion of an unnamed book on Indian affairs he learned about from a "creditable source":

"It is just such a work as one would write who loves justice; it is actuated by the noble sentiments of charity and mercy for the oppressed, condemned and injured Redman. It tells most plainly the thoughts and feelings of every Indian's heart; it un-bosoms his silent anguish and counts his burning tears; it portrays in terms most true and touching some of the many grievous wrongs which the almost helpless son of the forest is obliged to endure at the powerful hand of the heartless and ever-grasping Anglo-Saxon race."

The venerable missionary Father De Smet sent his last letter to Father Bouchard in 1872. De Smet was worn out from his many missionary years, having made eight known visits to the Indians along the Missouri and Kaw between 1851 and 1867, plus three extended visits to the Indians of the Rockies–all this before his friend John Baptiste Miege became bishop of the Indian Territory. Father De Smet also had traveled to Europe to solicit funds for the Jesuits more than twenty times!

In a tender missive which actually was a farewell letter to Father Bouchard, Father De Smet wrote, "I long to see you once more before I die." But Father De Smet breathed his last in 1873, without a final farewell hug from his fellow Jesuit. Father Bouchard would live lonely for his friend another 17 years.

1. McGloin, *Eloquent Indian*, pp. 47, 48.

2. Ibid, 74.

3. Wenzl, *Legacy of Faith*, p. 11.

4. McGloin, *Eloquent Indian*, pp. 75, 76.

5. Strecker, *Church in Kansas*, p. 54.

6. McGloin, *Eloquent Indian*, p. 75.

7

Rebellion with a Beard

Father Bouchard and his controversial beard.

As sometimes happens with eager young priests (especially converts), Father Bouchard bumped heads with his archbishop less than two years after his arrival in San Francisco. (The young priest managed to be both a saint and a sinner, giving hope to all!)

Father Bouchard had made known to his superiors his desire to serve American Indians, but the Delaware in Kansas held Father Bouchard in their midst for only a short time. The Indians didn't benefit for long from the ordination of one of their own. Father Bouchard's strongest impact in his early years as a priest in California was his devotion to the salvation of the Irish in the Golden City, where he drew huge crowds to hear his sermons at San Francisco's St. Ignatius Church. He was appointed assistant pastor in October, 1861, and delivered his first parochial mission at St. Ignatius in December of that year.

"His first sermon on the Pacific Coast was given to a crowded church, and the listeners were charmed by the sound of his silvery voice, by the power of his nervous eloquence, and by the pleasantness of his address, by the lucidity of his explanations and by the vigor of his stringent logic," wrote Father Richard Gleeson. [1]

The Jesuit historian Father Joseph Riordan later recalled: "Presently the little edifice (St. Ignatius Church) was taxed to its utmost, so that crowds stood without, unable to gain admission. Still his voice, which was remarkably powerful, reached even to these, and they stood in rapt admiration, for never before had they heard man speak like this man." [2]

Father Bouchard preached for the very first time in the presence of the Most Reverend Joseph Sadoc Alemany, Archbishop of San Francisco, on Sunday, January 5, 1862. Archbishop Alemany belonged to the Order of Preachers, but he was not known for his eloquent preaching. As the popularity of Father Bouchard's sermons steadily grew—among non-Catholics as well as Catholics--so did the consternation of the archbishop. So popular was the young priest who drew large crowds to hear his sermons that only a few months later, the pastor of St. Ignatius announced plans to build a new and larger brick church and college adjacent to the site. The laying of the cornerstone occurred May 11, 1862, less than a year after Father Bouchard's arrival. The young priest would serve the students of the new St. Ignatius College.

"The number of people that come to our church is incredible," an Italian Jesuit wrote from San Francisco in 1862. "Last Sunday more than a thousand people left because they could not find a seat."

An unsigned article in the University of Santa Clara *Redwood* (January 1906) noted: "The West had never heard such soul-stirring, feeling eloquence…. The church was altogether too small to contain the crowds anxious to drink in the burning words of the new Orator of the Golden City…. Father James Bouchard, S.J., Apostle of California."

Father Bouchard began to be known far and wide as "the eloquent Indian." He first drew scorn from Archbishop Alemany because of two sodalities of St. Ignatius Church that were founded under Father Bouchard's leadership in 1861 and 1862. The archbishop complained that the sodalities were drawing attendance from San Francisco's other five parishes. (Actually, it was Father Bouchard's fiery preaching that emptied the pews and offering baskets of other churches every Sunday.)

Another annoyance to the archbishop was Father Bouchard's beard, which the young priest grew *not to annoy* Alemany, but for the protection of his much-used voice in winter. He suffered the wrath of Alemany, however, when he refused to shave if off. Facial hair is unusual for a full-blood Indian, but Father Bouchard was half French--and his beard flourished in all its glory. (All five of my brothers and my son have been bearded men at some time or another.)

Not only did Father Bouchard *not* shave off his beard when requested to do so by the archbishop, he allowed it to grow like a creeping vine, further and further down his chest. Other people admired the Jesuit priest's beard, however.

"Although Father Nicholas Congiato, as Bouchard's local superior, was ever to the fore in defense of his fellow Jesuit, he evidently considered it but the part of prudence to remove him from

San Francisco from time to time, so as not to make his presence obnoxious to Archbishop Alemany," Father John McGloin explained. "In this case, San Francisco's loss was the obvious gain of Roman Catholicism throughout the Far West." [3]

Father Bouchard began his far-flung travels to other states to preach his powerful missions that drew thousands and made him one of the most famous Jesuits in the history of California and the Northwest. The first mention of his beard was contained in a *San Francisco Monitor* newspaper report of one of Father Bouchard's missions given in Austin, Nevada, in 1868:

"It has been seven years since we have seen Father Bouchard. His appearance is much changed since then but, to our mind, for the better. The venerable beard which he has permitted to grow till it sweeps down his breast adds a peculiar dignity and even majesty to his figure." [4]

Eventually, the Jesuit superior sent a petition all the way to Rome regarding the issue of Father Bouchard's beard. Rome responded favorably because Archbishop Charles Seghers of Portland, a close friend of Father Bouchard, later wrote to one of his priests who also sported a beard, informing him that Father Bouchard had obtained a papal dispensation from the Holy See to wear his beard. But no, the Portland priest could not keep his beard.

Archbishop Seghers "became quite an authority on shaving" in the Catholic Church, and even wrote an article on "The Practice of Shaving in the Western Church" that appeared in the *American Quarterly Review* in April, 1882.[5]

"One wonders if the bearded Father Bouchard, happy possessor of a papal dispensation and good friend of Archbishop Seghers, ever read this article!" Father McGloin mused.

"One final point concerning the beard of Bouchard: not only was it never shaven, but it was allowed to grow and prosper until it became quite a distinctive and personal trademark of the Indian Jesuit in his journeyings throughout the Far West," Father McGloin added. "With it he lived and with it he died!" [6]

The second archbishop of San Francisco, the Most Rev. Patrick W. Riordan, who served from 1884-1914, was another bishop favorably impressed by Father Bouchard – with or without a beard. Riordan said that Bouchard "... was a man who was to become the most famous Jesuit on the Pacific slope."

A studio photograph of Father James Bouchard, the first American Indian ordained a Catholic priest in the United States, a Jesuit and a relative of the author.

Courtesy of the Midwest Jesuit Archives, St. Louis, Mo.

1. McGloin, *Eloquent Indian,* p. 103.

2. Ibid.

3. Ibid, p. 114.

4. *San Francisco Monitor,* Oct. 24, 1868.

5. *American Quarterly Review,* Volume 7, No. 26, pp. 278, 310.

6. McGloin, *Eloquent Indian,* pp. 122, 123.

8

Speaking against Women and Chinese

The American Indian priest Bouchard lived forty-one years as a Jesuit. His parish was the entire vast Northwest. But even as his Indian race had been slurred by whites for so many generations, Father Bouchard surprisingly attacked not only the gender of women in his sermons, but also another race of people different from his own, the Chinese.

Considered the greatest pulpit figure of the West in his day, Father Bouchard claimed that "Woman is man's inferior in mental scope and capacity, as she is his superior in moral refinement and emotional susceptibility."

Father Bouchard had decided to share his controversial views on Woman's Suffrage (views that would be an embarrassment to the Jesuit Order today) with proceeds from his speech to help pay taxes on the Presentation Convent for nuns (women!) in San Francisco.

"One is at a loss as to whether to admire the courage or deprecate the foolhardiness of Father Bouchard, when one reads of his willingness in San Francisco, in 1872, to discuss the explosive topic of 'Woman's Suffrage,'" wrote the Jesuit Father McGloin.

"There are, I admit, individual women who are the individual superiors of individual men, but facts--relentless, uncompromising--will perversely array themselves on the side of masculine supremacy in the aggregate...." Father Bouchard said, plunging into his outlandish views at St. Francis Church in San Francisco.

"In the bright and beautiful galaxy of artists, we behold the names of women who have distinguished themselves as painters, but Raphael, Michael Angelo [sic], Van Dyke and others shine sublimely the highest!" he insisted.

Then he asked his audience: "How do women ... politicians or statesmen ... compare with Webster, Palmerston, Bismarck, and William H. Seward?" He next turned to literature, admitting "Women have composed beautiful verses," but adding, "Where will you find a female Shakespeare, a female Milton, or a female Byron?"

He further alienated women in his audience when he concluded, as reported in the *San*

This is the full Spiritus Magis mural created by Boris Koodrin of San Francisco. The mural portrays Father James Bouchard, S.J. and his French mother, Marie Bucheur, at left.

Francisco Monitor: "The day the rebellion of women becomes constitutional in the United States, I would advise all true men, who are not disposed to deck themselves in female attire and feed the baby with molasses candy, to emigrate to some more hospitable portion of the globe!" [1]

Father Bouchard did not make many friends among women that day. The venerable writer Father McGloin did not record the reactions of the women to Father Bouchard's tirade. (Had she been in the audience, my saucy red-headed Irish grandmother, my father's mother, would have burned the ears of Father Bouchard with her retorts, but she wasn't born yet.)

Father Bouchard later took on the Chinese at another benefit February 25, 1873 at St. Francis Church for the Presentation Convent in San Francisco. Fifty years old at the time, he was asked to speak because it was well known that he would draw a huge crowd. He chose as his well publicized topic *Chinaman or White Man, Which?* He knew that the subject was a sore one among the more than 100,000 Irish residents of San Francisco, who would flock to church to hear what *he* thought about it.

After gold was discovered in January, 1849, large numbers of Chinese were imported as "peon labor" into California. By 1860, there were 40,000 Chinese in the state. Simmering prejudice against the "yellow scourge" finally erupted in the popular outcry: "Chinese must go!" (If my Irish grandmother had been alive at the time, she unfortunately would have agreed with this sentiment, although still standing fast to her allegiance to women.)

Father Bouchard picked up on that slogan "The Chinese Must Go!" On Feb. 25, 1873, he delivered an obnoxious lecture, describing the Chinese as "pagan, vicious, immoral creatures,"

calling them "of low intellect" and accusing them of being "an idolatrous, vicious, corrupt, and pusillanimous race ….

"These pagan, these vicious, these immoral creatures, they are incapable of rising to the virtue that is inculcated by the religion of Jesus Christ, the world's Redeemer," he thundered.

"It is the white race we want!" (Cruel words coming from a priest whose ancestors also were of another race: the proud Delaware chiefs and warriors, mothers and wives.)

Father Bouchard called the white man "the head of all his kind in bone and muscle, in pluck and endurance, in intellect, a head and shoulder above all the other races …. The only race that has ever proved itself capable of self-government or really progressive civilization." [2]

Those were shocking words, but the Delaware Indian Watomika (Father Bouchard) apparently had identified himself completely with the white race. His skin was white, and his appearance was that of a white man. He refrained from publicly calling attention to his Indian heritage throughout his life. It was apparent that he wished to be taken for a white man; perhaps the temptations of white skin privileges were too strong for him.

As Father McGloin pointed out, "Although Bouchard never denied the facts concerning his Indian origin, it is abundantly clear from contemporary evidence that he did not stress this fact in his apostolate in the Far West." Father Bouchard was "seemingly obsessed with the thought of the inferiority of the Chinese race," McGloin added later. [3]

Unfortunately, Father Bouchard exhibited the same xenophobia as that of most of the Irish Catholics to whom he spoke. It was left to Protestant ministers to rebut his hurtful words.

"How should we treat the Chinese?" roared the Rev. George Morris of Dixon, California in response. "Let us remember that God 'hath made of one blood all nations of men to dwell on the face of the earth,' Leviticus 19:33-34.

"He [Father Bouchard] has dared to exclude one-third of the human race from all the benefits of the scheme of human redemption through Jesus Christ, our Lord!"

The San Francisco Methodist Preachers alliance passed a resolution calling for the Rev. O. Gibson to answer the lecture delivered by Father Bouchard on '*Chinaman or White Man, Which?*' Rev. Gibson was a missionary in China for ten years, and as superintendent of the Methodist Episcopal Chinese Mission in San Francisco was much beloved by his congregation and other Chinese in the city.

Ironically, only a few years after the Delaware Indian priest drew his last breath, a new bishop blessed the congregation of the church in which Father Bouchard had lambasted the Chinese. The bishop who spoke that Sunday, February 13, 1927, was another Jesuit: the Most Rev. Simon Tsur, *a Chinese priest*! By 1876, the number of Chinese immigrants had mushroomed to 116,000, many of them living in San Francisco.

The Lord always has the last laugh, which reminds me of the saying of Maya Angelou, the black poet and historian: "No human being can be more human than any other!"

Father Bouchard somehow survived the brouhaha caused by his beard and his views on women and Chinese, and in 1886, *The Nevada City Daily Transcript* wrote of him, "He is a grand looking old man (he was 63) with a long, white beard, and is loved and respected by people of all classes and denominations."

Father Bouchard's portrait was hung in the Church of St. Mary of the Mountains in Virginia City, Nevada's oldest church.

For thirty years, Father Bouchard had preached and taught the people of Upper and Lower California, Montana, Oregon, Nevada, and the territories beyond the Sierras, Washington Territory and British Columbia. He preached with equal fervor in cathedrals and in tiny wooden wilderness churches and while serving the mining camps of the Mother Lode and Comstock Lode.

In his book, *Indian and White in the Northwest, a History of Catholicity in Montana,* Father Lawrence B. Palladino, S.J., wrote: "Shortly after the sad event just recorded [the death of a pastor] Father James Bouchard, so well known all over the Pacific Coast as a zealous missioner and eloquent speaker, arrived in Helena [Montana], having come at the invitation of the Rt. Rev. Bishop for the purpose of giving retreats and missions throughout the Diocese.

"He commenced his apostolic labors by opening July 4 a ten-day mission in the Cathedral. He then passed to other places, spending two months and a half in this ministry and meeting…. He returned a year after and spent several weeks among our people reaping, with God's blessing, no less fruit from his preaching than he had on the previous occasion." [4]

(Father Palladino celebrated the first Mass in the Catholic Church in Livingston, Montana in 1883. My first newspaper job at the age of 20 was as a reporter for the *Livingston Enterprise*, and I used to attend daily Mass at Livingston's humble but lovely church.)

When Father Bouchard preached at the dedication of the church in Chico, California in 1872, the *Marysville Weekly Appeal* described his sermon as "one of the best of this talented orator's efforts; the church was filled to repletion [sic]."

Nearly a century later, my youngest brother, David, would be a rancher in the town of Chico, where Father Bouchard also had led numerous missions. In 1888, a year before his death, the indefatigable priest was still on the road, preaching in Sonora, California, where the local newspaper noted that the Jesuit priest was known thereabouts for his "elegant language, glowing eloquence and unsurpassed oratory."

After Father Bouchard's death at the young age of sixty-six on Dec. 27, 1889, the Most Rev. Archbishop Patrick W. Riordan, the second archbishop of San Francisco, declared: "To *no* man in all the West is the Church of God more beholden than to Father James Bouchard of the Society of Jesus. He kept the faith in the mining districts; he sustained the dignity of God's Holy Church in the midst of ignorance and misunderstanding, and everywhere he championed her rights. My debt to him, and I speak for my brother Bishops, is incalculable." [4]

Father Bouchard, the missioner of the Pacific Coast who grew up in a Kansas wigwam, is buried in the Jesuit Cemetery at Santa Clara, California. His dear friend, Father Florentine Boudreaux, one of the Jesuits who accompanied him to California in 1861, summed up the best of his friend's life, I think, when he wrote:

"He certainly was a powerful and fascinating speaker. His language was choice and beautiful and that without any visible effort on his part to make it so. His lively faith, for which he was remarkable, made him unspeakably earnest and effective. He went straight to the hearts of poor sinners and made them return to God, and many Protestants placed themselves under instruction and were baptized." [5]

Watomika, the Indian boy who became the Jesuit priest Father Bouchard, and his French mother Marie would be immortalized in books and in an historic 40-foot mural, *Spiritus Magis*, painted by California artist Boris Koodrin. The mural was completed June 4, 2005 for the sesquicentennial (150th) anniversary of St. Ignatius College Prep School in San Francisco.

Father Bouchard had gathered up converts as easily as the wild flowers he picked as a Delaware boy for his French mother, Marie, who was adopted by the Comanche and named "Monotawan" by Buckongahelas before she married his son, Kistalwa.

He was not the first missionary priest to or from Kansas (Father Joseph Lutz, a diocesan priest of St. Louis, was the first to attempt resident missionary work in the territory, and Jesuits followed him), [6] but Father Bouchard became the most famous Native priest from Kansas.

1. Bouchard, *Biographical Sketch of Watomika*.

2. Strecker, *Church in Kansas*, p. 53.

3. Ibid, p. 54.

4. Ibid.

5. Killoren, *Come Blackrobe*, p. 182.

6. Wenzl, *Legacy of Faith*, p. 11.

9

Origin of the Lenni-Lenape

A Lenni-Lenape woman
Art by Dennis Ray Scott

Who were the ancestors of Father Bouchard—and the ancestors of my family as well? We know little about Watomika's French relatives, and much more about his Indian forefathers and mothers. Who were the Lenni-Lenape, and who came and went before them thousands of years ago?

Scientists have decided that our Planet Earth is 4.6 billion years old. But the first true settlers in northeastern North America did not arrive until quite recently: at least 20,000 years ago. (Some archeologists believe it was as long ago as 100,000 years.)

The immediate ancestors of the Jesuit priest Bouchard were known as the Lenni-Lenape (the People), approximately 200,000 of them who made their homes on the central eastern seaboard. The People lived there for thousands of years before "the white skins," the Europeans, arrived in the Land of the Lenape, "Lenapehoking," which came to be called the Delaware River Valley.

At one time, the Algonquian-speaking nations occupied territory covering nearly one-third of the North American continent. Ten to twenty million American Indians populated the country north of Mexico when Europeans arrived.

Delaware Chief Charles Journeycake, a Baptist minister in Oklahoma and grandson of Buckongahelas, had his own version of the origin of the three races of people known to his Indian ancestors:

"In the beginning, the Great Spirit created three men and placed them on the earth. As they were all made in the image of God, they were all *white*," Charles declared, as related by Norman Wood in his book *Lives of Famous Indian Chiefs.*

God, wishing to test the three men, sent them on a journey that led to a wide and muddy stream, Charles maintained.

"Here two of the men hesitated, but the third plunged bravely in and made for the opposite bank. Seeing that the stream was sufficiently shallow to wade, the others followed … When the first man reached the further shore he was still *white*, being only slightly discolored by the muddy water. The second man came out *red or copper-colored*, while the last, crossing behind the others after the stream was thoroughly stirred up, came out *black*."

According to Charles, the men found three packages on the opposite shore. The *black man* chose the largest, which contained a shovel, spade and hoe.

"The *red man* chose the next largest, which contained a tomahawk, bow and quiver of arrows; this left the smallest for the *white man*, and behold it contained a book, pen, ink-horn and paper; and as the pen is mightier than the tomahawk or spade, it indicated that *he should rule over both the red and black man*." [1]

Charles' story would be frowned upon today, especially in light of the fact that the origin of the *entire* human race has been traced to Eastern Africa around Ethiopia.

James Fenimore Cooper, born in 1789, had a different viewpoint. In the preface to his book *The Last of the Mohicans*, published in 1826, he declared: "It is generally believed that the aborigines of the American continent have an Asiatic origin…. The color of the Indian, the writer believes, is peculiar to himself; and while his cheekbones have a very striking indication of a Tartar origin, his eyes have not. Climate may have had great influence on the former, but it is difficult to see how it can have produced the substantial difference which exists in the latter."

Cooper had another theory linking American Indians to Asians:

"The imagery of the Indian, both in his poetry and his oratory, is Oriental…. He draws his metaphors from the clouds, the seasons, the bird, the beasts, and the vegetable world…. The North American Indian clothes his ideas in a dress which is different from that of the African, and is Oriental in itself. His language has the richness and sententious fullness of the Chinese." [2]

The Indian Chief Pleasant Porter came closer to the truth in 1906.

"Pleasant Porter, the wise old mixed-blood chief of the Creeks, made a thoughtful analysis to a committee of the United States Senate," Angie Debo wrote in her *History of the Indians of the United States*.

"It is a complex problem, gentlemen…." Porter said. "You are the evolution of thousands of years, perhaps…. We both probably started at the same point, but our paths diverged, and the influences to which we were subjected varied, and we are the result." [3]

Chief Porter's remarks sounded as if he had been reading Darwin's *Origin of Species*, published in 1859.

Archaeologist-paleontologist Louis Leakey, who with his British parents grew up in East Africa, was convinced that *Homo Sapiens* began in Africa nearly two million years ago. His wife, Mary, discovered a skull, "Zing," at the Olduvai Gorge in Tanzania, Africa in 1959. This fossilized skull later was dated to be 1.75 million years old. In 1964 the Leakeys found another Tanzanian skull, Homo habilis, a species of the genus Homo that had a larger brain capacity and was estimated to have lived 2.3 to 1.4 million years ago. With his long gangly arms, Homo habilis appeared less like modern humans than Homo erectus skulls, which were discovered in 1891 on the Indonesian island of Java and in 1961 in Chad, Africa. Other such skulls were found in Europe, Vietnam, and China, proving that Homo erectus was a world traveler.

Louis Leakey believed that the ancestors of American Indians began trickling onto the North American continent 100,000 years ago.

According to the recent *Out of Africa Evolutionary Theory*, small groups of people began to travel out of the continent to Australia 50,000 years ago. Ice Age climatic changes had reduced their wildlife sources of food and created deserts from formerly lush African lands. Population geneticist and anthropologist Dr. Spencer Wells, author of *The Journey of Man* and *Deep Ancestry: inside the Genographic Project*, has traced the DNA of the nearly seven billion people living today to a common African ancestor, "Mitochondrial Eve."

"This Eve is the only female who has descendants who are now living in the present day," reported Wells, director of the *Genographic Project*, the largest genetic study of human migration ever. [4]

Wells followed the mitochrondrial DNA (mtDNA traces the maternal line of ancestry) of Eve's descendants who abandoned Africa in the first migration some 50,000 years ago, traveling along the coasts of Arabia, India, and Southeast Asia into Australia.

Other African descendants of "Eve" (including my earliest ancestral grandmother to whom Wells traced my mtDNA through the National Geographic Genographic Study in 2006) left East Africa from the area of present-day Ethiopia in a second migration 45,000 years ago. Their descendants spread across Eurasia (the large land mass that comprises Asia and Europe) for thousands of years before moving on to Siberia, Alaska, Canada, and the Americas. Archeologists unearthed the bones of sheep in the foothills of the Zagros Mountains that stretch across Iran and Iraq 9,000 years before Christ was born.

Our African Many Greats-Grandmother

"We all have an African great-great … grandmother who lived approximately 150,000 years ago," Wells explained in *The Journey of Man, a Genetic Odyssey*. [5]

Mitochrondrial Eve represents the root of the human family tree. Wells also has traced the presence of the Y-chromosome marker, M60, which is passed from father to son, to 60,000 years ago in Africa. The male ancestor of most western Europeans and American Indians–traced through the Y-chromosome--was a man who lived in Central Asia around 40,000 years ago.

"From here his descendants moved westward into Europe and eastward until they encountered Beringia and ultimately the New World," Wells wrote. "It is poignant to consider that when Columbus encountered Native Americans on his 1492 voyage, he was reuniting two branches of the human family tree that shared the same great-great- … grandfather on the steppes of Asia 40,000 years before." [6]

Doug Wallace, a geneticist, has focused on the origins of American Indians, using the mtDNA of women as a tool to track the origin of the first Americans back to particular populations in Asia. The first major publication of this work, in 1992 with Antonio Torroni, showed that Native Americans could be divided into at least two waves of migration.

"The earliest migration led to the settlement of both North and South America, while the latter wave of migration left genetic traces only in North America…. The results confirmed that Native Americans and north-east Asians shared a recent common mitochrondrial ancestry." [7]

In a 1996 study by Peter Underhill, a single nucleotide change on the Y-chromosome (M3) in men was found to be common throughout the Americas. More than ninety per cent of South and Central Americans examined were M3, as were fifty per cent of North Americans. M3, however, is not found in Asia. Later studies by Fabricio Santos and Chris Tyler-Smith at Oxford and Tanya Karafet and Mike Hammer at the University of Arizona showed independently that the ancestor of M3 was defined by a marker named 92R7, present in populations throughout Eurasia and distributed from Europe to India.

This finding pinpointed Siberia as the source population for some American Indians. And while the ancestors of modern Europeans entered Eurasia within the past 40,000 years, Wells believes the haplogroup Q clan from Asia entered the Americas only 20,000 years ago.

According to Wells, evidence is emerging from the genetic analysis of American Indians that the Siberian clan emigrated from southern to eastern Siberia within the past 20,000 years. Ice blocked a mass migration out of Alaska from 15,000 to 25,000 years ago, yet a small number of people managed to move through the frozen mass to North America, where they lived south of the ice sheets 11,500 years ago. The Laurentide ice sheet--two miles thick in some areas–covered most of eastern Alaska, northern Canada, and northern North America, stretching for five million miles 20,000 years ago, reaching as far south as present day New York City and Chicago.

The Siberians of 20,000 years ago would have been barred from southward expansion by this continuous sheet of ice. It was only as the Ice Age began to abate around 15,000 years ago that it would have been possible to flee a freezing world and enter the warmer, more pleasant North American plains via an 'ice-free corridor' that some palaeoclimatologists believe ran along the eastern edge of the Rocky Mountains.

The long treks of hunters in pursuit of giant mammoths, musk ox, and herds of caribou began during periods when the Ice Age glaciers caused sea levels to drop as much as 300 feet, allowing a land bridge to appear. It was around 15,000 years ago that grizzlies first lumbered into North America from Siberia. The aborigines–who were partial to bruin meat--must have followed close behind as Asians reached North America by traversing the 620-mile wide Beringia land bridge over the Bering Strait from northeastern Siberia into Alaska. Some anthropologists think Asians lived on the land bridge until it was submerged under water when the glaciers began to melt.

Other anthropologists believe the Polynesians, the Irish, and even the Jews found their way to the Americas hundreds, perhaps thousands, of years before Columbus. We do know that "Grains have been found dating back some 25,000 years in the land that is now France. Some have been found in the United States dating back 10,000 years. In the prehistoric collections of the British Museum there are exhibits of peas, beans, and even cakes made of barley and millet." [8]

And we mustn't forget Leif Erickson, the first known European to visit North America 500 years before Columbus. Small numbers of aborigines from Asia settled in Canada, and believed that their ancestors had been animals as well as men, so they carved totem poles with figures of people and animals. (Some Canadian tribes ate humans, but fortunately, people around the world switched from hunting animals or each other to foraging for food and then on to agriculture some 10,000 to 7,000 years ago.)

The Lenape ancestors of Father Bouchard and his grandfather Buckongahelas migrated from Canada, but their future did not bode well. Jay Wertz, author of *The Native American Experience*, explained: "The story of the Delaware (the name is completely European in origin) is a sad one. Battled into submission by the Iroquois Confederacy and swindled in land dealings with colonists, they were also one of the tribes hardest hit by European diseases." [9]

1. Wood, *Lives of Famous Indian Chiefs*, p. 676.

2. Cooper, *Last of the Mohicans*, p. xxvii.

3. Debo, *History of the Indians*, p. 6.

4. *Genographic Project*, National Geographic, Genetic History, p. 3.

5. Wells, *Journey of Man, a Genetic Odyssey*, p. 33.

6. Wells, *Deep Ancestry –Inside the Genographic Project*, pp. 101-102.

7. Wells, *Journey of Man*, p. 137.

8. Standard, *Our Daily Bread*, p. ix.

9. Wertz, *Native American Experience*, p. 9.

10

Family of Buckongahelas

Buckongahelas, the grandfather of Watomika (Father Bouchard), was born in western Ohio, the son of the Delaware War Chief Wendocolla, meaning "one employed as an important messenger." The Buck's mother was a Delaware woman, a daughter of the famous Chief Netawatwees of the Turtle or Unami Clan.

Netawatwees was the son of a Chief Tamanend of Canada, and his mother the daughter of Chief Owechela Weheeland, brother of the famous Chief Taminent or Tamened (named "Tamany" by whites), who signed the treaty with William Penn.

Born about 1686 in the Delaware Valley, Netawatwees signed the treaty of Conestoga in 1718. He also was known as "King Newcomer," despite the fact that most tribes detested the label "king" that was foisted onto chiefs by Europeans who thought that all leaders of distinction must bear the title.

The Buck's grandfather, the Principal Chief Netawatwees or Skilled Advisor," was the founder of the largest Lenape town in Ohio Territory, Gekelmukpechunk ('the water that is always still'). Inhabited by 700 people, the village stretched a mile and a half along the south bank of the Tuscarawas River. Gekelmukpechunk became the site of the present day Newcomerstown, which derived its name from Netawatwees, who became principal chief of his people after 1758.

Netawatwees and his people were forced from Pennsylvania into Ohio, and settled on the Cayuga River. He died in Pittsburgh, Pennsylvania in 1776, and was succeeded by White Eyes.

Buckongahelas married the daughter of the notorious Delaware War Chief Captain Pipe, whose Delaware name was Hopocan (tobacco pipe). He was the nephew of Chief Custaloga, who in his old age nominated Pipe as his successor as chief in 1773. Chief Buckongahelas spent many happy hours hunting in the forests of West Virginia, until his son was murdered there. He and his people lived in a sleepy Delaware village with a *human* scarecrow wildly painted and perched on a wooden platform to wave away hungry birds swooping down upon a cornfield.

When the great chief left his hut, a dozen dogs came running, squealing and whining to join him. The Lenape kept hordes of dogs– probably the first animal ever domesticated as long ago as 10,000 B.C. They loved their dogs as pets, and unlike some other tribes, didn't eat dog unless in dire danger of starvation.

The Buck and his family would stoop to crawl inside the small opening of a circular domed hut covered with birch bark. The living quarters of The Buck and his family would have been dampish and smelled of the smoke that twisted its way to the top of the hut to escape through a large hole. For religious ceremonies and meetings, the Delaware met in a large wooden longhouse.

A Delaware Indian (Lenni Lenape) long-house board given to the author by her husband, David Scott Myers.

The tawny young men of the family, decorated with tattoos, squatted on mats of woven cornhusks against one wall. The head of each male was shaved, except for a lock of hair on top where two feathers were attached. Their bodies were streaked with red ocher and white clay, and they wore nothing but breechclouts and moccasins, whether the weather was warm or chilly.

They were three of the four sons of Chief Buckongahelas: Mahonegon ("Running Wind"), Kistalwa, and Whapakong. A fourth son, Soloman, would be born later.

The three brothers and their two sisters set aside their morning bowls of boiled mush with maple syrup when their father entered. The family rose to greet Chief Buckongahelas with warm hugs from the women and much jolly back-slapping from the sons.

Chief Journeycake's two unnamed daughters included my family's ancestor, whom I have named Little Leaf. I imagine her as being small-boned and delicate, as are all the women in our family. Her cheekbones and eyelids would have been rouged with berry juice as red as the morning fire that scattered chill from the hut, her hair as dark as a moonless night. Perhaps she was as striking as my proud grandmother, Edna, also a descendant of The Buck, or maybe she very much resembled my lovely daughter, Anne.

The mother of this brood may have been heavy-set and only an inch or so shorter than her husband, Buckongahelas. The Delaware were taller than Europeans, though usually not as lofty as their ancestors, the Adena Indians, who occupied the Ohio Valley 2,200 years earlier. Adena men were more than seven feet tall; their women stood at least six feet from the ground. But even the Adena were not as tall as some Tallegewi or Tsalagi (Cherokee), who were giants and early enemies of the Lenape.

The face of the Buck's wife would have been streaked with red ocher (the white men's label "redskins" first referred to the Lenape). She probably wore a necklace of dyed porcupine quills–and an obvious air of authority. Perhaps she moved slowly (like many middle-aged and older Indian women hobbled with arthritis) to stand beside her petite daughter.

I can imagine the mother telling the story of her daughter's name: "When this daughter was born, the wind was high, and it blew a small leaf into our presence. My daughter was cradled in my arms, but she reached up and snatched the leaf from the air as it twirled past her. We named her 'Little Leaf' at that moment."

The wife of Chief Buckongahelas was the daughter of Chief Pipe, nicknamed "Hopacan" or "Tobacco Pipe," a war chief of the Delaware in Ohio and a captain of the Wolf clan. His Delaware name was Konieschquanoheel, "maker of daylight," and he led the pro-English faction of the Delaware against the colonists and the Continental Congress in the Revolutionary War.

Chief Pipe would present American scalps to the British at Detroit, although he later would do a confusing about-face and become a signer of a treaty with the Americans on Sept. 17, 1778. Buckongahelas also would haul a pole hanging with scalps to Detroit, proof of his success in battle against the white Americans, one of whom who had murdered his teenage son.

11

Lobes, Lips, and Nose Bangles

Among the most prominent of the Delaware leaders was War Chief Buckongahelas, "also spelled Pachgantschihlas, 'One whose movements are certain,'" historian C. A. Weslager wrote in his book *Delaware Indian Westward Migration*. [1]

Both of the ear lobes of Buckongahelas stretched down to his shoulder, his only somewhat alarming feature. Weslager wrote that "Buckongahelas had a heavy piece of lead decorating each lobe, which caused the skin tissue to stretch so far he could put it in his mouth." [2]

In his book, *The Middle Ground,* author Richard White also described the peculiar ears of Grandfather Buck, noting "Already of 'venerable appearance,' his

War Chief Buckongahelas Journeycake.
Art by David Roy Scott

appearance nonetheless shocked whites unused to Algonquian customs.

"Buckongahelas had long drooping ear lobes created from the Algonquian custom of piercing the ear and decorating the lobe with rings. The weight gradually caused the lobe to stretch until eventually it reached the shoulders. When listening attentively, Buckongahelas had the habit of sucking on his ear lobe." [3]

This nibbling on his ear caused one white officer who met him to voice his opinion that

65

Buckongahelas was "strange." Yet another strange face could be seen on his father, Chief Wendocolla, upon whose *lower lip* a sea lizard had been tattooed. The Buck's close friend, the Miami Chief Little Turtle, was known for the heavy silver bangles that dangled from his ears *and* from his nose. And another of the Buck's friends, Chief Blue Jacket, had large rings in his ears and his nose.

Shawnee Chief Blue Jacket

Kuki Gallmann, author of *"I Dreamed of Africa,"* has spent the majority of her life in Kenya. She tells the story of an ancient native woman she met, an expert in herbal medicine: "Many brass rings, discoloured by age, dangled from the elongated lobes and sides of her ears.... Her skull was shaven along the sides in the traditional way, leaving a crown of long, curly hair in tight ringlets, like a main on the top of her head." [4]

Historians decided that the face of The Buck resembled the young Benjamin Franklin. "Despite his somewhat fearsome appearance …, Buckongahelas was normally a mild-mannered and affable man," author John Sugden wrote. [5]

Buckongahelas also was known as Buckongahela, Buckongohanon "Giver of Presents," Petchnanalas "a fulfiller," Pachantschihilas or Pachgantschilias "One who succeeds in all he undertakes," and as Chief Journeycake.

It was not unusual for all Indians, especially warriors, to adopt many names, and white men seldom spelled an Indian's name the same way twice. The Delaware rarely went by surnames until the late 18th and early 19th centuries. As a boy, Grandfather Buck had been given the name "Journeycake" by his family, but he was widely known as Buckongahelas or simply "The Buck."

The Lenape were "the Real People" whom other Algonquian tribes believed were their family of origin. The Lenape were considered "the Grandfathers" because of their leaders' wisdom and reputation as peacemakers who were called to settle disputes among 35 to 40 different tribes in the great councils of the Algonquians.

Buckongahelas was a sachem (a clan leader) of the Wolf ("Took-seat") Clan of the Lenni

Lenape, re-named by the English as the Delaware Nation. The Lenape at that time were composed of three clans, which were groups of families who claimed common ancestors.

Delaware, Ruby A. Cranor, in 1974 wrote in her book *Talking Tombstones* that "Charles Elkhair was a member of the Turkey or *Pale* Clan within the Delaware Tribe ....") [6]

Robert S. Grumet further explained in *The Lenapes*, "It has been widely thought that the Lenapes were divided into only three tribal clans ever since the Rev. John (Johann) Gottlieb Heckewelder, a Moravian missionary who lived among them from 1754 to 1812, confused three Lenape tribal names with what are believed to have been their principal matrilineages."

"Thus, all 'Unamis' living along the Delaware River were thought to have belonged to the Turtle clan, all 'Wunalachticos' of the seacoast to the Turkey clan, and all 'Monsys' of the highlands to the Wolf clan. Today, most scholars agree that these names are most commonly regarded as only three of a much larger number of now-extinct matrilineages." [7]

The Lenni Lenape tribe originally consisted of three sub-divisions, the Unami or Turtle, the Minsi or Wolf, and the Unalachigo or Turkey Clans, according to Roberta Campbell Lawson, a Delaware. Born in 1878 in Indian Territory that would become Oklahoma, Larson was a granddaughter of the Rev. Charles Journeycake, one of the grandsons of Buckongahelas.

"Remote tradition tells of a fourth sub-division, the Crow, which has been out of existence for many years," reported Roberta, who married banker Eugene B. Lawson of Nowata and Tulsa, Oklahoma. (She was one of three major donors to the permanent collection of American Indian Art at Philbrook Museum of Art in Tulsa.)

"It seems that members of this division or clan could never rise in rank above that of a council fire lighter," Roberta wrote. "Perhaps a socialistic reform wave swept the country at that remote period and caused the elimination of the menial clan." [8]

When she was a child, Roberta came upon a little girl beside the road where the girl's impoverished family was camping. Roberta, whose parents were prosperous, asked the child why she didn't attend Sunday School. "Because I have no shoes," the girl replied with shame and embarrassment. Roberta immediately removed her own shoes and handed them to the girl. A barefoot Roberta trudged back to her surprised mother. Such were the kind hearts of even the children of the Delaware Tribe. [9] Roberta was inducted into the Oklahoma Hall of Fame in 1935. From her grandfather, she learned Indian legends and chants that she presented on stage and in music until her death in 1940.

Roberta's kindness to the girl with no shoes reminds me of the day that Chief Idquoqueywon greeted William Penn by extending his "heart-hand," *his left hand*, to shake hands with the famous Quaker, who became a "forever friend" of the Delaware.

"It is believed that shaking hands is an Indian custom, but before their knowledge of the whites they used the left hand," Weslager explained. "In the Engomween, or worshipping assembly, where ancient customs are said to prevail altogether, they always use the left hand." [10]

Buckongahelas extended his "heart-hand" to whites when they first appeared in Virginia, but the treachery of one white man broke the chief's heart. Still, in his later years, The Buck strove to further the welfare of his clan by seeking peace between the Delaware Nation and the United States.

1. Weslager, *Delaware Indian Westward Migration,* p. 42.

2. White, *Middle Ground,* p. 495.

3. Sugden, *Blue Jacket,* p. 93.

4. Gallmann, *I Dreamed of Africa,* p. 264.

5. Mitchell, *Indian Chief, Journeycake,* p. 8.

6. Cranor, *Talking Tombstones,* p. 12.

7. Grumet, *Lenapes,* pp. 15-16.

8. Lawson, *My Oklahoma,* p. 15.

9. Ibid.

10. Weslager, *Delaware Indians,* p. 498

12

By Land or By Sea?

The Lenni-Lenape believed that they were the first to colonize the continent that came to be called North America. They were certain they had existed on the northeastern corner of that vast land longer than any other Native People.

Some American Indians believe their ancestors originated in Australia and traveled by boat to South America, meandering into the southernmost parts of the continent. Others are convinced their forefathers and mothers followed a coastal sea route from the mainland of Asia. An American Indian DNA lineage has been traced to Europe, where the Solutrians lived in southwestern France and Spain 20,000 years ago.

The Clovis Culture in New Mexico, which dates from 10,800 to 11,200 B.C., long was thought to be the earliest evidence of humans in North America. There is speculation among anthropologists, however, that the Solutrians brought the Clovis spear point to America, and that Ice Age Europeans were among the first people to journey to America. A spear point at a pre-Clovis dig at Cactus Hill in southeast Virginia has been dated to circa 18,000 years ago (around the same time the Solutrian culture ended in Europe). There is even controversial evidence that the Vikings visited southern Oklahoma, and left behind a runic carving on Poteau Mountain near the town of Heavener.

Did the Vikings venture into Oklahoma, and leave these carvings as evidence of their visit?

The Younger Dryas minor Ice Age of bitter icy weather and heavy dust storms near the North American Great Lakes began about 10,900 to 12,000 years ago after the last great Ice Age. Perhaps caused by the impact of an enormous comet, the Younger Dryas brought about the extinction of many North American large mammals, including camels, mammoths, the giant short-faced bear, and numerous other species.

Some humans survived, but the impact event appeared at the end of the Clovis culture in northeastern North America. Surviving Natives must have fled west or south searching for more hospitable weather.

Indians living in the Americas between 13,000 to 10,000 B.C. (the end of the last Ice Age) are classified as Paleo Indians, whose remains in Florida date to 12,000 years ago. Their descendants hunted buffalo on the Great Plains and pushed them off cliffs in Colorado to kill them for food 8,000 years ago.

Regardless of their point of origin, the Lenape eventually migrated back to settle in the lush and undefiled river valley along the Middle Atlantic Coast, where after thousands of years, they were dispersed by hordes of white men.

"The most powerful Indian confederacy on the Middle Atlantic Coast was that of the Lenni Lenape, or Delawares," wrote Alvin M. Josephy, Jr., editor of *Indians*. [1]

According to writer Barry Pritzker, "The nations inhabiting the Northeast at about the time of the first European landings were for the most part divided among three language stocks: Algonquin, Iroquoian, and Siouan." [2]

The Eastern Tribes of the Middle Atlantic considered themselves older than the Plains Tribes and were known as the "Real People." American Indian tribes always had lived as separate nations on the vast North American continent, and the nearly 500 tribes never thought of themselves as one nation.

"The Lenni Lenape (Delaware), of whom William Penn wrote in his famous Account, were the most important tribe of the Algonquin-speaking Indians of the vast eastern North American woodlands...,´ noted John E. Pomfret in the foreword to the tercentenary edition of *William Penn's own Account of the Lenni Lenape or Delaware Indians*.

"The Lenni Lenape or 'original people,' about 8,000 in number when Penn arrived in 1682, held the territory from lower New York and Long Island to Maryland," Pomfret stated. [3]

The Lenape Nation was considered the "grandfather" of all the tribes who spoke different dialects of the Algonquin language group, the most widespread linguistic family in North America. The Algonquians made up the majority of the population along present-day Canadian and American shores of the western Great Lakes.

The Algonquian linguistic family in the Northeast Culture Area included the Lenape and their close friends, the Shawnee and Miami, as well as the Abenaki, Algonkin, Chippewa, Coree, Fox, Hatteras, Illinois, Kickapoo, Kitchigami, Machapunga, Mahican, Massachuset, Menominee, Mohegan, Ottawa, Potawatomi, Sac, Wampanoag, and several lesser known tribes.

Even some Great Plains tribes were included in the Algonquian linguistic family, including the Arapaho, Blackfoot, Cheyenne, and Gros Ventre. (The Arapaho and Cheyenne originally lived in present-day Minnesota and the Dakotas.) A few Sub-Arctic Culture Tribes, including the Cree, Montagnais and Naskapi, also spoke Algonquin dialects.

Snakes in the Grass

When Europeans first set foot on land that became the state of New York, the Algonquian and the Iroquoian were the two largest tribal groups, the Algonquian in the east and the Iroquoian in the remainder of the state.

The Iroquois were longtime fierce enemies of the Algonquian people, in whose language the word "Iroquois" means "snakes." (Perhaps that is where the derogatory term "snake in the grass" originated.)

"The Lenape … were part of a group of Algonkian speakers from North Carolina to New York," wrote Barry M. Pritzer.

"This central group of northeastern Algonkian Indians were referred to as 'grandfather' by other Algonkian tribes in recognition of its position as the group from which many local Algonkian tribes diverged." [4]

Early Lenni Lenape did not refer to themselves as "Indians." It was Christopher Columbus who named the Arawak whom he first encountered 'Los Indios' 200 years before the birth of Buckongahelas. The explorer for Spain mistakenly thought he had traversed a water route to India, but instead made his first landfall on an island in the Bahamas that he named *San Salvador.*

"It is generally thought that the Iroquoian tribes were more recent arrivals in the region than the Algonquians, and that they (the Iroquoian) probably migrated originally from the south…," author Carl Waldman noted.

"Both the Iroquois and Algonquians had strong tribal (or band) identities above and beyond the basic nuclear families, often living in palisaded villages. The Iroquois came to be known as the People of the Longhouse for their communal houses, whereas the Algonquians generally lived in wigwams." [5]

In *The Last of the Mohicans*, James Fenimore Cooper wrote that "In these pages, Lenni-Lenape, Lenope, Delawares, Wapanachki and Mohicans all mean the same people, or tribes of the same stock….

"The Mohicans were the possessors of the country first occupied by the Europeans in this portion of the continent. They were, consequently, the first dispossessed." [6]

The Delaware or Lenape, Cooper pointed out, "claimed to be the progenitors of that numerous people, who once were masters of most of the Eastern and Northern States of America, of whom the community of the Mohicans was an ancient and highly honored member." [7]

1. Josephy, Jr., *Indians*, p. 180.

2. Ibid, p. 163.

3. Myers, *William Penn's Own Account of the Lenni Lenape,* foreword, p. 7.

4. Pritzker, *Native American Encyclopedia,* p. 358.

5. Waldman, *Atlas of the North American Indian,* pp. 31, 32.

6. Cooper, *Last of the Mohicans*, p. vi.

7. Ibid, p. 182.

13

Iroquois, Jogues and Kateri

This painting of St. Kateri Tekakwitha is attributed to her friend Father Claude Chauchetiere, S.J., of Quebec, ca. 1685.

In the late 1500s, five Indian nations, the Seneca, Cayuga, Onondaga, Oneida, and Mohawk tribes, formed the feared and murderous Iroquois League. The confederation also was known as The Iroquois or the League of Five Nations. In 1722, the Tuscarora Indians would join, and the league then became the Six Nations.

"[The League was] founded in about 1570 by the Mohawk Indian Hiawatha and the Huron Indian Deganawida (the Peacemaker)," writer Carl Waldman explained.[1]

In vicious attacks, the Iroquois drove many tribes into the Ohio Valley between 1649 and the 1660s. The Algonquian family of the boy Wendocolla (aka Wewandochwalend), the father of Buckongahelas, was among those who fled from the fury of the Iroquois, who sought new lands for hunting animals for the mushrooming fur trade.

"Despite Algonquian predominance, which extended from the seacoast to the Mississippi River, these tribes faced a formidable foe in the Iroquois Confederacy …. whose homelands spread inland through the forests surrounding Lakes Ontario, Champlain, and George," explained editor James A. Maxwell.[2]

"The Six Nations have ever been a war-like people, unable to preserve peace," observed the Moravian missionary the Rev. David Zeisberger, who lived among the Iroquois before he began his ministry to the Delaware.

"There are few nations with whom they have not at some time had war. It is not too much for them to travel in parties five or six hundred miles into an enemy's country…. Had they not, with the captives taken, replaced those of their own numbers who had perished in the endless wars, they had, long ere this, died out."[3]

Cannibalism was known only among the Iroquois, Zeisberger further declared.

"The Iroquois, who inflicted hideous torture on their enemies, are depicted in fiction and folklore as cruel and vindictive," wrote Clyde F. Crews in his book *American & Catholic, a Popular History of Catholicism in the United States.*

"At the same time, the League of Five Nations was a great experiment in peaceful cooperation; Benjamin Franklin proposed it as the model for the union of the colonies when the constitution was being written." [4] (Franklin was intrigued by the organization of the Iroquois League–with representatives of each of its tribes at League councils. Franklin helped to draft the U.S. Constitution so that it would grant representation to each state in the U.S. Congress.)

After the Tuscarora joined the Iroquois League, the Six Nations ruled an even larger territory: present upper New York State, west to the St. Lawrence Valley and basins of Lakes Ontario and Erie.At the time of Kateri (Catherine) Tekakwitha's birth near Auriesville, New York (circa 1656), "The Mohawks were the fiercest [of the Five Iroquois nations]," a Kateri biographer, Marie Cecilia Buehrle, declared in her book *Kateri of the Mohawks.*

"The Oneidas lived to the left of them [the Mohawks, who resided at that time at Gandawague, the eastern gate to the Iroquois homeland]; then the Onondagas, who were at the center of the Federation …. The Cayugas lived beyond the Onondagas, and the Senecas, who bordered upon Niagara, guarded the western gate." [5]

Tekawitha (aka Takawita), grew up in upstate New York, the daughter of a Mohawk chief, Kenneronkwa (Beloved), and an Algonquin captive woman, Kahenta (Flower of the Prairie), who had converted to Catholicism.

When Tekakwitha was four-years-old, both of her parents and her younger brother died of smallpox. The pox disfigured Tekakwitha's face and diminished her eyesight, causing her to be nearly blind.. After her parents' death, she was adopted by her Mohawk uncle, the cruel Chief Iowerano. Her mother had been adopted into the tribe when its warriors captured her. Both mother and daughter had been appalled by the violence of the uncle's tribe.

"In the Mohawk village, drunkenness and loose living were the custom….," Buehrle explained. "Women, even children, participated in the torturing of enemies [on a scaffold in the center of the village] and fed upon their roasted flesh." [6]

The Jesuits converted Tekakwitha at the age of ten, and she was baptized a Roman Catholic at the age of twenty on Easter Sunday, April 18, 1676. At her baptism, she took the name *Kateri,* a Mohawk pronunciation of the French name *Catherine.* She left the Mohawks to serve a community of Christian Indians near Montreal. After years of weakening her frail body with severe penances for the terrible sins of her uncle and his people, Kateri died in 1680 at the young age of twenty-four.

Immediately following her death, the severe disfigurement of Kateri's face disappeared. Her face was reported "radiantly beautiful" by a priest, who witnessed her death and later painted a portrait of her. Her face was left uncovered until her burial so that all of the tribal members might witness her healing. Several miracles were attributed to her after her death. [7]

Kateri would be canonized in Rome by Pope Benedict XVI on October 21, 2012, becoming the first American Indian to be officially declared a saint by the Roman Catholic Church.

Isaac Jogues, a Predecessor in Sainthood

Only a few years before Kateri was born, "The first Jesuit name to be associated with the upper Great Lakes region is that of St. Isaac Jogues, who, in 1641, in company with Father Charles Raymbault, planted the cross at Sault St. Marie in what is now the state of Michigan…," the Jesuit historian Father Gilbert J. Garraghan wrote. [8]

Father Jogues experienced the merciless Huron in terrible ways. He was taken prisoner August 3, 1642, and after being tortured, he was carried to the Indian village of Ossernenon (where Kateri later lived), about forty miles above the present city of Albany. He remained there for thirteen months in slavery, but he finally experienced mercy.

"Women helped decide matters of war: To avenge the death of a husband or son, a matron could insist that her male kin wage war to bring back captives," Donna Lucey explained in her book *I Dwell in Possibility; Women Build a Nation, 1600-1920.*

"She could then decide the fate of those captured; she could either 'send them to the flames,' in the words of horrified Europeans, or adopt them into her own family." [9]

Father Jogues experienced the power and mercy of American Indian women when he was taken prisoner.

"Father Jogues, a captured Jesuit, had his finger cut off at the behest of one Iroquois woman, but was eventually given to another woman as a replacement for her dead brother…. She took him as her own…. treated him affectionately as a family member, tending to his finger and giving him clothes and a blanket."

After Father Jogues was rescued by the Dutch and returned to France, he revealed what had happened when he was given to the Indian woman.

"As soon as I entered her cabin, she began to sing a song of the dead, in which two of her daughters accompanied her…. I became aware that I was given in return for a dead man… causing the departed to come alive again in my person."

The fingers of Father Jogues' hands not only had been chopped off, but also burned and chewed off. Pope Urban VIII gave him permission to celebrate Mass with his mutilated hands. Despite all of his previous sufferings and like my Oklahoma friend Father Stanley Rother, who returned to his mission in Guatemala under death threats and was murdered July 28, 1981, Father Jogues went back to Canada in the spring of 1644 to negotiate peace with the Iroquois, following the same route over which he had been taken as a captive.

"In the autumn of 1646, near Auriesville, New York, he was seized by a band of Mohawks," writer Clyde F. Crews revealed. "Three months shy of his fortieth birthday, he was tomahawked to death. A lay companion, Jean de la Lande, died in the same way. Another lay assistant, physician Rene Goupil, had met a remarkably similar fate near the same locale in September, 1642." [10]

On October 18, 1646 (only ten years before Kateri was born), Father Jogues was decapitated, his head fixed on the Palisades, and his body thrown into the Mohawk River. Pope Pius XI canonized him June 29, 1930, along with seven other North American martyrs, including Lande and Goupil.

Kateri—who did penance for the tortures and deaths of Father Jogues and others--became the first American Indian recommended for canonization in 1844. Pope Pius XII declared Kateri venerable on January 3, 1943, and Pope John Paul II beatified her June 22, 1980, all steps in the canonization process. Kateri, known as the "lily of the Mohawks," is revered especially by the Native and Aboriginal Catholics of North America.

1. Waldman, *Dictionary of Native American Terminology*, p.111.

2. Maxwell, *America's Fascinating Indian Heritage,* p. 113.

3. Zeisberger, *History of Northern American Indians*, p. 27.

4. Crews, *American & Catholic*, p. 26.

5. Buehrle, *Kateri of the Mohawks*, p. 27.

6. Ibid, p. 16.

7. Garraghan, p. 2.

8. Ibid, p. 189.

9. Lucey, *I Dwell in Possibility*, pp. 22, 26.

10. Crews, *American & Catholic*, 26.

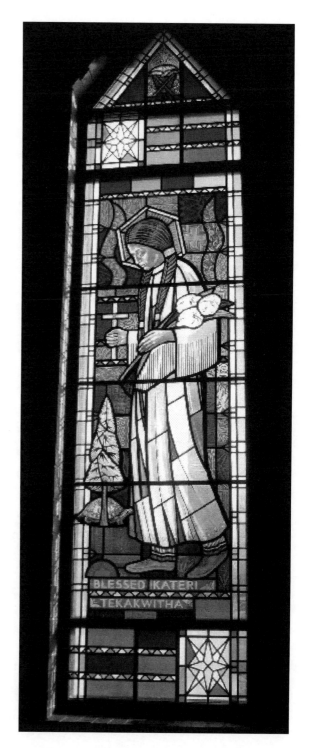

St. Kateri Tekakwitha was the daughter of a Mohawk chief and an Algonquin captive woman. The Mohawks were fierce enemies of the Lenape (Delaware). This stained glass window can be seen at the Mary Queen of Peace Chapel of Christ the King Church in Tulsa, Oklahoma.

Photo by Charlene Scott-Myers

14

A Sniff of Snappes

In 1609, prior to the birth of Kateri, Englishman Hendrik Hudson, on behalf of the Dutch government, had sailed up the Noord River for 150 miles "seeking the Northwest Passage to the Orient." [1]

Instead he encountered the Lenape Nation living near present day Catskill, New York. At that time, tribal bands dominated the Atlantic Coast region all the way from Newfoundland to below Albemarle Sound.

"When Hendrik Hudson anchored his ship, the *Half Moon*, off New York Island in 1609, the Delaware stood in great numbers to receive him, exclaiming, 'Behold! The gods have come to visit us!'" author Helen Hunt Jackson wrote in 1881. [2]

More than 200 years after Hudson's arrival in the New World, the aged Moravian missionary Heckewelder revealed in 1818:

"I at one time, in April, 1787, was astonished when I heard one of their orators, a great chief of the Delawares, Pachgantschilias [Buckongahelas], by name, go over this ground, recapitulating the most extraordinary events which had happened, and concluding in these words:

"'I admit that there are good white men, but they bear no proportion to the bad; the bad must be the strongest for they rule. They do what they please. They enslave those who are not of their color, although created by the same Great Spirit who created them…. I know the Long Knives. They are not to be trusted.'" [3]

Hudson piloted the **Half Moon** on the river he "discovered" that later would bear his name, and claimed the region for the Netherlands. While exploring the valley that also would be named for him, "He traded with bands of Algonquian Indians and brought the furs back to Europe." [4]

In the modern world, which offers consumers all kinds of natural and synthetic fabrics, "It is difficult to appreciate the obsession for furs that was manifest throughout Europe in the seventeenth century," historian Weslager wrote.

"No fabric could equal the warmth, wearability, and glistening beauty of natural furs that were widely in demand for both men and women's clothing. Persons of importance wore furs to display their rank and wealth, and kings and princes set the style by wearing robes of priceless white ermine." [5]

Europeans wanted "fur coats, muffs, wraps, and gloves" – and the soft feel of beaver fur for men's caps, especially after Hudson brought news of the abundance of furs in North America. Thus was born the Hudson Trading Company.

Hudson had sailed to shore in an Indian canoe with an old man who was chief of a tribe of forty men and seventeen women. They led Hudson to a circular oak bark house with a vaulted ceiling that contained a large amount of maize and beans. He and the chief sat upon two mats and were served food in red wooden bowls, including a pair of pigeons which had just been shot.

Pigeons were killed by the thousands in the mountainous regions of West Virginia where Buckongahelas lived in the 18th century, but in 1873, they deserted the region, flying southward in such great numbers that they darkened the sky for an hour over every town they passed.

Louise Erdrich, who is of Chippewa/German descent, has written about this extinct species of birds – *Ectopistes Migratorius*, in her charming book for children, *Grandmother's Pigeon*.

"These are passenger pigeons. Once upon a time, these birds were so abundant that they traveled in flocks that took three days to pass overhead, 300 million birds per hour.

"Their nesting colonies sometimes stretched forty miles long…. The lesson they teach is this – nature is both tough and fragile. Greed destroyed them. They were killed for food by the millions, and their nesting trees were burned. The last known pigeon, whose name was Martha, died in 1914 in the Cincinnati Zoo." [6]

Hudson, having consumed some of these pigeons and experienced the Indians' hospitality, concluded that the Natives were "very good people." When Hudson and his men prepared to leave, he noticed that the natives thought the white men's departure was caused by fear. The Indians then broke their arrows into pieces, and threw them into the fire as a gesture of peace.

As he would introduce Europeans to American Indian furs, it was Hudson who first introduced the Natives of North America to European liquor, serving them snappes.

At first, no Native, including the chiefs, would touch the stuff; they only sniffed it. But finally a man who was bravest drained the cup and fell into a stupor. The Indians thought he was dead, but when he emerged from his hangover, he was surprised by how sublime he felt under the influence. His brothers then were eager to partake of the strange liquid, and they also succumbed to it. The Indians named the place where they first tasted snappes Mannahattnik, also spelled as Manahachtanenk or Mannahattoe.

"They said the name Mannahattnik meant 'the place where we were all drunk'...," Oklahoma writer Angie Debo explained.

"The first taste of alcohol was more significant than anyone could have foreseen. The European had developed some immunity to its effects or restrain in its consumption through millenniums of use. To the Indian it was wholly ruinous. As tribe after tribe encountered it, it became a large factor in their history." [7]

The Dutch changed "Mannahattoe" into Manhattan, and a Dutchman, Peter Minuit, purchased the island in New York Harbor from the Lenape on May 6, 1626 for 60 gilders' ($24 or $72 in today's prices) worth of piddling trade goods: cloth, beads, and hatchets.

"He [William H. Seward] bought Alaska from the Russians [in 1867] for two cents an acre – a deal almost as fantastic as that of Peter Minuit who bought Manhattan Island for trinkets worth $24 ...," author Bruce Ramsey commented wryly. [8]

More than 300 years later, the esteemed writer Avram Davidson insisted on calling Manhattan "Mannahattoe," as testified by his friend Robert Silverberg, who received a letter from Davidson dated July 17, 1971, which stated:

"We – you and I – first met in an apt in Mannahatoe; but whose?"

"I quote this," Silverberg wrote in his foreword to *The Avram Davidson Treasury*, "to illustrate that Avram was capable of forgetting things occasionally too, but also to demonstrate certain notable idiosyncrasies of the man and of his style. Consider his use of the archaic term 'Mannahattoe' for 'Manhattan' – the original uncorrupted Native American name for that island in New York Harbor, which the Dutch twisted into the form used today, and which Avram, of course, knew, paying me the compliment of expecting that I would know it too. (I did)." [9]

More Bushy Beards

The Indians who met Hudson were intrigued by the white man's facial hair, as full-blood Natives rarely have beards or mustaches. A courageous Indian ran up to one of Hudson's officers and tugged at his bushy beard, which he expected would pull off the white man's face. When the beard remained steadfast, the Indian and his friends broke into surprised laughter.

The white men also introduced the Natives to guns and changed the name of the Lenni Lenape and their river, the Lenapehanna. In the white man's vocabulary, the Lenni Lenape came to be known as the Delaware Indians, and their river was titled the Delaware River. The new names were bestowed upon the Lenape (whether they liked it or not) and their river in honor of Thomas West, baron de la Warr, a governor of the Virginia colony from 1610 to 1611, who probably never even met any Lenapes.

France had founded trading posts in North America as early as 1600, and made friends and spouses of the Indians, in contrast to the English, who let the American Indians know from the beginning that they considered them inferior.

The State of Delaware also would be named for the Delaware, and would become the first of the thirteen original states to ratify the Constitution of the United States.

1. Athearn, *New World*, p. 46
2. Jackson, *Century of Dishonor*, p. 32.
3. Ibid.
4. Hirschfelder, *Native Americans,* p. 30.
5. Weslager, *Delaware Indians*, p. 104
6. Erdrich, *Grandmother's Pigeon*, p. 17.
7. Debo, *History of the Indians,* p. 43.
8. Ramsey, *Under All Is the Land*, p. 60.
9. Silverberg and Davis, *Avrfam Davidson Treasury*, p. 12.

15

Chief Tammany

Chief Netawatwees (aka "Newcomer") was one of the three sons of Chief Tamenend of Canada. The mother of Netawatwees was the daughter of the Lenape Chief Owechela Weheeland, brother of the famous Chief Tamany (aka Tameney or Tamine, called "Tamanny" by some whites).

"Contrary to popular belief, Tamany was not a king over *all* the Delawares, for in William Penn's time the Delawares did not have a single leader." [1]

Chief Tamany signed the first known land sale of land to William Penn by the Lenni Lenape or Delaware Indians on April 12, 1682, but the deed also was signed by three other chiefs, King Tangorus, King Swanpes (Swampisse), and King Hickoqueon.

The Delaware Indians also deeded Southern Bucks County in Pennsylvania to the Quaker William Penn on July 15, 1682, "the first of the Indian grants to him in that county, signed at the Falls of the Delaware, now Morrisville." [2]

Tammany Hall in New York was named for him, and Chief Tamanny was the uncle of Netawatwees.

The Walam Olum, a collection of pictographs which some Delaware believe to be a documented history of the Lenni Lenape, includes a fragment at the end of the book on the history of "the Linapis [sic] since abt [sic] 1600 when the Wallamolum [sic] closes." The fragment states that "Netawatwis became king of all the Nations in the West...." [3]

"This chief [Netawatwees] was born about 1677 and died in 1776 in Pittsburgh. He was chief of the Unami or Turtle division and consequently head chief of the tribe. He was the keeper of all contracts between his people and William Penn and other provincial officers." [4]

The Delaware Chief Wendacolla ("one who is brought this way") married a daughter of the illustrious Chief Netawatwees or Newcomer. Their son was Buckongahelas Journeycake, chief of the Delaware tribe in Ohio, West Virginia, and Indiana. Thus Buckongahelas was the grandson of Netawatwees ("skilled adviser") and the great-grandson of Weheeland, and a great-nephew of the famous "Chief Tammany," for whom Tammany Hall in New York was named.

Netawatwees was born about 1676. He signed the treaty of Conestoga in 1718, and he and his people were forced by the white skins from Pennsylvania into Ohio, settling on the Cayuga River. Netawatwees founded the largest Lenape town in Ohio Territory, Gekelmukpechunk ("the water that is always still"). Inhabited by 700 people, the village stretched a mile and a half along the south bank of the Tuscarawas River. Gekelmukpechunk became Delaware Nation's capitol and the site of the present day Newcomer's Town, which derived its name from Netawatwees.

"Lenapes living in scattered settlements throughout Ohio formed a nation under the leadership of powerful chiefs such as Shingas, Beaver, and Netawatwees…," Robert S. Grumet wrote in his book, *The Lenapes*.

"As an independent people, the Delawares sent their warriors east with Shawnees, Wyandots, and others to attack the English," explained Grumet. [5]

"Delaware war parties ambushed unwary travelers and struck isolated homesteads as far east as New Jersey. They killed hundreds of settlers. Many woman and children were taken back to Ohio as captives," J. C. McWorter recorded. [6]

Netawatwees, who became principal chief of his people after 1758, died at the age of 100 years in Pittsburgh, Pennsylvania in 1776. He was succeeded by the famed Chief White Eyes of the Turtle clan, a friend of George Washington who served as a colonel with the colonial army during the American Revolution in 1778.

By the 1770s, Chief Buckongahelas and his family were living during the hunting season in the western mountainous part of Virginia that eventually became West Virginia. One of his sons would be murdered by a white man while hunting in the area's lovely, lush forests.

Hunting Grounds of Buckongahelas

Several years after my dream, we strolled through the beautiful town of Buckhannon, the bubbling, curvaceous Buckhannon River, and the bountiful Buckhannon Valley with its lush forests that were named for my many-greats-grandfather.

The Buck welcomed early white settlers, the Pringle brothers and their friends, to his favorite hunting grounds in the heart of what later became north central West Virginia, among the foothills of the Appalachian Mountains.

Somewhere in the dark forest, the great horned owl issued its last hoot of the evening, but otherwise the fading twilight was silent. It was nearing Pooxit, "the time of the falling leaves," and Tachquoak (autumn) was nearly upon us, as it had been upon the Delaware people living nearby nearly 250 years ago.

We visited the beautiful town of Buckhannon, located along the Buckhannon River (the right fork of the Tygart River). The Buckhannon Valley is nestled in the heart of the foothills of the Allegheny Mountains. Here Buckongahelas and his men hunted for game, while his family resided in his village at Tygart Junction north of the Great Kanawha Valley.

In Buckhannon, the Upshur County Seat, we met the artist Ross Straight, who sculpted the town's powerful statue of Buckongahelas cradling his murdered son, Mahonegon. As a boy, Straight heard the story of Buckongahelas from his grandmother, whose family was among the original settlers in the area. He told us that two Delaware families still live nearby in the town of Philippi, and attended the dedication of the 650-pound statue of Buckongahelas and his son in Jawbone Park in Buckhannon in 2000.

West Virginia came into existence as a result of the Civil War. The early victory of the Union's General-in-Chief George B. McClellan at Rich Mountain in June, 1861 drove 4,500 Rebels back into the Shenandoah Valley. After that invasion, the folks in western Virginia decided they favored the Union Cause. West Virginia became *the only state to secede from the South's Confederacy.* Congress carved the new state from Virginia in 1863, as Charles Flato reported in his book *The Civil War.*[7] (Popular with his troops, but unpopular with Lincoln, the president removed McClellan from his command. McClellan unsuccessfully opposed Lincoln in the 1864 election.

The next day we stood in a dazzling, frost-covered meadow that sparkled in the first morning light like a million bright eyes. Before us was a thickly wooded area of silver-birch trees near the mouth of the Buckhannon River. The silence was heavy at first; then the air was choked with a chorus of birds' songs, the most melodious I had ever heard. A multitude of birds sang their trills with the brilliance of a coloratura. We listened in awe as thousands of winged creatures greeted the new day.

We began to walk, crunching the leaves beneath us. A younger and more vigorous Buckongahelas than the man who appeared in my dream would have hunted in these very woods. His muscles would have been strong, his face un-lined, his gaze friendly to all who looked upon him.

In that dark and ancient forest of the Buckhannon Valley that once was the favorite hunting grounds of Buckongahelas, it was a pleasure to see Rhododendrons that live only in the woods and to learn that black bears sometimes stroll along the mountain paths. (Like the bears of Colorado, the bears actually are brown in color, the only species of bruin found in that part of West Virginia.)

Before us was a thickly wooded space of silver-birch trees near the mouth of the shimmering Buckhannon River, "the waters of many bends." The river has been romantically described as "silently flowing with the sheen of molten silver beneath the arch of the overhanging trees." With its embarrassment of nature's riches, the valley was another Garden of Eden. When snows began to sprinkle the ground, Delaware men and their ancestors the Lenape would roam this pristine valley to hunt bear, deer, buffalo, elk, and smaller creatures for winter food.

When they returned home, the chief, his elders, and warriors gathered for council meetings in a large and long oval-shaped, domed hut about 40 feet in length and 20 feet in width. The council house or 'Big House'" was covered with bast (birch bark peeled off of trees in the summertime). The men sat inside on split logs during their councils. (My husband gifted me with a relic of an old Delaware Big House, a small piece of weathered wood that stood the strain of time and weather.)

Delaware wigwams were domed dwellings with a pole frame covered with cattails, reed mats, or bark from birch and elm trees. The wigwams were built over shallow pits, with earth piled around the bases to keep out the wind. In winter, heavy animal skins over the frame were a barrier to the biting cold.

Dozen of dogs hovered near the wigwams, waiting for scraps or a scratch behind their ears. The Lenape, I learned, had owned hordes of dogs–the first animal ever domesticated--as long ago as 10,000 B.C. Were the frisky mutts we saw scrambling over the hills during our visit descendants of the mutts of the Lenape?

1. Weslager, *Delaware Indians*, p.168.

2. Myers, *William Penn's Own Account of the Lenni Lenape*, p. 73.

3. Rafinesque, Walam Olum, p. 213.

4. Hodge, *Handbook of American Indians*, part 2, p. 58.

5. Grumet, *Lenapes*, p. 54.

6. McWhorter, J. C., *Scout of the Buckongehanon*, p. 73

7. Flato, *Civil War*, p. 32.

16

The Walking Purchase

William Penn, friend of the Delaware

In 1681, the English King Charles II nobly granted the Quaker religious reformer William Penn a large territory west of the Delaware River and north of Maryland, land that became the colony of Pennsylvania and now comprises most of the state of Pennsylvania.

The grant of land was made in lieu of payment of a debt of $38,400 owed to Penn's late father, Admiral Sir William Penn.

"During William Penn's humane administration of the affairs of Pennsylvania, the Delawares were his most devoted friends," author Helen Hunt Jackson observed. "They called him Mignon, or Elder Brother." [1]

The Delaware nickname for Penn was "Miquon" (quill or pen), but he was later known as "Onas, the Truth Teller," the name the Iroquois gave him. Penn, who arrived in the New World in 1682, was a good friend of the 8,000 Lenape who lived in lower New York, Long Island, and Maryland. He learned their dialects and walked among them without fear, weapons or guards. The deep sounds of the Delaware water drums always welcomed him.

Penn offered the Indians not only peace, but religious freedom. He was a just man who had been imprisoned in the Tower of London for his religious beliefs. He also vowed he would not steal land in the New World from its Native inhabitants, but rather purchase portions of land from the Indians to sell to the colonists.

"One of Penn's greatest achievements was in his fair dealings with the Indians. He held their loyalty for long years…. He sat in council with the Indians many times, and, in less than a year, he had mastered their language." [2]

Tamanend (the Affable)--sometimes called "Tamanen" and later "Tammany" by whites-- was referred to as "King Taminent" in an English record in 1692. (His brother Weheeland was our ancestor.) Lenape chiefs usually were required to be 50-years-old at that time.

Tamanend was the sachem (chief of a clan) who sold twenty thousand acres of land on Neshaminy Creek north of Philadelphia in Buck's County, Pennsylvania to Penn's cousin William Markham one month after Markham arrived in June, 1681. The chief signed his name as "Tamanen" on the deed. William Penn purchased land north of Philadelphia from Chief Tamanen and Chief Metamequan on June 23, 1683.

That same year in October, 200 Quaker converts from England, Ireland, and Wales embarked on the ships *John*, *Sarah*, and *Factor*, arriving in Delaware Bay two months later. Thirty more shiploads of immigrants arrived within a year. (Many ships carried the diseases of smallpox and cholera as extra passengers to Eastern ports in the late 1600s and early 1700s.)

Penn bestowed on the Indians many gifts of guns, hoes, blankets, beads, and articles of clothing. The pipe of peace that Penn smoked with Chief Tamanend was among a collection of Joe Bartles, a great-grandson of Buckongahelas. Bartles loaned the collection to the Oklahoma Historical Society.

The purchase was signed in the Friends Meeting House in Philadelphia. The chiefs had dinner with Penn and stayed overnight. They presented Penn with a wampum belt when he negotiated for Pennsylvania. The belt would last longer that the Indians' friendship with the Penn family. (Charles Journeycake, grandson of Buckongahelas, was said to own a belt identical to the one Penn received in 1683.)

Penn penned a letter that was read by an interpreter to the Delaware and other tribes: "I intend to order all things in such a manner that we may live in Love and Peace with one another. I have already taken care that none of my people will wrong you...." [3]

Chief Tamanend's response was gracious and cordial. More than a century later in 1817, the Rev. John Gottlieb Ernestus Heckewelder, a Moravian minister, wrote that Chief Tamanend was endowed with wisdom, virtue, prudence, charity, affability, meekness, hospitality, "every good and noble quality that a human being may possess."

Two hundred years later, the Democratic Party in New York City would name its headquarters "Tammany Hall" for this esteemed friend of William Penn. Tamanend died at age 97 in 1750.

The total Lenape population of the Delaware Valley was more than 20,000 when Tamanend was chief. (The Delaware Valley is the region on either side of the Delaware River. Ancestral lands stretched from southeastern Pennsylvania, central and southern New Jersey, and the area that became the state of Delaware. Each Lenape community had its own sachem, however, and Tamanend was principal chief of only a portion of the Lenape.

It was said that when Penn's Quakers or Society of Friends were nearby, the Indians could sleep in peace. The Truth Teller's peace lasted for more than 50 years, until his stepsons broke the peace. The great French philosopher, Voltaire, wrote that Penn's treaty was the only treaty between white men and Indians that was never sworn to and never broken.

On August 16, 1683, Penn had written a letter to members of the Free Society of Traders in London: "For their original (origin), I am ready to believe them (the Indians) of the Jewish race; I mean of the stock of the Ten Tribes…," Penn declared. [4]

For all their wanderings across country in the years ahead, the Lenape People indeed would become like the lost Tribe of Israel. By the year 1700, war and the white man's diseases of smallpox, measles, venereal diseases, diphtheria, and influenza had withered the Delaware Nation from a population of more than 20,000 to a mere 4,000 in number.

In the early 1700s, the Six Nations (the Iroquois) settled some of the Delaware and other tribes into Pennsylvania, where the Quaker Pennsylvania Assembly supported the Six Nations' domination of the Indians. Iroquoians usually lived in communal longhouses, while Algonquians preferred summer wigwams, with long houses serving as council or ceremonial buildings.

The Lenape began to move from the Delaware River Valley to the Susquehanna River around 1709. (Three hundred years later on April 19, 2011 in Pennsylvania, a natural gas well blew out, spewing 10,000 gallons of toxic wastewater into a tributary of the Susquehanna.[5]) Chief Owechela Weheeland, the great-great-grandfather of the un-born Buckongahelas, was among those who settled at the Susquehanna when its waters were flowing pure and undefiled. Wendocolla, who would father Buckongahelas circa 1720, eventually also bid farewell to his village on the Delaware River and followed the migration of the Lenape into Pennsylvania's Upper Susquehanna Valley, which was Iroquoian territory.

Death of Onas and Dire Consequences

After the death of Onas (William Penn) on July 30, 1718, his offspring cheated the Delaware out of much of their property in Pennsylvania. Penn had drafted a deed in 1686 stating that the northern boundary of land between Chester and Pennypack creeks could be determined by "as far as a man can go in one day and a half." But that deed was unsigned and the boundaries never set (although some historians record that Penn himself paced off the land for the day and a half and covered 30 miles). Penn set the deed aside, and the proposed transaction was forgotten.

Nineteen years after Penn's death, his stepson, Thomas, discovered the old agreement and determined to see it fulfilled. (Most of Penn's estate went not to William Penn, Jr., but instead to his half-brothers Thomas, John, and Richard. Thomas, a scheming scoundrel, acquired three-fourths of the family's assets, and became governor.)

Thomas and his brothers devised a scheme to cheat the Lenape and acquire more than thirty miles of land. The Delaware Chief Lapowinsa sat for his portrait by Gustavus Hesselius in 1735, and supposedly signed the "Walking Purchase" Treaty.

The year of the actual walk was 1737, nearly 20 years after William Penn passed to his heavenly reward.

"By cutting a path through the woods in advance, and using three fast walkers who had been specially trained and rehearsed for their mission – followed by horses carrying provisions – the whites began the walk, accompanied by two Indian observers," historian Weslager explained. [6]

The fastest runners to be found were persuaded to participate. The skilled walkers

WALKING PURCHASE
Starting here at sunrise, Sept. 19, 1737, Marshall, Yeates, and Jennings set out on the "Indian Walk." In one and a half days, Edward Marshall reached a point beyond present Mauch Chunk, some 65 miles to the north and west.

were Solomon Jennings, Edward Marshall, and James Yates, who lined up on the west bank of the Delaware River. The prize was five pounds sterling and 500 acres of land for the man who walked the fastest and the farthest. The Lenape would be required to sell all of the land covered in the race to the Pennsylvania Province.

As the sun rose on the morning of September 19, the three tall athletes began to walk. Actually, the trio took to trotting as fast as their long legs could carry them. When obstacles such as a river or a stream blocked their way, horses, also carrying provisions, were waiting to transport them swiftly to the other side.

By sunset of the first day, only one man, Edward Marshall, remained in the race. Yates had fainted or suffered a heart attack along the way. He died three days later. Jennings dropped out and blamed the race for his poor health the rest of his life.

By noon the next day, Marshall had covered 65 miles instead of the expected 30 miles. At the end of 18 hours, he too collapsed. He had reached the foothills of the Blue Mountain. The northern boundary had been established, and 1,200 square miles–twice the distance the Lenape had agreed to 50 years previously–would have to be sold to the whites.

Realizing the deceit that had perpetuated upon them, the Lenape were bitter. The stepsons of William Penn were not fair and honest as their step-father had been.

"You run, that's not fair, you was [sic] to walk!" grumbled one of the two Indian observers who accompanied the three runners.[7]

Twenty years after the Walking Purchase, Chief Teedyuscung, born 1700, (He Who Makes the Earth Tremble), denounced the transaction, muttering, "This very ground that is under me was taken from me by fraud…." The chief eventually moved his family to live with the Moravians at Gnadenhutten.

"Teedyuscung worked to preserve the lands for the Indians, and his group was active in fighting the English," explained W. C. Vanderwerth in his book on Indian oratory.

"Some sources say that jealousy of the leaders of the Six Nations figured in his death, which occurred on April 19, 1763. His cabin was destroyed by fire, with him inside it. It was thought he was murdered and then the cabin set on fire." [8]

By 1740, Thomas Penn had slashed into pieces the property acquired in the fraudulent walk, selling the lots to more than 100 white families, the beginning of a practice that would continue for the next century.

"In 1742, the last band of the tribe whose villages were at the junction of the Lehigh and Delaware Rivers (at present Easton, Pennsylvania) were forced to move to the Susquehanna, as a result of the infamous 'Walking Purchase' of 1737, through which the Delawares were fraudulently deprived of the last of their lands on the upper Delaware River." [9]

Buckongahelas was a young man of about twenty-two winters when the last of the Lenape left behind 1,200 square miles of their land. A year prior to the Delaware dispersion, another indigenous people, the Aleuts, also began to suffer.

Peter the Great of Russia sent explorer Vitus Bering seaward through Kamchatka in 1729. (The sea and strait he sailed still are named for Bering.) But in 1741, Bering charted a different course from the southeastern tip of Alaska along the Aleutian chain.

"His ship was driven ashore on an uninhabited island—his name is fixed on this also—of the Commander group, still belonging to Russia," writer Angie Debo explained.

"Here were found the web-toed, five-foot-long sea otters, bearers of the most beautiful fur in the world.

Russia's Peter the Great sent explorer Vitus Bering and others to rob the Aleuts of their furs. Thousands of the island people were murdered.

Bering and a number of his crew died there, but the survivors made their perilous journey back to Kamchatka. They carried nine hundred sea otter pelts, which brought eighty dollars apiece in the Chinese market."

Hordes of Russians rushed to the lucrative island chain, and from their first ship they netted furs worth a million dollars. Ten years later, a ship's cargo sold for nearly two and one-half million.

"They [the Russians] started at Bering Island, then moved east along the Aleutians, stripping each island as they passed," Debo added. "By the end of the French and Indian War, they had fur-gathering posts on the Alaska Peninsula."

The Aleuts were gentle, trusting folk, much like the Lenape had been before they were duped by the descendants of their friend, William Penn.

"The Russians treated them [the Aleuts] with unspeakable cruelty: They raped the women and held them as hostages until the men ransomed them with furs; they destroyed settlements and murdered people from sheer barbarity. It is estimated that the population when they came was 25,000; a count made in 1885 showed 3,892." [10]

Alarmed by the Russian advance, Spaniards sought to secure California from San Diego to San Francisco, where one day a Delaware Indian Catholic priest by the name of Father James Bouchard, S.J. (Watomika), grandson of Buckongahelas, would serve.

1. Jackson, *Century of Dishonor*, p. 33.

2. Myers, *William Penn,* pp. 8, 9.

3. Ibid, p. 62.

4. Ibid, p. 41.

5. Kelly, *National Wildlife*, p. 16.

6. Weslager, *Delaware Indians,* p. 189.

7. Ibid.

8. Vanderwerth, *Indian Oratory,* p. 12.

9. Weslager. *Delaware Indian Westward Migration*, p. 12.

10. Debo, *History of the Indians*, pp. 82, 83.

17

Wearing Women's Petticoats

As the feet of more Europeans touched the ground of the "New World," they deprived the Delaware of their lands east of the Alleghenies, just as Peter the Great had robbed the Aleutians. Many Lenape were pushed north from New York to Canada.

Others headed west around 1690 to the Eastern Ohio Valley, where Buckongahelas Journeycake was born around 1720 while the Lenape were still "wearing women's petticoats."

Penn had forbidden the sale of alcohol to Indians, but following his return to England and death in 1718, thousands of gallons of spirits were traded for trinkets to the Indians. No longer respecting the wishes of Penn as to the welfare of the indigenous people, white authorities convinced the Iroquois to conquer the Lenape.

The Iroquois of central and western New York (the confederacy of Five Nations or the Hodesaunee) was a deadly foe of all the Algonquian tribes. The league had been a thorn in the side of the Algonquian since its inception, and had subjugated northerly Lenape bands in the early 17th century. When joined by the Tuscaroras of North Carolina in 1722, the Six Nations boasted a population of some 16,000 Natives.

The old enemy of the Lenape attacked and defeated them when they lived in the Delaware Valley, invading as far south as Virginia and beyond the Ohio, claiming ownership of the Susquehanna Valley. Many Lenape were driven into the Ohio Valley, among them the father of Buckongahelas.

The Iroquois included the murderous Mohawk and brutal Seneca tribes and was so powerful that it lasted for two centuries. (Four so-called "kings" of the confederation paid a visit to London in 1710.)

Even prior to Penn's arrival in the New World, the league attempted to emasculate the Lenape men. They 'made women of them,' forbidding them to wage war and accusing them of 'wearing women's petticoats.' The Lenape were ordered to raise crops like their womenfolk, and no longer could they be warriors. This was a curse to Lenape men, who believed they had the right to defend their families and leave farming as the prerogative of the women.

"This is what the Indians call 'making them women,'" wrote Charles Thomson, director of the Quaker school in Philadelphia who was friendly to the Delaware.

Chief Teedyuskung, a one-time gypsy and basket maker, "gave Brother Onas (Penn) the kind of Delaware king that a succession of English governors had long sought. He maintained that the Delawares were now independent of the Six Nations, that … formerly we were accounted women, and employed only in women's business, but now they have made men of us…." [1]

The Six Nations insisted the Lenape were beholden to them because of their earlier defeat, and ordered them to pay tribute, but the Six Nations could not keep Lenape men from hunting, both for food and for profit.

By 1750, Wendocolla, aka Windaughala, the father of Buckongahelas, took his people down the Ohio River by boat and built a village at the mouth of the Little Scioto in Shawnee country. After 1750, most Southern Unami Delaware were to be found in the lower Allegheny River Valley and in the upper Ohio River valleys.

The respected Turtle Chief Netawatwees, a Unami Lenape, was born in 1678 in Pennsylvania. The grandfather of Buckongahelas, he had signed the treaty of Conestoga in 1718, and established his people at Gekelemukpechunk or Newcomer's Town in the early 1750s.

This is the face of Chief Netawatwees on a 26-foot-tall carving by Joe Frohnapfel that was dedicated on July 5, 2004 in Cuyahoga Falls, Ohio. The chief settled where the Schwebel Baking Company later was built.

Netawatwees was the recognized leader of the Delaware Nation, but was unacceptable to the Six Nations, who installed Shingas of the Turkey Clan to head the nation in June, 1752. Known as Shingas the Terrible, he had a reputation of extreme cruelty to his enemies, as opposed to Buckongahelas, who was known for fairness in his treatment of captured whites or Indians.

"Pennsylvania had offered a reward of 700 pieces of eight for any person who brought the scalp of Shingas the Terrible to Philadelphia, and Virginia also offered a reward of 'an Hundred Pistoles' for Shingas's death." [2]

In the fall of 1753, the governor of Virginia sent George Washington, only 21 at the time, to visit French forts in Pennsylvania and attempt to dissuade the French from further encroachment in that area and in Virginia. After dinner and too much wine, the French foolishly bragged of their intention to gain control of the entire Ohio Valley. In the spring of 1754, nearly a thousand heavily armed French soldiers and Canadian Indians floated down the Allegheny River under the command of Sieur de Contrecour. They attacked Virginia militiamen, and Major Washington was ordered to march against the French.

With the increase of hostilities in 1754, the Six Nations had second thoughts about "making the Delaware men women." The Iroquois needed the strength of the Delaware to make war, and issued a message to the governor of Pennsylvania stating that "The Six Nations have ordered their cousins the Delawares to lay aside their petticoats and clap on nothing but the breech clout."

"We are Men!"

Delaware warriors spread fear and death in eastern Pennsylvania, southern New York, and New Jersey, throwing back a strong warning to the Six Nations: "We are men, and are determined not to be ruled any longer by you as women...." [3]

The Six Nations got the message when the Delaware added, "Say no more to us on that Head lest we cut off your private Parts, and make Women of you, as you have done of us!"

The Delaware definitely had cast off their petticoats forever. No longer "wearing women's petticoats," the young Lenape men who dreamed of glory on the field of battle now found an outlet for their ambitions – and the position of war captain became a dramatically more significant one.

Buckongahelas, approximately thirty-years-old, would discover his destiny as one of the greatest war chiefs of his people.

The Rev. John Gottlieb Ernestus Heckewelder, a Moravian minister to the Delaware, wrote about their wisdom in his *Historical Account of the Indians*. Historian Charles McKnight in 1876 recorded Heckewelder's account of an event that happened a year earlier.

"'In the beginning,' he [Heckewelder] says, 'of the Summer of 1755, a most atrocious murder was unexpectedly committed by a party of Indians on fourteen white settlers, within five or six miles of Shamokin, Pa.

"The surviving whites, in their rage, determined to take their revenge by murdering a Delaware Indian who happened to be in those parts…. He was a great friend to the whites, was loved and esteemed by them, and in testimony of their regard, had received from them the name of Luke Holland, by which he was generally known.

"The Indian told the enraged settlers that the Delawares were not in any manner concerned in it, and that it was the act of some wicked Mingoes or Iroquois, whose custom it was to involve other nations in wars with each other by clandestinely committing murders….

"But all his representations were vain; he could not convince exasperated men whose minds were fully bent upon revenge. At last, he offered that if they would give him a party to accompany him, he would go with them in quest of the murderers, and was sure he could discover them by the prints of their feet and other marks well known to him, by which he would convince them that the real perpetrators of the crime belonged to the Six Nations."

Luke Holland did just that. He demonstrated to the white men where the murdering Indians had disturbed the rocks as they ran, had loosened leaves by dragging a blanket over the rocks, and numbered in eight by their footprints that he found. Finally approaching the enemy encampment, the surprised whites saw for themselves the scalps that had been taken, hanging up to dry.

"'See!' said Luke Holland to his astonished companions, 'There is the enemy! Not my nation, but Mingoes, as I truly tell you.'" [4]

1. Weslager, *Delaware Indians*, p. 233.

2. Ibid, p. 237.

3. Ibid, p. 236.

4. McKnight, *Our Western Border*, pp. 647, 648.

18

War Over Stolen Lands

The French and English went to war in July, 1755, killing each other for the vast lands in the Ohio Valley, lands that did not belong to either nation. In the midst of two foreign nations at war fighting over their homeland, the Delaware chose to become allies of the French, who had proven better friends than the English and usually fought only against the Fox Tribe.

"The French seem to possess a greater share of the good will of the Indians than the English, being regarded by the Indians as being more akin to themselves, probably because they enter more easily into the Indian manner of living and appear always good-humored," missionary Zeisberger wrote.

"Indians have more faith in the French than in other Europeans." [5]

Sir William Johnson

It was the Englishman Sir William Johnson, a negotiator for peace with the Lenape in 1756, who had officially removed the petticoats from the Lenape men, hoping that they would join the British in warring against the French.

"I do in the name of the Great King of England, your father, declare that henceforward you are to be considered as Men by all your Brethren, the English, and no longer as Women, and I hope that your Brethren of the Six Nations will take it into consideration, follow my example, and remove this invidious distinction which I shall recommend to them," Sir Johnson said. [6]

"We have already noted the wonderful success the French had for winning the hearts of the untutored redmen of the forest; it was as remarkable, in its way, as the genius of the English in repelling and alienating them," wrote historian Charles McKnight in 1876. "Thus the native population shrank back from before the English as from before an advancing pestilence...." [7]

Many Indians crossed over the Allegheny Mountains to Western Pennsylvania to fight the English along the frontier. Buckongahelas was among those warriors. In his mid-thirties, the young war chief cut his teeth on this war that raged for more than a decade. This war included the drunken Paxton Boys' slaughter of peaceful Christian Indians in Lancaster County, Pennsylvania in December, 1763.

Chief Netawatwees, "ye great man of the Unamie nation," (the grandfather of Buckongahelas) refused to sign a treaty with Colonel Henry Bouquet in 1763. (Bouquet was the officer who had been instructed to infect the Natives with smallpox.) In retaliation, Chief Netawatwees was captured and not restored as chief until peace later was established.

Bounties for Scalps of Adults and Children

The English army destroyed most of the remaining Lenape villages in Pennsylvania in the fall of 1764, a fearful year for Indians because one of Penn's descendants, John Penn, reinstated bounties for scalps of "enemy Indians."

Pennsylvania offered 130 pieces of eight for the scalps of Indian boys and girls under the age of ten; 134 pieces of eight for the scalps of Indian males over the age of ten; and 50 pieces of eight for the scalps of Indian females older than ten.

The Algonquian coalition of tribes had been driven from their ancestral homelands in Eastern Pennsylvania and split into several small bands. In 1768, those Lenape who had remained on the Susquehanna joined their kin in Western Pennsylvania. The Shawnee, whom the Delaware called their "little brothers," also were pushed westward with their "older brothers." The Shawnee settled in the southern part of Ohio, and established towns on the Lower Muskingum that were destroyed by Angus McDonald in Dunmore's War in 1774.

At the beginning of the American Revolution in 1775, many Delaware were living along the Tuscarawas River, a tributary to the Muskingum River, in the Ohio Valley.

The non-Christian Delaware population lived at Newcomer's Town during the early days of the Revolution. In 1775, Chief Windaughala ("council door"), father of Buckongahelas, lived at New Hundy. Buckongahelas and his father, Wendecolla (aka Windaughala), joined the Delaware faction that sided with the British, led at first by Captain Pipe and then by his son-in-law

Buckongahelas. Most of the Indians' trade now was with the British.

Count Grigory Potemkin

Buckongahelas and his father, Wendocolla, very nearly fought alongside the Russians in the American Revolution.

The British approached Count Grigory Potemkin--Catherine the Great's friend and political partner--in Moscow with an urgent request. In 1775, Britain's American colonies rebelled against London. Britain had the finest fleet in the world, but a poor army, so the British sought to obtain Russian troops to help fight the Americans.

By September 1775, the British desperately needed help from the Russians, and requested 20,000 infantry as soon as ships could sail the Baltic after the winter thaw.

General Count Peter Ivanovich had no intention of helping the British, so Sir Robert Gunning, the English envoy, approached Potemkin. Potemkin was interested, but Catherine, the Empress of Russia (who actually was of German birth), refused. Catherine, who admired Peter the Great's reforms of Russia, had her hands full bringing her own new reforms to the vast country over which she ruled.

The disappointed British then hired mercenaries from the army of Hesse, where Frederick II ruled from 1760-1785. He rejuvenated the treasury of his poverty-stricken nation by loaning 19,000 soldiers, known as Hessians, to Great Britain to fight during the American Revolutionary War, 1776-1783.

Could the Russians, joined with the British, have beaten the Americans in the Revolutionary War? It is difficult to imagine the

Catherine the Great

United States today with the Tory rule of 1775: a monarchy that favored the Church of England and was opposed to reform.

1. Zeisberger, *History of Northern American Indians*, p. 77.

2. Weslager, *Delaware Indians*, p. 234

3. McKnight, *Our Western Border*, pp. 15, 16.

4. Weslager, *Delaware Indians,* p. 248.

5. Ibid, pp. 294-295

6. Viola, *After Columbus*, p. 109.

7. Montefiore, *Life of Potemkin*, pp. 146-147.

19

Pringle Brothers

Buckongahelas and his family lived peaceably for a time in their village in what is now Upshur County, West Virginia, near the mouth of the Buckhannon River named for him. The forests of the Buckhannon Valley were the chief's favorite hunting grounds.

There were approximately 100 million natives living in North and South America when the Europeans first set foot in the Americas. The first known white men to enter the Buckhannon Valley in what later would become West Virginia were the Pringle brothers, who had arrived in 1762. It was the same year that the English-born John Heckewelder, only nineteen years

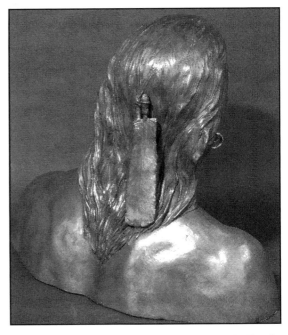

The back of the bust of Buckongahelas is shown on this sculpture of the Delaware war chief by artist Ross Straight.

old, traveled with the Rev. Christian Frederick Post across Pennsylvania to Ohio country to become a Moravian teacher of Delaware children on the Tuscarawas.

Heckewelder would devote his life to the Delaware as a missionary and receive the honorable name "Piselatulpe," (Turtle), by which he was known by all the Delaware.

Heckewelder wrote that he met Buckongahelas "at Tuscaroras as early as 1762: and the Chieftain accordingly reminded him of the fact when, in 1781, he visited the settlement of the Christian Indians in Ohio [a year before their slaughter at Gnadenhutten]." [1]

The Pringles set up residence inside a gaping hole in a large sycamore tree at the mouth of Turkey Run. The tree was near the site of what would become the lovely town of Buckhannon, which we visited while I was writing this book. Eventually, even Fort Buckhannon, built in 1773, would be named for great chief, The Buck.

"'While the Pringles were domiciled in the mighty sycamore at the mouth of Turkey Run," said [John] Cutright [the last surviving scout of western Virginia], 'there was an Indian village located at or near the mouth of the river. The chief of the Indians of that village was Buck-on-go-ha-non, renowned in the border wars of the times. The first white settlers conferred the name of this chief to the beautiful stream on which he lived.'" [2]

When they first arrived, the Pringles were aware that Indians were about, and even pilfered some food the Natives had put away for winter. The brothers were unaware, however, that they were camping in a tree in the midst of the favorite hunting grounds of the famed Indian scout Chief Buckongahelas.

Not wishing to participate in the French and Indian War, Samuel and his younger brother, John, had deserted from the British garrison at Fort Pitt in 1761. They kept track of the passing months inside their sycamore tree-house by the number of full moons that came and went (just as American Indians did), and cut notches on a stick to mark the moons.

The brothers survived panthers and bears – Samuel was mauled by a bear and attacked by a panther – but after two years, their ammunition was running low. A distance of 200 miles separated them from the nearest white settlement. Three days after the thirty-sixth notch was etched upon their wooden calendar, the brothers were desperate. Now their food supplies were low, usually not a problem in winter when hunting of some animals actually was easier because heavy snows slowed them down. But without ammunition, the brothers were rendered helpless.

Now the Pringles were starving. John set out in 1765 to seek additional ammunition and supplies while his brother Samuel recovered from his bear-inflicted wounds.

The West Virginia artist who

The Pringle Brothers at the Pringle Tree was sketched by Robert B. Smith to look like a woodcut, based on an original woodcut by Diss Debar done in the mid-1800s.

sculpted the stunning statue of Buckongahelas and his son Mahonegon that stands in Jawbone Park in Buckhannon told me that his great-grandmother, Rita Herron Chewning, often spoke of the chief and the Pringles.

"My great-grandmother was the great-great granddaughter of John Cutright, one of the first settlers in this area," he revealed. "Her grandmother told her stories about 'Ole Buck.' She said that when Samuel Pringle was starving, Buckongahelas came to him in the hollow Sycamore tree and fed him to keep him alive."

Four moons passed, and Samuel was near death by the time his brother returned with food and news that the French and Indian war was over. Now the Pringles could return east, which they did. But eventually Samuel longed for the upper Monongahela, and his tales of its great beauty drew several men and their families to accompany him back to the sycamore tree.

Samuel Pringle, his wife Charity Cutright, her brothers Benjamin and John Cutright (Ross Straight's ancestor), Jesse Hughes, and William Hacker reached the tree's branches on June 10, 1768 – and soon also encountered my ancestor, whom they called "Buck-on-ga-ha-non."

The first permanent settlement on the Upper Monogahela was in 1769, on the Buckhannon River. The first clearings for the town of Buckhannon were completed in 1769, and the village prospered until 1774, when its inhabitants fled the bitter border wars. The West Virginia town of Buckhannon was established much later in 1816 on land owned by Elizabeth Jackson, mother of Colonel Ed Jackson, who plotted the town in 1815. His grandson was Thomas J. "Stonewall" Jackson, the famed general who served under Robert E. Lee in the Confederate Army during the Civil War.

More than forty white men had married Indian women, and several white women had married Indian men only a few years after the Pringles and friends made their homes in Virginia in 1768. Many persons of black ancestry also came to live among the Lenape, either as slaves or as free men.

1. Thatcher, *Indian Biography*, p. 172.
2. McWhorter, *Border Settlers of Northwestern Virginia*, p. 162.

20

Kill Every Buffalo You Can

In 1491, millions of bison were moving eastward in North America. Buffalo even were to be found on the Monongahela and throughout the region between that river and the Ohio River, southward to the Kanawha. The Spanish introduction of horses onto the continent made buffalo running possible for Indians.

A French lieutenant, Joseph DeLery, wrote in his notes on March 26, 1755 that he saw the dung of Illinois buffaloes near the Conchake River on his way to Fort DuQuesne at the junction of the Allegheny and Monongahela rivers in Ohio.

Buffalo – although not in great multitudes as on the plains – roamed throughout the Trans-Allegheny and West Virginia, but they became nearly extinct there and throughout the vastness of North America after an orgy of destruction by whites. The white man identified the buffalo with the continued existence of their enemies, the Indians, and adopted cattle as their favorite source of meat. (Only a few thousand buffalo remain alive today.)

One of the earliest references to the existence of buffalo in West Virginia was written in 1772 in the journal of a Baptist minister, the Rev. David Jones, who traveled to the Indian tribes west of the Ohio River and spent nearly a year unsuccessfully struggling to convert the Delaware and Shawnee in Ohio.

"Under date June 18, 1772, he writes: 'Went out to view the land on the east side (of the Little Kahana) to kill provisions. Mr. Owens killed several deer and a stately buffalo bull.

"In speaking of that part of the Valley of Ohio near the mouth of the 'Great Guiandot,' he says under date of January 1773: 'Here are great abundance of buffalo, which are a species of cattle, as some suppose, left here by the former inhabitants.'"

Describing the country around Wheeling, the Baptist minister recalled: "The wild beasts met with here are bears, wolves, panthers, wildcats, foxes, raccoons, beavers, otters, some few squirrels and rabbits, buffaloes, deer and elk, which are called by the Delaware 'moos.'" [3] (The Lenape word for elk was "mus," which Rev. Jones heard as "moos;" the Lenape word for deer was "ahtu.")

Twenty years later, Capt. Nathan Boone killed his first buffalo on the Kanawa in Virginia when he was a boy. He also killed buffalo on New River and on the Big Sandy in Virginia in 1797-98.

Chief Buckongahelas and John Anderson surely hunted together, but not for "moos." Shooting at low-flying ducks headed south for the winter, the chief's sons would have carried decoy ducks they designed from woven reeds, painted with berry juices and decorated with feathers. The hunters fooled many live fowl into becoming moist, delicious meat for supper with those decoy ducks.

It was believed by Indians that the sacred buffalo wandered north from Mexico. There were 40 million buffalo in North America at their peak, the chief source of food, clothing, shelter, weapons, and tools for Indians. In 1811, Major George C. Sibley toured the southwestern section of Indian Territory that would become Oklahoma. Near the Cimarron River, he and his party sighted some 30,000 buffalo grazing near a stream that flowed into the river from the north.

A mountain of buffalo skulls.

"It is interesting to note that at the Cooper site only a few miles to the south on Beaver Creek, archaeologists recently have uncovered a buffalo (bison) kill site dating back 10,800 to 10,200 years earlier," author Stan Hoig explained in his book *Beyond the Frontier*. "These were giant buffalo, nearly half again as big as present-day buffalo." [4]

Before the railroad, the buffalo ranged from the Colorado River in Texas up to Canada, but buffalo would not cross over railroad tracks (just as my dog Sarah will not walk across grates on sidewalks).

The white man would slaughter the great herds of American bison that stretched across the continent–as he would destroy the American Indians of many nations. An ambitious buffalo hunter could earn more than $100 per day slaughtering buffalo during the late 1800s. During the 1870s, buffalo hides were selling for $3.50 each, even south of the Arkansas River where the Medicine Lodge Treaty was drafted in Kansas in 1867 to protect the buffalo and the rights of Indians.

"Every Buffalo Dead Is an Indian Gone."

"Kill every buffalo you can," Colonel Richard Irving Dodge, the U.S. Army commander of Fort Dodge (near present-day Dodge City, Kansas), had urged his troops. "Every buffalo dead is an Indian gone."

That statement of the man for whom Fort Dodge was named actually was true because American Indians depended on the buffalo for life itself and did not waste any portion of their favorite animal.

"Buffalo meat, cut into thin strips, was dried in the sun," Sydney E. Fletcher wrote in his book *The American Indians.* "Then it was stored in rawhide cases to be used for food in the winter.

"Buffalo hide was made into moccasins, ropes, shields, snowshoes and tent covers. Pelts taken in the winter when the buffalo's hair was long, were used for bedding, and for clothes of extra weight and warmth. The sinews furnished bowstrings and thread for sewing. The horns were made into spoons and drinking cups. Buffalo hoofs furnished glue for mending. In fact, to many Indian tribes, the buffalo symbolized their very existence, and was considered the greatest gift that could have been bestowed upon them." [5]

A sickening photograph in Dodge City's Boot Hill Museum shows gigantic mounds of 200,000 slaughtered, skinned buffalo piled up in Dodge City, Kansas, a shipping point for five years for the hides of some three million buffalo. Buffalo Bill (William Cody) bragged that he had killed 4,280 buffalo to feed the builders of the Kansas Pacific Railroad. By 1867, buffalo were fast disappearing from the West. Other hunters slaughtered more than 850,000 buffalo in only a two-year period between 1872 and 1874.

According to the National Wildlife Federation, "the uncontrolled killing and conversion of prairie habitat to agriculture reduced the U.S. bison population to less than 600."

Indians were forced to survive on small animals like squirrels and rabbits that were difficult to find during winter months.

Whites who had no respect for the lives of buffalo could not be expected to have respect for a darker race of people. In another sinister attempt at genocide of American Indians, the British deliberately introduced smallpox to the Delaware Tribe in 1763. English General Jeffrey Amherst, appointed Governor-General of British North America, approved the distribution of blankets from whites infected with the dread disease to members of the Delaware Tribe.

Amherst regarded Indians as "more nearly allied to the Brute than to the Human Creation," and did not hesitate to say, "I am fully resolved whenever they give me an occasion to extirpate [to destroy completely] them root and branch," Angie Debo noted in *A History of the Indians of the United States.*[6]

Historian C. A. Weslager reported that Amherst wrote to Colonel Henry Bouquet: "You will do well to try to inoculate the Indians by means of blankets, as well as to try every other method that can serve to extirpate this execrable race."[7]

Captain Simeon Ecuver at Fort Pitt obeyed those words and gallantly presented three deadly gifts to his next Indian visitors, Turtle's Heart and Mamaltee. The Indians took away two blankets and a handkerchief which Ecuver had obtained from smallpox patients at the fort. This deliberate infection of Indians with the disease has been called "the first use of biological warfare in history."

The disease of the pox spread among the people like a ghostly wind. Over the years, thousands of Indians would perish in agony from smallpox and other white men's diseases for which the Indians had no immunity.

Close living quarters of Natives contributed to the spread of typhoid, cholera, tuberculosis, and smallpox. In only one year, 1816, four thousand Comanches died from smallpox. Out of the population of 1,600, only 100 members of the Mandan Tribe survived the epidemic. The tribe later became extinct. The pox killed half of the Blackfoot Indians, while cholera wiped out the majority of Kiowa and Comanche Indians. Germ warfare served the white men well.

Gigantic mounds of 200,000 slaughtered, skinned buffalo were piled up in Dodge City, Kansas, a shipping point for five years for the hides of some three million buffalo.

1. McWhorter, *Border Settlers of Northwestern Virginia*, p. 379.

2. Hoig, *Beyond the Frontier*, p. 331.

3. Connell, *Son of the Morning Star*, p. 135.

4. Ibid, p. 132.

5. Fletcher, *American Indians*, pp. 4, 5.

6. Debo, *History of the Indians*, p. 81.

7. Weslager, *Delaware Indians*, p. 245.

21

The Buck Meets George Washington

Buckongahelas was born in western Ohio around 1720, and George Washington only twelve years later in Tidewater, Virginia on February 11, 1732.

The Buck in his maturity as a war chief and diplomatic leader would be called "the George Washington of his people," and representing his people, he would meet with George Washington.

When the late Helen York Rose, the Delaware historian, traced her family tree, she discovered that she was, as am I, a descendant of Chief Buckongahelas Journeycake.

Delaware Chief Taminend or Taminet, born 1676-d 1776 "is the start long ago of our family," Rose wrote. "In the *Wilderness Trail* it states that he had three sons. He also had a daughter who was the mother of Chief Natawtwees [Netawatwees]."

Chief Taminend supposedly was a cousin of the woman he married, and not the famous Chief Tamany who sold land to William Penn. Chief Tamany was an uncle of our ancestor Chief Taminend's wife.

"Chief Natawatwees/King Newcomer of the Turtle Clan …was a small lad of about eight years age when the Penn Treaty was signed [in] 1682," Rose wrote.

"His birth year was 1676 and death 1776. He died while on the way to make a treaty with the colonists in 1876 and was buried at the forks where the Ohio River starts, under the Treaty Tree.

"His daughter married Chief Wendacolla…. Chief Buckongahales [sic] was the son of Wendacolla and Netawatwees' daughter; therefore, he [The Buck] was the grandson of Chief Netawatwees and a descendant of Chief Taminand. His [Buckongahelas'] wife was a daughter of Captain Pipe, a war chief of the Wolf Clan."

The Buck's notorious father-in-law was *not* his favorite relative, although they both fought together and would become wanted men with a price on their heads listed on poster nailed to trees.

Captain Pipe, head of the Munsee was nicknamed "Hopacan" or "tobacco pipe." He was a controversial war chief of the Lenape Wolf Clan in Ohio, nominated Wolf Clan chief by his uncle, Chief Custaloga, whom he succeeded. Pipe's Indian name was Kogieschquanoheel, "maker of daylight." (Small wonder that he went by the nickname of "Pipe.")

Pipe and his brother, Joshua, a Moravian Christian, were the great-grandsons of Chief Pokonga, and sons of Gideon Maw Weher (Captain Pach Got Goen), chief of Scotacooks when he was baptized February 13, 1743.

Delaware Captain Pipe (Hopocan), father-in-law of Buckongahelas.

Historian Weslager called Pipe "a bold and ambitious schemer and a man of courage." Pipe led the pro-English faction of the Delaware against the colonists and the Continental Congress, presenting American scalps to the British at Detroit. His son-in-law Buckongahelas joined him, and having chosen the losing side of war, they would be forced to sign a treaty with the victors on September 17, 1778.

The Buck was known widely as Buckongahelas, but there is a record of him under the name "Chief Journeycake." Helen York Rose gleaned this bit of information from a man by the name of Greg Schoof, who sent her a "documentary report and history of Absentee Delaware, as narrated by Willie Thomas, written by Henry Chisholm [of Anadarko, Oklahoma, a descendant of one of the two daughters of Buckongahelas]."

In Rose's manuscript at the Denver Public Library, she quoted from a statement by Chief Thomas of the Absentee Delawares:

"In 1793 a Chief Journeycake (as he was sometimes called) of the Delaware (also called Roosner or the Delaware name Buckongelah, Pulcoagelah) and an ancestor of the now deceased Will Thomas, was given a friendship medallion to wear around his neck as a symbol of trust and friendship toward all White Fathers…. There is, also, a buffalo muzzle loading gun given to them which is still in the possession of the Absentee Delaware Tribe at the present time."

"From the dates on this document, it could not be speaking of Solomon Journeycake, as he was born about 1790," Rose explained.

"This Chief Journeycake of 1793 would have been Solomon's father, and, no doubt, the little lad who was stolen by the other tribe of Indians and returned to his father's village—and was given the name Journeycake."

Rose talked to Chisholm, who confirmed that "Yes, he knew about the friendship

Seneca Chief Red Jacket wearing his enormous medal.

medallion—he has it! Yes, he knew about the buffalo gun, his nephew has it at Lawton, Oklahoma!" [1]

In his book *Lives of Indian Chiefs*, Norman Wood also talks about the enormous medals (seven inches long by five inches broad) that George Washington handed out like candy to the Indian chiefs, but he lists the date of the chiefs' meeting with the president as 1792.

"Red Jacket [the Seneca chief] was one of fifty chiefs who visited President Washington at Philadelphia, then the seat of government, in 1792," Wood wrote.

"While there, the president presented him with a silver medal, on which Washington, in military uniform, was represented as handing a long peace-pipe to an Indian chief with a scalp lock decorated with plumes on the top of his head, while a white man was plowing with a yoke of oxen in the background.

"This last figure was probably intended as a hint for the Indians to abandon war and the chase, and adopt the peaceful pursuits of agriculture." Wood went on to say that the chiefs preferred ornaments of silver to those of gold, "for they are more becoming to their red skin." [2]

The Son of Chief Wendacolla

The writings of historian C. A. Weslager also verify that The Buck was the son of Wendacolla. In his book *The Delaware Indians, a History*, Weslager talks about "Old Hundy, a Munsie town on the north side of the Walhonding between the mouths of the Killbuck and Mohican Creeks; [and] "New Hundy, built two or three miles west of Old Hundy, where in 1775 the Chief Windaughala ("council door"), father of Buckongahelas, had his residence." [3]

Chief Windaughala, aka Wendacolla, a war chief who served under Chief Beaver, also was known as "one employed as an important messenger," The Buck's father also was known as Wendocolla, Wandaughhala, Wandohela, Windochelas, Windaughalah, Wiendugh-weland, and Tweegachschage).

"A reference in the Pennsylvania records in 1758 before he took over the principal chieftaincy calls him [Wendocalla] 'ye great man of the Unamie nation,'" Weslager wrote. [4]

The Buck's mother was an "unnamed Lenape (Delaware) woman," the daughter of the "skilled advisor" Chief Netawatwees, who also was called Netahutquemaled or Netodwehement of the Turtle Clan.

Buckongahelas and Captain Pipe would become bitter enemies in future years. One of The Buck's two unnamed daughters, whom I have named "Little Leaf," married John Anderson, my many-greats-grandfather.

1. Rose, *I Walked the Footsteps of My Fathers*, pp. 134, 138.
2. Wood, *Lives of Famous Chiefs*, p. 251.
3. Weslager, *Delaware Indians*, p. 243.
4. Weslager, *Delaware Indian Westward Migration*, p. 27.

22

John Anderson, Trapper and Trader

Long before Chief Buckongahelas met George Washington, the Delaware threw leftovers from their meals onto the sacred fire in the center of their huts, believing that the fire was an old Indian woman who issued from the sun.

They dared not spit upon the fire or throw water upon it, because they believed such disrespect for the Fire Woman would bring upon them a scary sickness.

"The sun is our greatest God, also a woman," The Buck's wife would have instructed their four sons and two daughters. "In ancient times, the mother of the Sun God was named 'White Woman.'"

The Delaware and their ancestors the Lenape believed in only one supreme God.

"The Lenape acknowledged the existence of a great god or supreme force whom they called Manitou," explained Weslager in his book *Delaware's Buried Past*.

"They were taught to believe that he made the world, sun, moon, stars, plants, animals, and all living things." [1]

"The *Gam'wing* was the Lenape annual meeting of worship that lasted for twelve nights, ending on the thirteenth day," M. R. Harrington noted. [2] The meeting included singing, drumming, praying, and preaching. The Lenape also highly reverenced dreams.

"Our Creator has many helpers whom we call *Man-it'to-wuk*, and people pray to them for help. Sometimes a *Man-it'to* will appear in a dream or vision to a person in trouble and give him some power or blessing that will help him all through life." [3]

Little Leaf's mother would have been a typical Lenape woman, busy with cooking and gardening, dropping a heated rock into water to boil for mush or stew in a tightly woven egg-shaped basket propped on rocks. Little Leaf would eat the stew flavored with venison or squirrel; then throw the leftovers of her meal into the embers, which blazed up as the Fire Woman gobbled her gift.

At one Algonquian site, their food remains included beaver, dog, red and gray fox, black bear, mink, harbor seal, deer, loon, great blue heron, mallard, black duck, red-tailed hawk, bald eagle, great auk, snapping turtle, stingray, sturgeon, sea bass, sculpin, sea robin, scup, wolf fish, bay scallop, mussel, quahog, surf clam, long clam, moon snail, thick-lipped drill and channeled conch. [4]

Into the life of the Indian maiden Little Leaf would stride a tall, robust gentleman with a fine beard and mustache, wearing buckskins and a fox-skin hat that failed to hide a firm strong jaw on a young, excited face. The man so eagerly working as a trapper and trader in the New World was the Dutchman John Anderson, one of my ancestors. He was a sandy-haired Quaker born at Warwick, Pennsylvania in 1716, the eldest of the eleven children of Eliakim and Elizabeth Anderson. (John Anderson would die after 1776.)

Seeking religious freedom, many Quakers migrated to Rhode Island, Delaware, New Jersey, North Carolina, Pennsylvania, and Maryland-- lands the Lenni Lenape had occupied for thousands of years. Anderson and his relatives would have avoided Massachusetts, where Quakers were imprisoned, tortured, and executed.

Puritans in Massachusetts Bay Colony imprisoned, tortured and hung Quakers, both men and women.

John journeyed to Europe to sell beaver pelts to customers in Amsterdam and other cities. The fur trade had begun between the Lenape and the Dutch and Swedes in New York around 1610. In 1626, the Dutch purchased the Island Manhattes from the Manhatesen Indians (probably a northern branch of the Lenape) for sixty guilders or what at that time amounted to twenty-four dollars. The Dutch and the Swedes purchased thousands of acres of land from the Lenape.

The talented Chippewa author Louise Erdrich, who grew up in North Dakota, has written many moving and humorous stories about American Indians. While a student at Dartmouth College in Hanover, New Hampshire, enrolled in a Native American Studies seminar, she asked to submit a story instead of a research paper.

"She wrote a story based on what had actually happened when the Swedish colonizers first encountered the Delaware Indians," authors Paula Gunn Allen and Patricia Clark Smith reported in their book, *As Long as the Rivers Flow*.

"The vain colonial governor thought he would really impress the Delaware people if he had a whole suit of clothes made out of wampum, the lustrous pieces of shell Eastern Native Americans used for money. The Delaware made the suit for him, but the governor was very fat, and as soon as he took a deep breath, the whole suit burst apart!" [5]

The Swedes did not hold sway for very long with the Delaware, and the Dutch would make even less of a good impression upon the Indians.

"The Swedes claimed land along Delaware Bay from 1638 until 1655, when they were ousted by the Dutch," [6] Arlene Hirschfelder wrote in the book *Native Americans*.

In 1637, a party of Puritans set fire to a Pequot village and burned or shot to death 500 Indians, and in February, 1643, in unprovoked attacks, the Dutch murdered 500 Lenape at Pavonia (now Hackensack, New Jersey) and at Corlears Hook on Manhatten Isle. In response, the formerly friendly Lenape of the Delaware Valley attacked Dutch settlers at Swanendaelael, and began their first migration west along the Susquehanna River, where tribes of the Six Nations lived.

Despite the enmity between them, by the 1650s, the Lenape and other tribes were supplying Dutch traders with more than 35,000 beaver pelts a year to sell in Europe.

The young Dutch trader John, who was a Quaker, arrived at the wigwam of Chief Buckongahelas, inquiring about pelts and hides for sale. For a century, the Lenape had traded with the French, but the Scots, Dutch, and Brits offered better quality goods and prices. By 1760, the French fur trade would come to an end, and the beaver--with its soft, thick fur–would be scarce; the animal had been nearly hunted out of existence by the 1730s. Europeans were crazy for furs of all kinds from America during the seventeenth and early eighteenth centuries.

Only deer and bearskins were plentiful by the time John began his career. In exchange for pelts, he would pay the chief with gunpowder, tools, trinkets, cloth, items of clothing, and cooking pots and utensils. Woolens were becoming popular among the tribes and began to replace fur garments. Iron pots were considered priceless by Native women.

John may have emerged from the wigwam of Buckongahelas as the chief's daughter, Little Leaf, sauntered past, her skin bare of clothing from the waist up, her arms laced with copper and beaded bracelets and piled high with wood for her father's hungry fire that simmered night and day. The Dutchman must have been struck by the beauty of the girl he beheld, even though she was of a tender age of fourteen, an age at which Indian girls often married. After their first menstruation, Indian girls were considered women, since they were able to bear children. Menstruation brought its drawbacks too, however.

"Among the Delaware and in many other tribes it was believed that a woman herbalist lost her power to cure while she was menstruating, and she was not allowed to prepare remedies during that time," noted Carolyn Niethammer, author of *Daughters of the Earth.* [7]

"The Reverend John Heckewelder wrote in the 1800s that wives of the white missionaries ministering to the Iroquois often appealed to the native women for help for what were then termed 'female complaints.'

"Heckewelder also gives a story of his own cure: 'I once for two days and two nights suffered the most excruciating pain from a felon or whitlow [tissue inflammation] on one of my fingers which deprived me entirely of sleep. I had recourse to an Indian woman, who in less than half an hour relieved me entirely by the simple application of a poultice made of the root of the common blue violet.'" [8]

William Penn observed the marriage customs of the Lenape:

"When the Young Women are fit for Marriage, they wear something upon their Heads for an Advertisement, But so as their Faces are hardly to be seen, but when they please; the Age they Marry at, if Women, is about thirteen and fourteen; if Men seventeen and eighteen; they are rarely elder." [9]

Chief Buckongahelas no doubt invited John to sup with him and to draw from the long pipe upon which he slowly smoked his precious tobacco. Perhaps the canny chief noticed the white man's frequent glances at his daughter, but he would not have been surprised.

"The European would have found the Indian women very shy, modest, and desirous of pleasing their men," wrote historian Weslager. "In their knee-length skirts of deerskin, their breasts bare, and long braided tresses setting off their soft features, the young women would have been highly attractive to the white visitor." [10]

Later Buckongahelas and the young white man hunted together, accompanied by the chief's sons, who wore animal skins and antlers on their heads when searching for buffalo and the more solitary moose during rutting season in the fall. Anderson one day appeared not as a hunter or trader, but bearing gifts of silver, ginger, nutmeg and cloves, and brightly colored cloth. John asked Chief Buckongahelas for the hand of his daughter Little Leaf in marriage.

It was the custom that women and men of The Buck's clan were joined in wedlock to members of other clans. Many Indians followed the law of *exogamy*, which forbade the bonding of a woman and a man from the same clan. Harsh experience of dimwitted, sometimes malformed children had taught people of all races not to mix their blood too closely. Incest was one of the Lenape taboos.

In fact, the Delaware Indians were more cautious than whites regarding inter-marriage of blood relations, Moravian missionary David Zeisberger pointed out.

"Blood relations do not marry; in this particular they are even more strict than the whites. They claim that division of the race into tribes came about in order to make it more readily certain that a man in taking a wife was not marrying a near relative. " [11]

Zeisberger further noted that "No Indian will marry a person in his own tribe, as he is too closely related to all in it." [12]

Intermarriage among the Lenape Turtle (Unami), Turkey (Unalachtigo) and Wolf (Muncy) clans was wise because it added to the strength of each group. The tribe gained additional land wherein the men might hunt and women plow the ground to grow their precious maize, which had become a staple for Mexican Indians as early as 1,000 years before Christ and a crop in the Eastern woodlands by the year 800 B.C.

John was a man whose skin, though browned by the sun, paled in comparison to Little Leaf's creamy dark complexion. Little Leaf was "pilsu" – spirit pure. John was a white man, son of a race that had proven itself treacherous to American Indians many times in the past. But at least four white frontiersmen are known to have married into Indian tribes and become so respected that they were named tribal chiefs. Thousands of white men, who enjoyed the free and adventurous life of the Natives, linked their lives to Indian women before the Eastern and Western lands finally were stolen from the first Americans.

Little Leaf's mother might have been disturbed by John's proposal; no white man had ever lived under her roof. If anyone should wed the hairy-faced trapper, she believed it should be a white woman, not her lovely dark-skinned daughter, Little Leaf. This reminds me of an old Indian saying, "Every crow thinks *theirs* is the blackest."

An Indian Solution to Marital Disagreements

Chief Buckongahelas disagreed with his wife, but retiring to his bed on a blanket on a woven mat, he would sing himself to sleep, a habit of many Native peoples. Perhaps his wife punished him that night by sleeping at the opposite end of their spacious domed hut. The mighty chief–feared in war and respected in peace--treasured his wife (and perhaps even feared her wrath a little).

After she fell asleep that night, perhaps he awoke and sprinkled tobacco mixed with his spit upon her snoring body, an old Indian custom of harassed husbands. Singing incantations softly, he would pray that his wife's love and obedience would return to him. Next day, his wife would relent, not realizing why, and the future marriage of their daughter, Little Leaf, and John would be announced to tribal elders.

Invitations were issued to neighboring clans, in whose hands were placed small pouches of precious tobacco leaves as a welcoming gift when their ears heard the news. Many would hurry to the wedding feast because they respected Chief Buckongahelas and were curious about the tall white man whose family originated in a faraway land.

Traditionally, a Lenape groom-to-be would go hunting for three days to obtain game for his bride's family. If he met with success and returned with fine meat for the table, it would be a good omen for the marriage to take place. If he rode into camp empty-handed, his prospects would be less than favorable.

John was no slouch, and bravely attempted to fulfill every Lenape tradition. On the evening of the third day, he tromped to his future father-in-law's camp on a horse hauling a *travois* heavily laden with meat. He unloaded the meat at the entrance of the home of Buckongahelas. If accepted, the young man would wed Little Leaf.

Later that evening, the meat would be missing from in front of the hut, as a smiling John spied from his horse hidden in a nearby grove of trees. He returned with happiness to his lean-to, making a nest of dried grass and setting fire to it with flint and steel, gently and patiently blowing on the first flicker of flame. He tied together the ends of a long trade blanket--a trick the Delaware taught him--and, voila! He had created a sleeping bag for the night. He would cover the coals of his fire with dirt, and throw the sleeping bag on top of the embers. The oils in the trade blanket's unprocessed wool would keep it from catching fire–and John would be cozy and warm all night long, another lesson learned from his future in-laws.

For her splendid wedding, I imagine Little Leaf gowned in a butter soft deerskin skirt dyed deep blood red (as my dear Choctaw-Cherokee sister-in-law appeared on the day of her wedding to my brother.) Red was the color of the Sun God and the sacred fire, the color of life. Glass beads on the bride's fringed leather skirt dripped like syrup down the front (early English traders traded glass beads for furs, but by 1850 seed beads from Venice would be popular with Indians).

If they married in warm weather, Little Leaf's body, with no shame, would have been naked from the waist up, although adorned with beads and necklaces. If the wedding were in winter, she would have worn a robe of soft feathers, deerskin leggings, and moccasins. Perhaps her neck was decorated with a choker of white carved bones and pearls connected to a circle of silver in the center. A strip of leather finished with colorful feathers might hang from the sparkling silver. (Odette long ago created such a necklace for me to wear to a powwow.) North American Indians often preferred silver over gold, as they believed that silver reflected more strikingly against their dark skin.

The green stone turquoise is popular with American Indians today, and when the Delaware were forced to migrate to the Plains, they became enamored with turquoise too. Indians artists shape turquoise stones like kernels of corn in honor of the annual Corn Harvest Ceremony. The Delaware also loved pearls, and designed their own earrings, bracelets, and necklaces of both seeds and pearls. Centuries earlier, they had fashioned their jewelry with porcupine quills, sea shells, and coral.

The real jewel at the family wedding long ago was Little Leaf herself, her face alight with joy. Head held high, she proudly approached the tall Dutch trader who would be her husband. Her silky black hair reached past her tiny waist (my Grandmother Edna's waist-length ebony hair probably resembled Little Leaf's shiny jet-black hair). Little Leaf's dainty feet were clad in red-beaded moccasins created for the wedding.

As the sun peered above the horizon that morning, Little Leaf rose from her woven mat and sipped a tea of white water lily roots--the Lenape "love medicine."

The faces of the young Indian bride and the tall white groom were painted with bright colors. The bridegroom was dressed in a buckskin shirt and elk skin pants, with fox and wolf tails wound around his heels and knees. On his feet were soft deer skin moccasins that Little Leaf fashioned for him as a wedding gift. Buckongahelas removed the tall beaver hat from John's head – replacing it with an eagle's tail feather tied to a ribbon to wear in his thick blond hair.

A soft drum that pounded like the beat of a human heart beckoned the young couple to come together in the presence of their beloved ones to honor Mother Earth, who gave them life and all that sustains life. A medicine man offered tobacco to the Great Spirit, *Waka-Tanka*, as well as the skin of a beaver that had been sacrificed for the sake of the bride and groom, who would exchange two beaver skins at their wedding banquet.

Grandfather Buck strutted like a peacock in his regalia: an exotic, chocolate-colored cloak fashioned from brown and white turkey feathers, a garment he reserved for such grand occasions. Around his neck were heavy Chevron beads made of six layers of glass (the glass was from Czechoslovakia; Indian trade with the Czechs had begun before the voyages of Columbus). The chief's bonnet bore only one eagle feather, not many feathers as in other tribal chiefs' elaborate helmets. Carrying a fan of two turkey feathers, Buckongahelas proudly led the way to the wedding meal, which was a feast for the eye as well as the stomach.

Oversized platters that the pilgrims called "chargers" would have been piled high with plentiful food. Guests at such weddings consumed both Indian and English fare, as Lenape musicians sang and struck the drum. Later, dancers swayed to the joyful sounds of both flute and drum. (The only singers not at the drum were women, who were not allowed around the sacred instrument.)

Guests and the family no doubt dined on caviar, a favorite of New England Indians, who pulled thousands of sturgeons from nearby lakes and rivers every year, as Russians still do today. The wedding feast also would have offered quail, pheasant, ducks, geese, and turkeys stuffed with cranberries, baked yams, pies of bison and vegetables, puddings made of corn instead of flour, and custard apples. Roasted pig (first brought to these shores by my other relatives on the *Mayflower* 100 years earlier) was another delicacy the Indians served. Pork was a welcome change from jerky.

For their journey back home, guests received round, hot cornmeal "Johnnycakes" to slip into their pockets and nibble along the way, as the child Buckongahelas had done. It is said that the Lenape originally named their delicious concoction "journey cakes" for the corn cake that saved the life of the little boy lost to another tribe's family.

The Indian recipe for "journey cakes" called for two cups white cornmeal, two teaspoons sugar, one teaspoon salt, two cups boiling water, and one-fourth to one-half cup milk or cream. The water is added to the dry ingredients, and the mixture allowed to rest until it swells in size. Then spoonfuls are dropped on a hot, greased griddle to fry.

The white pioneer women's recipe, adapted from the Indian "receipt," included neither cornmeal, milk, nor cream, which were difficult to transport. Instead, cooks trekking cross country in covered wagons combined sugar, butter, apple cider or vinegar to flour and baking soda. If they had cinnamon and cloves, the cooks tossed those into the batter as well. These cakes were baked over a campfire on a flat wooden shingle called a "journey board," served with a hard sauce of butter, brown sugar, and nutmeg.

For their wedding night, John surely spirited his bride away to a spot deep in the woods near the lovely Buckhannon River that sang softly to them as they became one as man and wife. John whispered to his bride tenderly in Algonquin (the Delaware language), speaking in the Unami dialect he was learning. As he held her close, her heart beating wildly like a winded animal caught after a long chase, he would have calmed her with his gentleness.

In the late 1800s, the weddings of native couples would not be recognized by the federal government, which ruled that all Delaware tribal marriages were null and void. Married Delaware

This is the Delaware payhouse near Alluwe, Oklahoma where the Rev. Charles Journeycake performed Delaware marriages after the United States declared the Indian marriages null and void.

Photo courtesy of Bartlesville Area History Museum.

couples were forced to remarry in a Christian or civil ceremony, as happened at the Delaware payhouse near Alluwe, Oklahoma when the Rev. Charles Journeycake, a Baptist minister and Little Leaf's nephew, performed "one marriage after another, standing on the porch of the payhouse as couple after couple came before him."

1. Weslager, *Delaware's Buried Past*, p.161.

2. Harrington, *Indians of New Jersey*, p. 49.

3. Ibid, p. 149.

4. Kopper, *Smithsonian Book of North American Indians*, pp. 134-135.

5. Allen and Smith, *As Long as the Rivers Flow*, p. 300.

6. Hirschfelder, *Native Americans*, p. 32.

7. Niethammer, *Daughters of the Earth*, p. 146.

8. Ibid, p. 147.

9. Myers, *William Penn*, p. 27.

10. Weslager, *Delaware Indians*, p. 54.

11. Zeisberger, *History of Northern American Indians*, p. 52.

12. Ibid, p. 63.

23

Birth of Another Ancestor

An Indian man who married a Delaware Indian woman in the 1700s was expected to move in with his mother-in-law. It would be no different for this white man, John Anderson, who would strive to please both his wife and his mother-in-law, so that the latter would not evict him.

Kin relationships with the Delaware were determined by the mothers of the tribe.

"Supreme in every longhouse was the oldest woman, 'mother' of the household in the sense that it exclusively belonged to her and her female relatives," James Maxwell wrote.

"When she died, the next oldest woman took over. All males left home as soon as they married, and went to live in the longhouses of their wives. Conversely, when a woman married, her husband immediately moved into her longhouse." [1]

John, husband of Little Leaf, would have carried his sparse belongings from his cramped lean-to into Chief Journeycake's spacious wigwam that was considered the property of the oldest woman in the household, the wife of Buckongahelas. John may have brought with him marigold seeds from Dutch New Netherlands for his mother-in-law to plant in the field behind her dwelling. The bright orange blossoms would bloom throughout the summer, and Delaware women would pluck the flowers to season their stews and soups.

The newlyweds would have been afforded a modicum of privacy behind a curtain of softened animal skin at one end of the wigwam, and soon, Little Leaf was with child. The young wife, Little Leaf, and her husband, John, were joyous and met with the tribal holy man as each month passed. The holy man concocted an herbal drink for Little Leaf to guarantee her safe delivery. She was forbidden to eat squirrel, speckled trout, and rabbit. The Lenape did not eat rabbit because *Nanapush*, the Creator's holy representative on earth, changed himself into a rabbit when he left the Lenape. Warriors and men preparing for games of competition with other clans also disdained rabbits because the creatures were timid and fearful, and it was assumed that their meat would render a warrior afraid and weak as well.

"Remember the rabbit has large eyes," the holy man would have cautioned, stretching his own eyelids wide as a warning. "The squirrel goes up a tree, but your baby must fall down. And speckled trout will give your infant marks (birthmarks)."

Little Leaf would have avoided even glancing at squirrels, trout, or rabbits. She, like other Delaware mothers, prayed that her child would drop easily down the birth canal, be free of marks, and be born with normal eyes. When it came time for the baby to be born, a Delaware woman doctor would deliver the infant.

"One never thinks of an Indian woman doctor, yet the practice of obstetrics in the old days was wholly confined to women doctors," wrote Roberta Campbell Lawson, an Oklahoma Delaware.[2]

Little Leaf's baby was born around 1753 in Perquimans, North Carolina. She was christened "Mary" when her father, John, and her grandfather, Chief Buckongahelas, plunged the yelping, complaining child into the chilly waters of the Perquimans River, an Indian custom of purification.

"Of their Customs and Manners, there is much to be said; I will begin with Children," William Penn wrote in his *Account of the Lenni Lenape or Delaware Indians*.

"So soon as they are born, they wash them in Water, and while very young, and in cold Weather to Chuse [sic], they Plunge them in the Rivers to harden and embolden them." [3]

Since John was a Quaker, he would not have had his infant daughter baptized, as many Catholic, Lutheran, and Episcopal pioneer fathers did. Quakers, The Society of Friends, did not require baptism as a rite of membership. The first Quaker missionaries had arrived in Carolina in 1671, although some missionaries had reached Virginia as early as 1652. The first recorded Quaker service in North Carolina was held in Perquimans in 1672. Several of my ancestors lived in Perquimans.

Perquimans County, the first permanent English settlement in North Carolina, was settled around 1650 by Virginians who had heard of its rich bottom lands, abundant timber, and good climate. The meandering Perquimans River, with its more than 100 miles of shoreline, was the main highway through the area. The source of this and other nearby rivers was the Great Dismal Swamp, where the water was a deep blood red color, having passed through cypress tree roots. This water was said to have a powerful diuretic effect on anyone who drank it.

At four months of age, it became obvious that baby Mary would have her father's eyes--not a hare's--only her eyes were darker than his pale blue. Her complexion was lighter than Little Leaf's chocolate brown skin, but her nose bent slightly to the side. The infant's dark "dishwater" blonde hair was frizzy with fat, puffy curls, inherited from her father's side of the family.

The baby was placed on a stiff cradleboard, decorated by her Delaware grandmother with hundreds of bright beads and colorful ribbons. The cradleboard would be carried on her mother's back or hung from a tree while her mother worked in the fields. The family presented the infant with several gifts: a tiny gourd rattle filled with stones, a comb of silver birch wood to untangle her mass of curls, and a beaded turtle charm to bring long life to the papoose.

Her rowdy Grandfather Buck certainly spoiled the little girl, hoisting her up onto his shoulders, tickling her tiny feet, making faces to watch her giggle. As a toddler, she and her grandfather would play hide and seek, weaving in and out among the rows of corn that were taller than she was.

Mahonegon, the son of Buckongahelas, was born two years after baby Mary in 1755. He adored his niece, who was more like an older sister. The relationship of Mary to Mahonegon was similar to my relationship with my beloved uncle, Stan, my mother's half-brother who was born several years after me. I remember wickedly teasing the younger boy about being my "uncle," so I could see his cheeks blush a lovely apple crimson.

1. Maxwell, *America's Fascinating Indian Heritage*, p. 122, 124.

2. Lawson, *My Oklahoma*, vol. 1, August, 1927, pg. 36.

3. Myers, *William Penn*, p. 26.

24

Death of a Beloved Son

Returning to the 1700s, the year is 1773. American Indians of different nations have been at war with the white border settlers along western Virginia, but Chief Buckongahelas has not been among them. He has been a friend to the Virginians, as he was a friend to the two Pringle brothers and their families.

"It was well known that the great Delaware Chief (the Buck) was friendly to the settlers, and had, on more than one occasion, exhibited this friendship in substantial ways," John C. McWhorter wrote in 1927.

In his book, *The Scout of the Buckongehanon*, McWhorter describes the son of Buckongahelas, Mahonegon (Running Wind), as "a tall, handsome, athletic young Indian of fewer than twenty snows," adding, "Clad in buckskin and blanket, a few eagle feathers ornamenting his raven hair, the bronzed hunter was graceful and attractively dignified in his bearing.

"The proffered hand of Running Wind, son of Buckongahelas, was clasped by that of the great Scout [Captain William White] with all semblance of friendship. The Captain felt secure in the presence of the two tribesmen, knowing as he did the splendid reputation of the Delaware Chief [Buckongahelas] for sincerity and integrity." [1]

Photo by Charlene Scott-Myers

Buckongehelas and his murdered son, Mahonegon, created by sculptor Ross Straight, can be seen in Jawbone Park, Buckhannon, West Virginia.

127

In the densely forested hillside near where the town of Buckhannon now stands, the young, well built, dark-skinned man of less than twenty years, Mahonegon, reclined on his stomach on the ground near a salt lick, his rifle and a spear resting on the log by his side in the June twilight shadows. The spear – decorated with a dew claw from the hoof of a deer and feathers from hawks and crows – might have been a wedding gift to his father, Buckongahelas, many moons ago.

"The claws signify the hope that you will see your enemy before they see you," Buckongahelas would have told his son. "The feathers are for good luck."

Mahonegon never saw the enemy who struck him down, and unfortunately, the feathers failed to bring him any luck at all.

Unknown to Mahonegon, a white man--the frontier scout Captain White--stalked the nearby woods searching for any Natives he could find. The man who would become notorious as an Indian killer crept stealthily into the thicket where Mahonegon lay on his stomach near a salt lick waiting for deer to appear. He came upon the young Mahonegon, but did not recognize the lad who had his back to him. White was the man who had taken the hand of the teenage Mahonegon "with all semblance of friendship."

According to McWhorter, Captain White sighted the boy, aimed and shot the unsuspecting lad in the back – always a coward's shot. The bullet punctured the lad's heart, murdering Mahonegon in cold blood.

"There, lying on his face, his gun resting across a log, reposed the body of a tall, finely formed young Indian, shot through the heart," McWhorter reported.

"The Captain stopped and turned the body on its back. He gave a perceptible start as he looked into the handsome features of the son of Buckongahelas! The face was un-streaked with war paint, and his garb was only that of an Indian hunter." [2]

The captain was shocked when he recognized the son of Buckongahelas, the great Delaware chief. It was obvious that Mahonegon was not waiting to do battle with white men in the forest, but rather to hunt in the early evening when deer would approach the salt lick.

"This does not bode well for the western border settlers," White admitted darkly to his friends who joined him at the salt lick after hearing the shot. It did not bode well for White either.

The white men dispersed in haste, fearing to face Buckongahelas and the fearsome rage that would consume him when he discovered his murdered boy.

The whites had heard the translation of one of Buckongahelas' other names, Poch-gent-she-he-los, "breaker-in-pieces."

Searching for his son, Buckongahelas beseeched the *Wematekanis* or Little People of the forest to assist him in locating Mahonegon. The Lenni-Lenape were as certain that the Little People existed as my Irish ancestors on my father's side were sure of their leprechauns.

"It was said that many of the old Irish families had fairies for ancestors," writer Sharon Moscinski recalled. "Numerous songs told of elves, sprites, or banshees, the Irish female spirit whose waiting warned of a death soon to come." [3]

The Little People of the forest did not warn Buckongahelas of a death soon to come. The gallant Delaware chief stumbled onto the scene, unsuspecting the stab of sorrow that would pierce his heart. When he spied his son on his back by the salt lick--his arms and legs askew like a discarded rag doll--The Buck experienced unspeakable fear for his beloved boy, a fear as painful as a metal-tipped arrow actually piercing his heart.

Running to the body, Buckongahelas knelt and bent his head to the boy's bloody chest, listening for a heartbeat, then lifted the limp wrist to find a pulse. Finding none, the Buck launched into a pitiful lament, lifting the mortally wounded boy into his arms.

Photo by David Scott Myers

129

Perhaps he remembered the first time he held his oldest son. Mahonegon, like all Indian babies, had been a red-faced, chubby little thing, hardly a handful when born screaming at the top of his lungs. He was silent now, his long body heavy and still.

As the baleful wails of the father washed over his boy, the sorrowful sounds drifted across the ancient forest. The father cradled his bloodied son on his lap, with the boy's lifeless eyes staring up at him. That scene would be immortalized 250 years later by sculptor Ross Straight in a statue that stands in Jawbone Park in Buckhannon, West Virginia, one of the loveliest spots on earth. (I visited Buckhannon in August, 2007.)

That morning, before he left on his hunt, Mahonegon probably grasped his father in a rough bear hug, laughing and jostling with his dad. (The young men in my family, especially my five brothers, always have been great teases.) When his sister, Little Leaf, spied her father's horse bearing the body of her dead brother, she sorrowfully shed the first of her three diamond tears.

The chief vowed to avenge his son's cruel and senseless death. He returned to his village in deep sorrow – probably the deepest sorrow he would experience during his long and painful life. He painted his face black (he and his family would appear with ash-covered faces for a year of mourning), and he painted his dead son's face. The father placed his son's medicine bag and other small belongings he might need in the next world beside his body on a tall raised bier. The boy's body later would be buried in a simple grave, lined and covered with bark and dirt, as Buckongahelas prepared to release his son to the ages.

Mahonegon had left his family and friends to walk the Star Path.

Metacom, the son of Massasoit (the chief whom Edward Winslow, another of our distant relatives, befriended after the *Mayflower* arrived in the New World) was similarly seized with grief 100 years *before* Buckongahelas lost his son. Metacom's wife and nine-year-old son were captured by the English, who no longer were friends of the Wampanoag.

"My heart breaks; now I am ready to die ...." Metacom, known to the English as King Philip, cried out when he learned of the capture. [4] His wife and son were among 500 tribal members sold as slaves and shipped away from Plymouth. The English later beheaded Metacom and displayed his head on a pole.

When Comanche Chief Pah-hah-yuco's son was killed in a fight with Mexicans in 1843--seventy years *after* Mahonegon's death–that chief was so distraught that he "had burned five of his six magnificent lodges, killed nearly all of his horses and mules, and thrown aside all of his ornaments and wearing apparel, keeping only his robe.

"I must cry and mourn till the green grass grows," the chief had said. 'I have scattered ashes on my head. I can do nothing during the season of my grief." [5]

And so grieved by the death of his son in the late 1860s was Kiowa Chief Setangya (called Satank by Americans) that "The grief-stricken old man thereafter bore his son's bones along with him on a lead horse wherever he went." [6]

Legend has it that Mahonegon, the murdered son of Chief Buckongahelas, is buried beneath the Buchhannon Court House.

According to legend, Mahonegon, son of Buckongahelas, is buried under the present Upshur County Courthouse in Buckhannon, West Virginia. The area's Boy Scout Camp is named for Mahonegon. Traces of the ancient village where he and his father lived still may be found near the town of Buckhannon.

Mahonegon's murder in 1773 was thought by many to be the beginning of Indian hostilities in the area, and perhaps, the opening shot of Dunmore's Bloody War of 1777.

"And that deadly shot, ringing out among the Monongahela hills on this quiet June day, striking with death the only son of Buckongahelas, the Delaware, was the opening gun on the Western Virginia border of 'Dunmore's Bloody War," J. C. McWhorter wrote.

"It is claimed by some historians that the battle of Point Pleasant fought October 10, 1774 was the first battle of the American Revolution. If so, then this shot of the border scout, Captain William White, was the first of that epochal struggle – the shot that was actually 'heard round the world.'" [7]

A Killer of Unarmed Indians

Who was this Captain White who so ruthlessly and needlessly murdered the young Mahonegon? A descendant of a doctor who lived in Frederick County, White arrived in the Buckhannon Valley sometime between 1769 and 1771. There is no record of White on War Department muster rolls or in Bureau of Pensions records in Washington. Each settlement elected its own captain, and he probably received his title in that way.

White was known for his deep hatred of Indians, any Indians anywhere. But he would not deliberately have murdered the son of Buckongahelas, as he had a healthy fear and respect of the chief.

Although he shot Mahonegon in the back, White was described as "a frontier hero" in J. C. McWhorter's book about the captain and The Buck, *The Scout of the Buckongehanon.* McWhorter's brother, historian Lucullus Virgil McWhorter, described White far differently, however, in his book, *The Border Settlers of Northwestern Virginia from 1768 to 1795.* Lucullus minced no words in declaring White's deeds to be those of a bloody and cowardly killer.

Lucullus told the story of White's murder of another unfortunate Indian after White chased the young man over a precipice into quicksand, into which both men sunk when White jumped down after him.

"The young Indian, who was wholly unarmed, made frantic efforts to escape, while White made strenuous attempts to strike him with his tomahawk. In the struggle, the warrior inadvertently flung out his arm toward White, who seized his hand, and drawing his helpless victim within reach, sank the hatchet in his head." [8]

Not long before Dunmore's War in 1774, during a visit to Colonel Crawford in the Allegheny (Talego) Mountains in 1768, White and an Irishman murdered two peaceable Indians on the Wappatomaka and were imprisoned in the Winchester jail. A Captain Fry led an armed mob of fifty to sixty men who forced the jailer to relinquish his keys. White was dragged out in irons and gleefully escaped justice and punishment for his crimes.

In 1772--exactly a year before he came upon Mahonegon at the salt lick--White also was the leader in the ghastly murder of Bull Town Lenape families in the county of Braxton, Virginia.

In June of that year, Shawnees from the Ohio had killed a family who lived on the Gauley River. In retaliation, White and four other men from Buckhannon and the Hacker's Creek settlement – including William Hacker, the scout Jesse Hughes, and John Cutright – headed for Bull Town, named for Captain Bull who had attempted to sway the Lenape away from the English.

The fifth killer was believed to be a notorious renegade by the name of Reeder from the Wappatomaka. He was known for his horrible method of murdering peaceable Indians by thrusting a rod full length up their rectums into their intestines.

Bull Town was a peaceful settlement on the Little Kanawha River of Indian families who manufactured and sold salt at the "Salt Licks" to white families. Capt. Bull escaped the slaughter only because of a previous tragedy: the death of his small child, whose body he had taken to be buried with his tribe north of Ohio after whites had offered no condolences.

"Mr. (Christopher T.) Cutright's statement was that sometime prior to the massacre, death entered the lowly hut of Capt. Bull, robbed him of his little child…. The parental affection in the Indian bosom is strong, and the grief of the stricken parents was most poignant." [9]

Christopher Cutright, speaking of his father, John Cutright, and his friends, later said: "When Billy (William) White and Jesse Hughes went on an Indian killing, they killed all with whom they came in contact, not even sparing women and children.

"My father was about as bad as they were, and Samuel Pringle of the sycamore tree, who married my father's sister, was scarce better." [10] (It was sad to learn of the involvement of Samuel Pringle, whom The Buck had befriended and whose life he had saved when he found him starving in the hollow Sycamore tree.)

After murdering the Bull Town families, White and his cohorts threw the bodies into the Little Kanawha and burned the Indian village. The slaughter of the peaceful Lenape Indians, who had nothing to do with the Shawnee attack, is known to this day as "a blot on the story of white pioneers of Western Virginia." The horrible massacre of the families at Bull Town "in treachery and cold blood" was "as repulsive as any reported by captives in Indian camps," reported historian Lucullus McWhorter.

Shortly after the Bull Town massacre, White was joined by Samuel Pringle and Jesse Hughes in another slaughter at dawn of thirteen peaceful Indian hunters from Ohio who were camped in the cave-like recess of Indian Camp Rock and could not escape when the attack began.

Capt. Bull returned to the Virginia area and was killed in 1781 by some of the same men who had destroyed the Bull Town families in 1772. A large party of Indians had attacked a white settlement and taken prisoners. Capt. White, Jesse Hughes and his brother Elias, and John Cutright were among the assembled company who sought revenge at the Indians' camp. Christopher Cutright again told the story:

"When the whites rushed upon the camp, one of the Indians struggling in the agonies of death was recognized as Capt. Bull, the founder of Bull Town on the Little Kanawha. Jesse Hughes seized the dying chieftain and dragged him through the campfire ... 'while he was yet kicking.' Not satisfied with this, he then flayed from the thigh of the dead chieftain pieces of skin, with which he repaired his own moccasins which had become badly worn during the pursuit. Upon the return of the company to the settlements, Hughes as a joke threw his moccasins with their ghastly patches into my mother's lap." [11]

White was not the "Hero of the Buckongehanon" as described by J. C. McWhorter in his romance novel that contained more fiction than fact. The Delaware believed White was possessed by an evil spirit that had taken over the captain's soul and turned him into a vicious, bestial man who would murder an innocent Indian boy and unarmed Indian families.

The murder of his beloved son kindled hatred in the heart of Buckongahelas, like the lodge fire that burns for a year until extinguished and re-lit for the next year. The Buck and his family lifted his son's body onto the raised bier so that the boy's soul might be free to travel on the twelfth day following his death. In later years, the Delaware would adopt the white man's custom of burial in a wooden coffin, but they would drill a hole into the top of it, so that the soul of the deceased might fly away freely to the Great Spirit in the sky.

Fifty years later, another great Delaware chief, William Anderson, also would lose his young son to death. Writing in deep grief to General William Clark, Anderson confided: "My brother: When I was in St. Louis I took the Osages a little by the hand. I had not been settled down at my home two months before the Osages killed my son.

"I asked you not to give the Osages any more powder, but they came and they killed my only one boy. They killed him with bow and arrow--Well, twice you have let us down--you say you never heard of the boy being killed before now. All my [people] know that he was killed.

"I am in pain," Anderson admitted. "I cannot think good in my heart--I can do no more--It is not many days since I called my warriors to me and they called all their grandchildren here. My brother: The other day you heard about it from me, now you will hear from my warriors."[12]

In the same manner, the white man who murdered the son of Buckongahelas, as well as his white friends, became the enemies of The Buck—and they would hear from him and his warriors. For his murder of Mahonegon, Capt. White would meet his death in 1782 at the hands of a Delaware warrior near the Buckhannon Fort—named for Buckongahelas. Great-grandfather Buck was not the murderer. He was away at a treaty council.

1. McWhorter, J. C., *Scout of Buckongehanon*, pp. 102, 74.
2. Ibid, pp. 101, 102.
3. Moscinski, *Tracing Our Irish Roots*, pp. 8, 9.
4. Josephy, Jr. *Indians*, p. 174.
5. Hoig, *Beyond the Frontier*, p. 210
6. Josephy, Jr. *Indians*, p. 381.
7. McWhorter, J. C., *Scout of Buckongehanon*, p. 104.
8. McWhorter, Lucullus, *Border Settlers*, p. 108.
9. Ibid, pp. 87, 88.
10. Ibid, p. 102.
11. Ibid, p. 135.
12. Cranor, *Kik Tha We Nund*, p. 10.

25

Clouds of War

It was following his son's callous murder that Buckongahelas became one of the most feared of all the war chiefs in the border wars. Previously, he had offered his left hand in friendship to Virginia whites, opposing young men of his clan who clamored for scalps of intruders on their lands in the vast region of the Great Kanawha Valley along an area that became West Virginia.

Now began the frightening Delaware war dances that preceded planned attacks upon their enemies. The Moravian missionary Zeisberger had witnessed the dances, and described them as "very wild and fearful to behold."

"One dancer carries his hatchet, another [dancer] a long knife, another a large club, a fourth a cudgel. These they brandish in the air, to signify how they intend to treat or have treated their enemies, affecting all the while an air of anger and fury." [1]

It was said of Buckongahelas that soldiers who fell into his hands as prisoners rejoiced because they knew they would be treated fairly instead of having their bodies tortured and brutally murdered.

"This chieftain was a fearless warrior, and tradition credits him with having led some of the war parties against the Virginia border," wrote historian Lucullus McWhorter. "This may be true; he opposed the settling of the Trans-Allegheny, but nowhere can there be ascribed acts of cruelty in the welfare of this lofty-minded chieftain.

"With his ability as a warrior was coupled a humane heart and a noble purpose. He sought not the injury of non-combatants, nor did he rejoice in the effusion of blood. He struck only in defense of his outraged people. His prowess was felt in the French and Indian War of 1763." [2]

Mahonegon was murdered in June, 1773, and in September, a little known hunter by the name of Daniel Boone and fifty others attempted to establish a settlement in Kentucky. Boone's oldest son, James, and a few men were attacked in the forest by a band of Delaware, Shawnee, and Cherokee who were opposed to the settlement. The Indians believed in blood revenge, an eye for eye–a son for a son–and James and another boy were captured and put to death, the first killings of whites that precipitated Dunmore's War in 1774.

The bloodcurdling cries of "Mahonegon, Mahonegon!" were the last words that many whites heard after Buckongahelas entered the fray. Blood flowed in the border towns across the valley the following year. In fact, the year 1774 became one of the bloodiest in the history of the area west of the Alleghenies as the Shawnee also resisted intrusion into their lands. In the conflict of Dunmore's War that raged on the nearly 400-mile-long West Virginia frontier, hundreds of whites were scalped and murdered, but more Indians actually died than whites.

"It must be said that most of the victims of murder on the border, from the close of Pontiac's War to the Dunmore War of 1774, were Indians," Lucullus McWhorter wrote. "Nor do we find that any of the murderers ever received just punishment." [3]

Wanted Dead or Alive

Buckongahelas, his father Wendacolla (aka Windaughala or Windochelas) and their warriors became known on both sides of the border as the "Windochelas Gang." Rewards for their capture were posted in town windows and "wanted posters" hammered onto neighborhood and forest trees of the Trans-Allegheny.

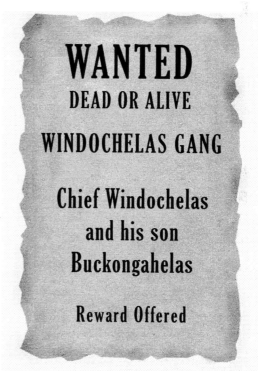

"Nowhere in the Anglo-Saxon conquest of the New World is there a territory so fraught with dramatic tragedy, personal prowess and adventure, as the Trans-Allegheny," historian McWhorter declared.

"For more than twenty years, embracing the Revolutionary struggle, amid the dark mazes of this mighty wilderness, the Red and the White warriors met in deadly conflict." [4] (Reds and Whites of another country, Russia, also would brutally slaughter each other by the thousands little more than a century later.)

A year after he murdered Mahonegon in 1773, Captain White showed up with Colonel John

Sevier of North Carolina at the Battle of Point Pleasant on October 10, 1774, the American colonists' first conflict and victory and the only major battle of Dunmore's War. Sevier also conducted two campaigns against the Cherokees, later becoming the first governor of Tennessee and a brigadier general of the United States Army in 1798.

Cornstalk, the most prominent predecessor of Blue Jacket (a close friend of Buckongahelas), led the Shawnee in Dunmore's War in 1774 after Virginia attacked the Shawnee. (Cornstalk would attempt to keep the tribe neutral in the American Revolutionary War.) The Delaware Chief White Eyes prevented many of his warriors from joining in the trouble started by Virginia's Tory Gov. John Murray, the Earl of Dunmore.

The Revolutionary War that began in 1775 would bitterly divide the Delaware Nation. After the murder of his son, Buckongahelas despised the American colonists more than the British, and in 1776, he and his father, Wendacolla, broke with White Eyes and Killbuck of the Turtle Clan, who promoted Delaware neutrality at the war's onset. Chief William Anderson also sided with White Eyes, much to Buckongahelas' disappointment.

There were American Indians and blacks who fought with the Continental Army, however, although Washington and many of his supporters at first had opposed the inclusion of blacks in the army.

"In response to concerns in Congress over how much of the army was in fact made up of old men and boys, as well as Negroes and Indians, General William Heath reported: 'There are in the Massachusetts regiments some few lads and old men, and in several regiments, some Negroes,'" historian David McCullough wrote in his book *1776*.

"Such is also the case with the regiments from the other colonies. Rhode Island has a number of Negroes and Indians. The New Hampshire regiments have less of both....

"Like most southerners, Washington did not want blacks in the army and would soon issue orders saying that neither 'Negroes, boys unable to bear arms, nor old men' were to be enlisted. By year's end, however, with new recruits urgently needed and numbers of free blacks wanting to serve, he would change his mind and in a landmark general order authorize their enlistment." [5]

The British Proclamation of 1763 had limited frontier settlement to the eastern side of the

Appalachians, but white settlers had ignored the proclamation. Friction escalated between the settlers and the Cherokees, as well as the Delaware. Virginia and both of the Carolinas began campaigns to crush the Overhill Cherokees in June, 1776. That year not only some of the Delaware still were fighting with the British, but troops from Scotland were recruited to join the Royal Navy's attack on American soil.

The 40-gun Phoenix warship was one of 120 ships in the British fleet that dropped anchor to land at Staten Island on July 2, 1776.

"The British fleet of 120 ships that had dropped anchor for the landing at Staten Island on July 2, 1776 included "the *Centurion* and the *Chatham*, of 50 guns each, the 40-gun *Phoenix*, and the 30-gun *Greyhound* with General [William] Howe [who had served in the French and Indian War] on board, in addition to the 64-gun *Asia*," McCullough wrote.

"In their combined firepower these five warships alone far exceeded all the American guns now in place on shore. Nathanael Greene reported to Washington that the total fleet of 120 ships had '10,000 troops received at Halifax, beside some of the Scotch Brigade that have joined the fleet on the passage.'

"And as Lieutenant Colonel Samuel Webb of Washington's staff further noted, an additional 15,000 to 20,000 could be expected 'hourly' on still more ships from England under the command of General Howe's brother, Admiral Richard Lord Howe." [6]

The British armada that sailed into New York Harbor eventually numbered more than 400 ships, "the largest naval force every seen in American waters, the largest sent out from the British Isles to defeat a distant foe," McCullough recorded. "With no fighting ships of their own, the Americans faced an almost impossible task of defending against such might." [7]

The Tories had at least two dangerous plans that were discovered by informants for the Americans, Katherine and John Bakeless revealed in their book *Spies of the Revolution*.

"The first plan was to kidnap George Washington from his New York headquarters…. The second plot was for a sudden uprising of armed Tories. This was to take place *behind* the American army in Manhattan, on Long Island, and also along the Hudson River as far north as the Highlands, near West Point.

"It was to be timed so that General Howe's soldiers and the ships commanded by his brother, Admiral Lord Howe, would be attacking the American front together." [8]

The British continued to supply arms to the sympathetic Indian Nations during the Revolutionary War, and the Overhill Cherokees began raids against the interlopers into their territory. State militias conducted raids of their own. Under the Treaty of DeWitt's Corner between the Cherokee and South Carolina in May, 1777, the Cherokees were forced to cede almost all of their land in South Carolina. This treaty ended the Cherokee War of 1776-1777, which began at the beginning of the American Revolution. Similar treaties between American Indians and states resulted in land cessions to North Carolina and Virginia.

Buckongahelas, his father, and a few followers also joined the British fighting with Wyandot Chief Half King in an assault on Wheeling in August and September of 1777. Buckongahelas then established a town on the headwaters of the Great Miami in Ohio near the village of Chief Blue Jacket and his other Shawnee friends, who also despised the colonists.

On September 17, 1778, some Delaware journeyed to Fort Pitt (presently Pittsburgh, Pennsylvania) to sign the first treaty the Continental Congress ever enacted with an Indian nation. Buckongahelas refused to sign this treaty in which the Indians promised to join American troops and allow them to travel through their lands to attack the British on the Great Lakes.

"From 1778 until 1871, the treaty was the principal instrument of US government Indian policy: over 370 treaties, 60 percent of which required tribes to give up their homelands to the US, were negotiated and signed between Indian nations and the U.S. government," Arlene Hirschfelder noted in her book *Native Americans.* [10]

In return for the Natives' signatures, the treaty of 1778 provided a promise for an Indian state to be established as the fourteenth state, with representation in Congress, which, of course, never happened.

On February 25, 1779, Congress instructed George Washington to deal with British, Indian, and loyalist attacks on frontier settlements in New York and Pennsylvania. Washington ordered an expedition under the command of General John Sullivan. During a series of savage raids and counter-raids between the British and the Americans, forty Iroquois villages and their farms lands and crops were destroyed.

The Iroquois rejoined the British and other tribes, including the Delaware, in a retaliatory invasion in the northwest. This was only the beginning of bloodshed between American Indians and whites, who considered themselves the only true Americans.

Despite the might of the British, the overwhelming odds, and defeat following defeat, the Continental Army, led by the brilliant George Washington, eventually would prevail in 1783. Captured Tories would be hung, sentenced to imprisonment, or tattooed in a similar manner as slaves and pigs.

"Sometimes Tories were branded with a hot iron in the form of the letter T—a form of punishment long used in England," the Bakeless authors reported. [9]

Eventually, the rebellious Delaware who sided with the British, including The Buck and his father-in-law Captain Pipe, also would be punished, losing millions of acres of their precious lands and removed to the faraway habitats of strangers.

1. Zeisberger, *History of Northern American Indians*, p. 77.

2. McWhorter, Lucullus, *Border Settlers*, p. 164.

3. Ibid, p. 104.

4. Ibid, pp. 26.

5. McCullough, *1776*, pp. 36, 37.

6. Ibid, p. 135.

7. Ibid, illustration 12, following p. 116.

8. Bakeless, *Spies of the Revolution*, p. 83.

9. Ibid, p. 112.

10. Hirschfelder, *Native Americans*, p. 58.

26

George Washington's Warning

My grandfather Sherman Taylor's great-great-grandfather, a captain, was an aide de camp to General George Washington. Sherman was the father of my mother. On the other side of the family were the Delaware descendants of Buckongahelas, including Sherman's wife, my grandmother Edna.

Many of the Delaware had become British allies during the American Revolutionary War under the leadership of Chief Buckongahelas and his father-in-law Captain Pipe.

Washington invited leaders of the Delaware nation who had written him to meet with him on May 12, 1779 at his headquarters at Middle Brook, New Jersey, hoping to consolidate waning Delaware support for the American side of the Revolutionary War. (His address to the Delaware Nation is one of several rare historic documents on display at Gilcrease Museum in Tulsa, Oklahoma.)

"Brothers," the commander-in-chief of all the armies in the United States of America began in a kindly manner. "I have read your paper. The things you have said are weighty things, and I have considered them well. The Delaware Nation have (sic) shown their good will to the United States. They have done wisely, and I hope they will never repent.

"I rejoice in the new assurances you give of their friendship," the white military leader added. "The things you now offer to do to brighten the chain prove your sincerity. I am sure Congress will run to meet you – and will do everything in their power to make the friendship between the people of those states – and their Brethren of the Delaware Nation, last forever.

"I am a warrior," asserted the man who would become the first president of the United States ten years later and serve two terms as the "Father of the Country."

"My words are fine and plain; but I will make good what I say," Washington continued, his tone becoming testier.

"'Tis my business to destroy all the enemies of those States and to protect their friends," he said. "You have seen how we have withstood the English for four years; and how their armies have dwindled away and come to very little; and how what remains of them in this part of our great Country are glad to stay upon two or three little islands – where the waters and their ships hinder us from going to destroy them.

"The English, Brothers, are a boasting people – they talk of doing a great deal, but they do very little. They fly away on their ships from one part of our country to another, but as soon as our warriors got together, they leave it and go to some other part. They took Boston and Philadelphia – two of our greatest towns, but when they saw our warriors in a great body ready to fall upon them – they were forced to leave them."

The mighty warrior went on with his long-winded speech to his audience: "We have till lately fought the English all alone. – Now the Great King of France is become our Good Brother and Ally. – He has taken up the hatchet with us, and we have sworn never to bury it, till we have punished the English and made them sorry for all the wicked things they had in their hearts to do against those States. And these and other great Kings and Nations on the other side of the big Waters, who love us and wish us well – and will not suffer the English to hurt us."

Washington paused to let the threatening words that would follow impress the minds and memory of his listeners.

"Listen well to what I tell you and let it sink deep into your hearts," he cautioned. "We love our friends and will be faithful to them – as long as they will be faithful to us. – Good brothers, the Delawares will always be so. – But we have sworn to take vengeance on our enemies – and on false friends. – The other day, a handful of our young men destroyed the settlement of the Onodagas. – They burnt down all their houses – destroyed their grain and horses and cattle – took their arms away – killed several of their warriors and brought off many prisoners and obliged the rest to fly into the woods.

"This is but the beginning of the troubles which those Nations, who have taken up the hatchet against us, will feel," Washington warned ominously.

Then suddenly changing his tone, he added, "I am sorry to hear that you have suffered for

143

want… or that any of our people have not dealt justly by you…. But as you are going to Congress, which is the great Council of the Nation and holds all things in their hands, I shall say nothing about the supplies you ask. I hope you will receive satisfaction from them. I assure you I will do everything in my power to prevent your receiving any further injuries and will give the strictest orders for this purpose. I will severaly (sic) punish any that shall break them."

Washington added another caution to the Delaware: "You do well to wish to learn our arts and ways of life and above all the religion of Jesus Christ. These will make you a greater and happier people than you are. – Congress will do everything they can to assist you in this wise intention; and to tie the knot of friendship and union so fast that nothing shall ever be able to loose it."

Washington concluded his admonitions to his darker-skinned "brothers" by saying, "There are some matters about which I do not open my Lips, because they belong to Congress, and not to us warriors – you are going to them – they will tell you all you wish to know. When you have seen all you want to see, I will then wish you a good journey to Philadelphia. I hope you may find everything your hearts can wish, that when you return home you may be able to tell your Nation good things of us – And I pray God he may make your Nation wise and Strong (sic) that they may always see their own best interest and have courage …." [1]

Sixteen Scalps to Detroit

The Buck was not swayed by the White Father's strong words. He believed the best interests of the Delaware were served by siding with the British. Throughout the Revolutionary War, the War Chief Buckongahelas would lead forays against the Americans. He moved his people to the upper Miami River, and proudly brought sixteen scalps on a long stick to the headquarters of the British or "regulars" at Detroit in 1781, seeking additional weapons, ammunition and other supplies. (Enemies were scalped after death by both Indians and whites as proof of a warrior's accomplishments. Only extremely cruel warriors scalped people while they still were alive.)

By 1781, most of the Delaware had entered the war on the side of the British redcoats. A few, including Gelelemend (John Killbuck, Jr.), remained friendly to the Americans. Gelemend later converted to Christianity and lived the remainder of his life at the Moravian Goshen mission with Rev. David Zeisberger, whom historian Russell H. Booth Jr. called "the greatest of Moravian missionaries."[2]

After the murder of White Eyes, who was killed by white soldiers whom he had supported, Buckongahelas' stance against neutrality grew in popularity among the Delaware who had sided with the duped White Eyes. As the war progressed, more and more Lenape joined Buckongahelas, and by 1781, a total of 240 warriors followed his leadership. By the time Buckongahelas rode into battle against the American General Arthur St. Clair ten years later, The Buck had accumulated more than 450 warriors.

Buckongahelas evacuated his people to Goscachgunk (now Ohio) to establish their capital in April, 1781 and live in peace. But the massacre of their brothers and sisters by Colonel Daniel Brodhead at the Delaware town of Coshocton in 1781, and a Pennsylvania militia's horrible butchery of nearly 100 Christian Delaware Indians at Gnadenhutten, Ohio in 1782 made that peace impossible.

"Suspected by the British of helping the Americans, distrusted by the frontiersmen because they were Indians, and located as they were between the contending parties, the Christian Indians were, quite literally caught between two fires," Zeisberger wrote in 1781.[3]

Bitter attacks between Delaware and other tribes against Americans continued for years after the Revolution ended in 1783. "It is estimated that, during the years from 1783 to 1790, as many as 1,500 settlers died in isolated frontier Indian attacks," historian Carl Waldman reported.[4]

"Finally, the Delawares were able to make a separate peace with the Americans, at a heavy price, in the Treaty of Fort McIntosh, signed on January 21, 1785," author Robert Grumet wrote. "Forced to give up the Tuscarawas River country, most Delawares moved to western Ohio."[5] Buckongahelas was present at Fort McIntosh, now Beaver, Pennsylvania, but he did not sign the treaty.

During 1785, the Delaware joined with thirty-four other Indian nations that still were supported by the British, and prepared for further war with the white Americans. Despite the danger to their lives, white settlers continued to pour into the Ohio Valley, and to demand that all Indians be expelled from the area.

"Delaware warriors led by Buckongahelas defended their villages and attacked invaders,"

[6] Grumet reported. But still the invaders came, like ants marching ever onward. Much death and destruction awaited the members of the Delaware and other Indian tribes.

Buckongahelas searched for the murderer of his son for nine years, but Captain White went on his way unmolested, accompanying his close friend Colonel William Crawford, a friend of George Washington, on many attacks against the Delaware. White also served as a lieutenant in Capt. George Jackson's Company of Volunteer Militia in 1781. White was captured twice by Indians, once on the Little Kanawha in September, 1777, when he was painted red, and forced to run a gauntlet before he escaped. Had his identity and evil deeds been known, he would have been painted black and put to death, as was his companion captured with him, Leonard Petro.

White finally was shot to death on the evening of March 8, 1782 in West Virginia within sight of Bush Fort (also called the Buckhannon Fort) in the vicinity of the Buckhannon River. His wife witnessed the shooting that occurred near a tree with upturned roots, but she was unable to identify the Indian warrior who escaped into the woods. It was rumored that the assassin was the father of the boy White murdered in the quicksand years previously. Buckongahelas never admitted to arranging the death of Captain White, who had accumulated many enemies besides the Delaware war leader. The notorious Chief Buck could not have done the deed himself, however, as he was in Ohio attending a treaty council at the time of the murder.

Captain White was killed on the same day that nearly 100 Christian Indians were chopped to death by Pennsylvania militiamen at the Moravian town of Gnadenhutten in Ohio on March 8, 1782, "the Year of Blood."

1. *George Washington's Speech to Delaware*, May 12, 1779, Gilcrease Museum of the Americas, Tulsa, Oklahoma.
2. Booth, Jr., *Tuscarawas Valley in Indian Days*, p. 222.
3. Ibid, p. 199.
4. Waldman, *Atlas of the North American Indian*, p. 114.
5. Grumet, *Lenapes*, pp. 74, 75.
6. Ibid, p. 75.

27

Sweet Moravian Music

Chief Netawatwees, grandfather of Buckongahelas, allowed the very first Moravian religious service in Ohio Territory to be held in his grand house at Gekelemukpechunk at noon on March 14, 1771, four years before the Revolutionary War began. A crowd of Indians and a dozen white men excitedly gathered to hear the first Moravian sermon delivered in the territory. The Moravians droned on for hours in their sermons, their words dropping like stones from their mouths after a spell.

Roberta Campbell Lawson, also a descendant of Buckongahelas, told the amusing story of a three-year-old Delaware girl who listened patiently for three hours or more to a monotonous Moravian minister, and then rose amid the congregation to shout: "Tachitgusseek!" (the Delaware equivalent of "shut up!"). [1]

Many Christians and non-Christians today never have learned of the Moravian missionaries and their history. The Moravian church originated in ancient Bohemia and Moravia in what today is the Czech-Republic.

Only eleven Moravians ventured to America at first with their mission to convert the Indians of the Six Nations. Settling in 1735 in Georgia, they tried for five years to proselytize the Creeks and Cherokees. Unsuccessful and unwanted by those Natives, the Moravians tried their luck with converting the Mohicans and Wampanoag at a mission in 1740 at Shekomeko in New York that lasted for six years.

The Moravians then moved to Lehighton, Pennsylvania, where they founded the first Gnadenhutten mission. Spurned by the Six Tribes, they concentrated their conversion efforts on the Lenape, named by whites the "Delaware," as they were known by that time.

"But how did Native Americans view the way Europeans treated their African prisoners?" author Katz asked in his book *Black Indians.*

"Two European missionaries, trying to convert the Delaware Nation, returned rejected, but with this report on the Delaware response to their plea: 'They [the Delaware] could not help recollecting that we had a people among us, whom, because they differed from us in color, we had made slaves of, and made them suffer great hardships, and lead miserable lives…. Now they could not see any reason, if a people being black entitled us then to deal with them, why a red color should not equally qualify the same treatment.'" [2]

Such skepticism was well justified. The Gnadenhutten missions of Christian Moravian Indians–the first in Pennsylvania, the second in the Ohio Valley--seemed cursed from the start.

Non-Christian Indians allied with the French attacked the mission in Pennsylvania in November, 1755. The survivors settled in Bethlehem, Pennsylvania, where my ancestor Little Leaf's great-aunt, Maw-We- Ha (Christina), lived as a youth. The attack on the Ohio Gnadenhutten mission in 1782, this time by Pennsylvania militiamen, would be an even more horrific slaughter on a much grander scale. Aunt Maw-We-Ha, unfortunately, would be at the Gnadenhutten in Ohio when that second brutality began.

Author Barbara Mitchell has written a delightful book, *Tomahawks and Trombones*, about the Moravians and their love of music. Some of her story comes from a 225-year-old diary kept by the Moravian "sisters." The book tells how the Moravians gave the New World its first orchestra, the Bach Choir. The tale is told that when the Moravians ventured across the vast ocean to America, their ship was so crowded that each family could bring only one chest.

"But tucked into the chests were violins and flutes, oboes and French horns. One instrument, though, would not fit: the trombones. So sadly, the Moravians left their trombones behind. And there were no trombones in the New World yet." [3]

Moravians settled in Bethlehem, Pennsylvania and were without their trombones for twelve years. Finally they wrote to their European brethren, begging for them to send a box of trombones. Four long boxes of trombones arrived a year later in the spring. By the next Christmas, relations between the Delaware and the Moravians were strained.

"But the New Year, 1755, was not so fine. Stories of Indian attacks filled the air. French settlers and English settlers both wanted all the fur trade in the New World. Each side took more and more land away from the Indians. They pushed the Indians off their best hunting grounds…. And in the fall, the crops were poor. There had been no rain. The Delawares had almost no corn. Fur trappers were taking their animals. The Delaware were starving." [4]

The Indians became angrier and angrier. They began to attack the settlers' homes. At last, it was Christmas Eve. The Delaware, armed to the teeth with tomahawks and bows and arrow, surrounded the missionaries' village. Four or five of the missionaries, armed only with their trombones, climbed to the top of a roof.

"Suddenly a loud sound cut through the air. It was clear and strong. It was beautiful. The Indians had never heard anything like it. The music echoed off the stone houses. It filled the morning sky. The Indians were frightened.

"'Music up in the sky!' they said. 'It must be the voice of the Moravians' God! Surely He watches over this place.' They lowered their tomahawks and walked quietly back into the woods." [5]

The Indians were astounded. Such powerful and unusual melodies surely had come from *Kishelamukonk*, the term used by the Delaware when they spoke of their Creator. The Indians cast aside their weapons, extending their hands in friendship to the white men and women with their strange but magnificent melodies.

Moravian leaders, such as the renowned David Zeisberger, born at Zeuchtenthal, Moravia in 1721, were fluent in the Delaware tongue and won the respect of most of the Indian leaders. Zeisberger journeyed to America in 1740 at age nineteen, and began his fifty years of work as a Moravian missionary to the Delaware following his ordination in 1749. (He had lived among the Mohawk prior to this time, and learned the languages of the Six Nations.)

Rev. David Zeisberger

"Perhaps in all the history of this famous Indian Nation there was no other man, with the exception of Sir William Johnson, whom they trusted as much as they trusted David Zeisberger," wrote Arthur Butler Hulbert of Marietta College in Ohio.

"Cheated on the one hand by the Dutch of New York and robbed on the other by the agents of the Dutch and the English, the Iroquois became suspicious of all men; and it is vastly more than a friendly compliment to record that in his mission-house at Onondaga, they placed the entire archives of their nation, comprising possible the most valuable collection of treaties and letters from colonial governors ever made by an Indian nation on this continent." [6]

"We Have a Different Skin"

Zeisberger was so admired that he became an adopted Munsee, a sub-division of the Lenape, and was accepted as a member of the Great Council. He served the Delaware for nearly fifty years until his death in 1808 at the Delaware settlement of Goshen in Ohio.

Chief Buckongahelas did not oppose the Moravians at first, but he recognized that they and their beliefs were a threat to his native culture that had developed over thousands of years.

"You yourselves see that we have a different skin," he told his ancient people, urging them not to abandon their traditional ways of worshipping the Creator as the Lord and master of all life.

The Moravians, however, baptized several of Netawatwees' grandchildren and a nephew, Gelemend, also known as Captain John Killbuck, Jr., although his father bitterly opposed the sect and divided the Delaware on the subject. Killbuck, Sr. was a member of the Wolf lineage, but his nephew was of the Turtle clan, since Delaware lineage was determined by the mother's clan. Sometimes the opinions of members of different clans within a tribe clashed with as much fury as those of different tribes.

Buckongahelas never moved with force against the Moravians, but to his death he opposed the conversion of his people to Christianity. Still, he went out of his way to warn the Delaware Moravian Christians of their impending danger at Gnadenhutten in Ohio during the American Revolution.

Since the Moravians felt a special call to minister to the Delaware, they founded several villages where the Christian Indians lived apart from their non-Christian brethren. The second Gnadenhutten was only one of three villages in eastern Ohio–the other two were Schroenberg and Selma--where the Delaware converts studied, prayed, farmed, learned German or English, cut their hair, and dressed in the same clothing as the whites.

Besides music, the Moravians brought the sounds of buzzing bees into the lives of the Delaware. Bees were unknown in Ohio until the Moravians arrived.

"Of bees, nothing was known when we came here in '72 [1772], now they are to be found in large numbers in hollow trees in the woods," the Moravian missionary Zeisberger reported in his *History of Northern American Indians*. [7]

The Moravian missionaries gave much to the Delaware Nation, but they also took away much. They did their best to strip the Delaware of their families of origin, their traditions, their culture, their language, and ultimately, their identities as members of an indigenous race. The fact that they failed was due, in large part, to the example of leaders like Buckongahelas, who embraced his religious and cultural heritage with all of his being.

"Religion for the Delaware, as with most Algonquian tribes, revolved around the Great Spirit, a term that evoked creation, godship, and a host of spiritual forces inhabiting all things in nature," James A. Maxwell, editor of *America's Fascinating Indian Heritage*, explained.

"To a Delaware, those forces were everywhere, warming him, feeding him, healing him. The spirits listened to prayers and answered in the form of sunsets and snowfalls, favorable winds and spring rains. All things had souls. A twig, a stone had a life of its own, just as men, women and animals did. Old age was regarded as a high honor by all Algonquians, and death released the spirit into regions where pain, sickness, and sadness did not exist." [8]

To the end of his life, Buckongahelas held fast to the religious beliefs of his ancestors, but his descendants would convert in great numbers to Christianity, with two of them becoming renowned men of the cloth in Kansas and Indian Territory (now Oklahoma) and the Pacific Northwest.

1. Zeisberger, *Indian Dictionary*, p. 153.

2. Katz, *Black Indians*, p. 108.

3. Mitchell, *Tomahawks and Trombones*, p. 16.

4. Ibid, pp. 30, 34, 35.

5. Ibid, pp. 48-51.

6. Zeisberger, *History of Northern American Indians*, p. 3.

7. Ibid, p. 96.

8. Maxwell, *America's Fascinating Indian Heritage*, p. 120.

28

Buck Warns the Christian Delaware

The Delaware Tribe was a house divided by the Revolutionary War. Captain John Killbuck Sr. of the Wolf Clan and Chief White Eyes of the Turkey Clan were pro-American, while Captain Pipe and and his son-in-law Buckongahelas of the Wolf Clan were loyal to the British.

White Eyes had offered to guide the Americans through Western Pennsylvania, but the Delaware were notified that he died suddenly of smallpox along the way, which was strange because he had survived the disease earlier in his life. The Americans had murdered one of their best friends among the Delaware.

Buckongahelas brought an urgent message of warning in February of 1781 when he visited the mission of Gnadenhutten ("Tents of Grace") in Ohio, speaking to its residents and those from the town of Salem prior to his exodus from the area two months later. The early historian Samuel G. Drake recorded the words of The Buck:

"Petchenanalas [Buckongahelas], at the head of 80 warriors, appeared suddenly at Gnadenhuetten [sic], surrounding it before day, allowing no one a chance for escape. Not knowing his object, the people were filled with terror.

"But he soon dispelled their fears, by telling them that he came to take the chief *Gelelemend*, and a few other head men, whom he would have, either dead or alive. As it happened, not one of those he sought after was there at the time. Having satisfied himself of this fact, the chief demanded that deputies from the three Christian towns should meet to hear what he had to say to them." [1]

The Buck warned the Christian Indians of the dangers that beset them, as their settlements were in the path of fighting during the Revolutionary War. The chief had learned that a militia intended to murder his peaceful baptized brethren, disobeying Colonel Brodhead's orders.

As an orator, Buckongahelas was reputed to rank with Little Turtle of the Miami, Tarhe (the Crane) of the Wyandots, Black Hoof of the Shawanese, and Tog Wane of the Senecas. The Buck explained that he had sided with the British in the Revolutionary War due to the many wrongs suffered by his people. This was so despite the fact that White Eyes, the successor of Netawatwees, had supported the United States.

Buckongahelas invited the Christian Indians at Gnadenhutten to travel "westward from the rising sun" with him, promising that he would safeguard them all.

"His deportment on that occasion was singularly characteristic of the man; for all writers agree in representing him as fearless, frank and magnanimous," Benjamin Thatcher wrote of Buckongahelas in his two-volume *Indian Biography*.

"It should be premised, that he lived on the Miami, and being rather in the British interest, was disposed to watch quite closely the movements of the peace-party. What he *did*, however, he did openly. And he never hesitated to explain himself with the same freedom." [2]

The principal men from Gnadenhutten, Salem, and Shonbrun assembled with ninety or so dark-skinned Christian Delaware to hear the voice of the strong and powerful Warrior Chief Buckongahelas thunder into their ears. The chief's words were fiery with passion as he spoke to the peaceful Indians.

"Have you not discovered the footsteps of the long knives [i.e., the Mechanshican, or Americans] almost within sight of your towns, and seen the smoke arising from their camps! Should not this be sufficient warning to you; and lead you to consult your own safety! ...." author C. A. Weslager recalled the words of Buckongahelas.

A Family Quarrel

Historian Drake had recorded more of Buckongahelas' speech to the Christian Delaware: "Friends and kinsmen, listen to what I say to you. You see a great and powerful nation divided," he told his kinsmen and their wives.

"You see the father [the British] fighting against the son [the colonists], the son against the father. The father has called on his Indian children to assist him in punishing his children, the Americans, who have become refractory. I took time to consider what I should do – whether or not I should receive the hatchet of my father to assist him. At first, I looked upon it as a family quarrel, in which I was not interested. At length, it appeared to me that the father was in the right, and his children deserved to be punished a little.

"That this must be the case, I concluded from the many cruel acts his offspring had committed, from time to time, on his Indian children, in encroaching on their lands, stealing their property, shooting at and even murdering without cause, men, women, and children: yes, even murdering those who at all times had been friendly to them, and were placed for protection under the roof of their father's house; the father himself standing sentry at the door at the time!

"Friends and relatives, often has the father been obliged to settle and make amends for the wrongs and mischiefs done us, by his refractory children; yet these do not grow better. No! they remain the same, and will continue to be so, as long as we have any land left us!

"Look back at the murders committed by the Long Knives on many of our relations, who lived [as] peaceable neighbors to them on the Ohio!" Buckongahelas advised. "Did not they kill them without the least provocation? Are they now, do you think, better now than they were then? No! indeed not; and many days are not elapsed, since you had a number of these very men near your doors, who panted to kill you, but fortunately were prevented from so doing, by the Great Sun [Colonel Broadhead and his army], who at that time, had by the Great Spirit been ordained to protect you!" [4]

The aged Moravian minister the Rev. John Heckewelder further recorded portions of the Gnadenhutten speech in 1818, as reported in Helen Hunt Jackson's book *A Century of Dishonor*:

"I at one time, in April, 1787, was astonished when I heard one of their orators, a great chief of the Delawares, Pachgantschilias [Buckongahelas], by name, go over this ground, recapitulating the most extraordinary events which had before happened, and concluded in these words:

Rev. John Heckewelder

"'They enslave those who are not of their color, although created by the same Great Spirit who created them. They would make slaves of us if they could; but as they cannot do it, they kill us. There is no faith to be placed in their words. They are not like the Indians, who are only enemies

154

while at war, and are friends in peace.

"They will say to an Indian, 'My friend; my brother!' They will take him by the hand, and at the same moment, destroy him. And so you (addressing himself to the Christian Indians at Gnadenhutten), will also be treated by them before long. Remember that this day I have warned you to beware of such friends as these. I know the Long-Knives. They are not to be trusted." [5]

The Buck surely thought of his son, Mahonegon, lying on the ground at the Virginia salt lick, a teenage boy shot in the back without the least provocation. The face of the dead Mahonegon – with his dark eyes starring blankly at his father – surely also was in the mind of Buckongahelas as he spoke.

"I admit that there are good white men, but they bear no proportion to the bad; the bad must be the strongest, for they rule," Drake reported. [6]

Heckewelder later wrote that the chief's speech to the Christian Indians was delivered "with ease and an eloquence not to be imitated," and described Buckongahelas as "mild and affable in his manners; friendly and humane."

The peaceful Christian Indians listened keenly to the words of Buckongahelas, but neglected to heed them. The Delaware believed in personal Guardian Spirits, as many Christians believe in guardian angels. Were they not one and the same? Would not the Guardian Spirits or angels protect the Moravian Christian Indians?

The Indians at Gnadenhutten and Salem declined the invitation of Buckongahelas to accompany him, and scolded The Buck and his pugnacious father-in-law Capt. Pipe, saying that they broke the Ten Commandments by going to war with the British to defend the Delaware people against the Americans.

Despite the resistance of the Christian Delaware, according to historian Drake, "The chief then spoke with respect of their peaceable mode of life, and commended their desire to live in friendship with all mankind; but said they must be aware of their exposed situation – living in the very road the hostile parties must pass over, in going to fight each other; that they had just escaped destruction, from one of these parties; that therefore no time should be lost, but they should go to the country on the Miami, where they would be entirely out of danger."

Deaf as Stones

The Gnadenhutten Indians had turned "deaf as stones," Buckongahelas later remarked.

"The Christian Indians replied, that, as they had never injured the Americans, they thought they need not fear injury from them; that if their friends at war wished them well, in truth, they would not make their settlement upon the path they took to go to war, as it would lead their antagonists the same way; and that they could not remove without great detriment; and therefore, as they were then situated, they could not consent to go," Rev. Heckewelder wrote.

"Pachgantschihilas consulted in the meantime with his chief men, and answered very feelingly to what the brethren had said. He observed that he was sorry that they should differ from him in opinion, but that he had no intention to use compulsion, and only requested that those might be permitted to go, whose fears prompted them to it. This was readily assented to, and the council broke up, and the warriors departed." [7]

But before he left, Buckongahelas "proceeded to the middle of the street, from whence he addressed the inhabitants of the place and thanked them for their hospitality, assuring them of his regard and good wishes for them, and adding:

"'If at any time they should hear it said, that Pachgantschihilas was an enemy to the believing [Christian] Indians, they should consider such words as lies!" Thatcher wrote. [8]

The Buck then proceeded to another Moravian village of the Christian Delawares, Salem, and Thatcher reported the kindly words of Buckongahelas to his men:

"Before entering which place he cautioned his warriors to leave their arms behind them, 'lest the women and children should be frightened. And destroy nothing,' he added, 'which belongs to our friends; no, not even one of their *chickens*.'" [9]

Drake addted: "Here [Salem] a family of old people joined them, through fear of what Pachgantschihilas [The Buck] had predicted, and the event justified the proceeding! The massacre of Gnadenhuetten [sic] will ever be remembered with the deepest regret and indignation.

"Nothing was feared from the good Petchenanalas; but the prowling monsters [Alexander McKee] M'kee, [Simon] Girty, the "White Savage," [Matthew] Elliot, and perhaps others, calling themselves white, were the plotters of the ruin of the innocent people at Gnadenhuetten [stet], which followed not long after." [10]

Buckongahelas moved his people who were not Christians to safety. They joined his father-in-law, Captain Pipe, along the Sandusky in Ohio in April, 1781, finding sanctuary for them from the border wars. As Thatcher told the story:

"'The Christian Indians,' said the Chieftain [Buckongahelas], "were a happy people; and he would never trouble them on account of their not joining in the war.

"Indeed, they could not with propriety join in wars, without first renouncing praying, 'meaning Christianity]. ---And every Indian, or body of Indians, had a right to choose for themselves, whom they would serve! – For him, [The Buck], he had hired himself to his father, the king of England, for the purpose of fighting against his refractory children, the Long-Knives; whilst his friends and relations, the Christian Indians, had hired themselves to the Great Spirit, solely for the purpose of performing prayers!' [meaning, attending to religion].

"He added that both were right in their way, though both employments could not be connected together." [11]

The Lenape established 14 towns in the vast Ohio lands. Old Town Hill was located southeast of what now is Muncie. A second town was erected on the present day Minnetrista Boulevard; a third was situated near the community of Yorktown. The Indians called the nearby stream "Wapihani."

Eleven months after his speech was delivered by the prophetic Chief Buck, the Christian Indians were chopped to pieces in what one historian termed "one of the foulest deeds ever to stain American history."

Ninety of the Gnadenhutten Indians--about 60 of them women and children--and six visiting Indians were murdered at the place where the Buck's words had been spoken, by the same men the chief had alluded to, and in the same manner he had foretold.

The horrible murders of so many Delaware Christians in such a cruel and brutal way reminds me of a line in the beautiful *Sketchbook of Thomas Blue Eagle*, written by Gay Matthaei and Jewel Grutman with elegant illustrations by Adam Cvijanovic:

"My heart had fallen to the ground, and I had no strength to pick it up." [12]

1. Drake, *Indians of North America,* chapter 4, pg. 43.

2. Thatcher, *Indian Biography*, pp. 172, 1873.

3. Weslager, *Delaware Indians,* p. 315.

4. Drake, *Indians of North America,* pp. 43-44.

5. Jackson, *Century of Dishonor*, pp. 32-33.

6. Drake, *Indians of North America,* book 5, pp. 43-44.

7. Ibid, p. 44.

8. Thatcher, *Indian Biography*, p. 177.

9. Ibid, p. 175.

10. Drake, *Indians of North America,* book 5, p. 44.

11. Thatcher, *Indian Biography*, pp. 174, 175.

12. Matthaei and Grutman, *Thomas Blue Eagle*, p. 38.

29

Lambs to the Slaughter

As I write this sad chapter, I am holding in my hands an old, old book, 756 pages long, with its pages as wrinkled and cracked as the skin of my ancient Grandmother Scott when she died. The book, *Our Western Front One Hundred Years Ago,* was written by historian J. Charles McKnight and published in 1876. McKnight chronicled the story of the Delware people, whom he greatly admired.

"The Delawares were a noble, intelligent and virtuous tribe, as compared with redmen generally, and peculiarly susceptible to Gospel teachings," McKnight wrote. "Among them the missionaries worked east of the Alleghenis for years, converting thousands; forming them into separate industrious communities; teaching all the arts of peaceful civilization, and assiting them to live pure, devoted and consistent Christian lives.

"Persistent invitations had been extended to the Moravians by the Great Council of Delawares in Ohio, to come further west and settle near them on the Muskingum [River]. The invitation was soon after more urgently repeated by the great and good Delaware chief, Netawatwees, backed by the Wyandot chiefs, who promised all the land they needed and constant protection." [1]

Netawatwees invited the Moravians to move from Pennsylvania to Ohio, and urged that their new village be located near the Delaware capital of Gekelmukpechunk. He granted the Christian Moravians the use of the Tuscarawas Valley in Ohio, extending from the mouth of the Stillwater Creek to what now is the Tuscarawas River.

The town of Gnadenhutten was situated alongside the banks of the Muskingum in the Tuscarawas Valley. Rev. Heckewelder counted 241 Indian converts and missionaries with their families

The reconstructed Gnadenhutten Moravian Christian village in Ohio.

who arrived in the valley on August 23, 1773. Construction of the town of Gnadenhutten began the following October.

Nine years later--in the fall of 1782—the troublemaker Captain Pipe, father-in-law of Buckongahelas, encouraged the British to arrest the Moravian missionaries and remove the Christian Indians at Gnadenhutten from the path of the Revolutionary War. Pipe took this action despite the fact that his brother was a Moravian convert. Both sides of the conflict, British and American, still were being assisted by Indians of different tribes.

The Moravian Indians left Gnadenhutten and were escorted by British-allied tribesmen, primarily Delaware and Wyandot, to Captive's Town on the upper Sandusky. Moravian missionaries Zeisberger and Heckewelder were arrested and taken to Detroit, where the British tried and acquitted them for treason. Thus they were not at their missions when the Christian towns were brutally attacked.

"In the spring of '82 occurred a dread and lamentable event, which not only rests as an indelible stain upon the fair fame of the western border, but which added for a long time a rancorous bitterness to all the subsequent savage warfare," McKnight wrote.

"We allude, of course, to the dastardly and execrable massacre of the Moravian Indians on the Muskingum [river]." [2]

In February of 1782, nearly 100 starving Moravian Christian Indians returned to their village along the Tuscarawas River to search for food. In Delaware traditional villages, it was a woman's job to harvest the fields, but the Moravians convinced the Christian Delaware men to do "women's work." Both men and women were scavenging what crops they could find when the western Pennsylvania militia approached them.

Their captor would be Colonel David Williamson, who had led an expedition in March of 1781 in which about ninety-three Indians were killed. Now Williamson was chosen as leader of a volunteer militia of rabid Indian-haters from Washington County, Pennsylvania.

The Pittsburgh militia began by terrorizing the countryside and chasing a Delaware war party that eluded them. Then the militia turned its premeditated venom on the innocent, pacifist Christian Delaware Indians who lived guilelessly in the Moravian village of Gnadenhuten.

The militia was enraged by a recent murder by different Indians of a woman and her infant along the frontier. The husband of the woman reportedly was a member of the militia. The Christian Indians were accused of "having stolen goods of murdered borderers in their possession, triumphantly pointing to pewter dishes and spoons, and to branded horses as proof of the alleged robberies. One of the witnesses to the slaughter at Gnadenhutten, the Rev. Edward Christy, denied that this was true.

"'Twas in vain that the branding irons made by native blacksmiths were shown, and that the astonished Indians accounted–as I heard their teachers do in each case–for every article in their possession–what had been made by themselves and what had been bought from traders or carried from the East." [3]

According to Russel H. Booth, Jr., author of Tuscarawas Valley in Indian Days, the rules of the religious mission, strictly adhered to by all who wished to remain, stated: "No man inclining to go to war–which is the shedding of blood, can remain among us. Whosoever purchases goods or articles of warriors, knowing at the time that such have been stolen or plundered, must leave us. We look upon this as giving encouragement to murder and theft." [4]

The charge that the Christian Moravian Indians were involved in the murders of the woman and her child later was declared an outright lie. The slaughter of the Delaware Christians at Gnadenhutten was premeditated. The killers came, mounted on horseback and heavily armed, and began their dirty work in the dark forest before they ever reached Gnadenhutten. They encountered and shot a single Indian, Joseph Schebosh (or Schebosch), in the arm. Begging for his life, he told the militia that he was the son of a white missionary, the Rev. John Schebosh. (He also was the son of Captain Pipe's sister, Maw-We-Ha, aunt of the wife of Buckongahelas.)

Rev. Christy explained the militia's treatment of Joseph, relating how the Moravians had gathered their corn and were planning to depart on the day the militia arrived. "The band [the militia] was divided into two equal parts; one to cross over about a mile below Gnadenhutten and secure [capture] those who were gathering corn, and the other, with which I was, to attack this village itself. The first party found young Shabosch about a mile from here out catching horses. He was shot and scalped by a Capt. Builderbeck." [5]

Delaware Indians later recognized Builderbeck as the murderer of Shabosch and the killer who fired the first shot at the Moravian massacre. They captured, killed, and scalped the captain in revenge.

The bloodthirsty militia chopped Joseph to pieces, and then murdered another Indian in his canoe. This also was witnessed by the latter Indian's brother-in-law, Jacob, who escaped. Jacob recognized some of the militiamen as killers who had captured and murdered Christian Indians the previous autumn at Schonbrunn. Four other Indians, including a woman and two men named Paul and Anthony, also were killed along the river bank before the militia entered Gnadenhutten.

At first, the killers feigned friendship as they greeted the Moravians gathering corn in their fields of 300 acres. Later, with the evil grins on their faces, they also would round up and murder the Indian inhabitants of the nearby Moravian village of Salem.

The whites urged all of the Indians to gather their belongings to move to Pittsburgh, where they would be safe. With total trust, the Indians of both villages relinquished their guns, axes, mallets, and knives to the militia, who offered to "protect" them. The Indians were as lambs going to the slaughter as the horror began to unfold.

The militia suddenly turned on the Christian Delaware, accusing them of taking part in raids in Pennsylvania, which they knew was untrue. The Indians were placed under arrest and their bodies bound. Cries of alarm issued from mothers who clutched their children close to their bodies, hoping for rescue.

The Wailing of Women Begins

But there would be no rescue for the twenty-nine men, twenty-seven women, and thirty-four children who lived at the Christian Delaware mission or for their six Indian visitors. All of the ninety-six Indians would die horrific deaths at Gnadenhutten.

Many of the Delaware, including the men, fell to their knees in prayer. They believed that the Great Spirit lived in the Twelfth Layer of Heaven, and so they repeated their prayers twelve times. Now, facing possible death, the Moravian Christians prayed their Christian prayers twelve times.

The wailing of women began, like Rachel weeping for her Jewish children in the Old Testament. The village had remained neutral during the border wars and offered food and drink to both white and Indian warriors, including some of the militiamen. Colonel Williamson chose to ignore that fact. Like Pilate, he was too cowardly to make the decision for death himself, and so he put it to a vote of his 160 militiamen.

The militia stood in lines. As their names were called, if they were in favor of life, they stepped out of line. Only eighteen men in the militia of 160 courageously came forward to disagree with the verdict of the majority. The eighteen objected to the proposed execution of so many innocent men, women, and children, and urged that the Delaware Indians be taken as prisoners to Fort Pitt. These eighteen men did not participate in the slayings, and one man, Obadiah Holmes Jr., rescued and later reared an eight-year-old Delaware boy named Benjamin. Rev. Christy also was one of the eighteen brave dissenters.

"This young divine, having lost his betrothed by Indians, had accompanied Williamson's slaughtering expedition, and was a protesting and horrified witness of the dreadful drama," McKnight recorded.

"Meanwhile, the assassins–for I can call them by no milder name–debated as to the mode of death. Some even advised burning the Moravians alive, as they were cooped up in the two cabins." [6]

As the militiamen voted, the Indians began to sing softly the Christian hymns they had learned from the Moravian missionaries. The eighteen men who had protested the proceedings withdrew in horror and fear of what was to transpire.

The band of malcontents barely escaped violence and moved to the edge of the woods, "protesting in God's name against the diabolical atrocity resolved upon," Rev. Christy recalled.

The decision was death, Colonel Williamson finally announced to the hushed Moravians as he appeared before them. He claimed later that he had not approved of the mass murder, but, like Pilate, his soul would be stained with blood the next morning and forever afterwards.

The Christian Delaware petitioned the captain for permission to spend the night in prayer, and the execution was delayed until daybreak so that the Moravian Indian Christians would have time to prepare their souls to meet their Maker. The militia would spend their night deadening their senses in a drunken orgy.

All night the Delaware and their visiting friends from other tribes prayed and lamented the fate of their loved ones. With tearful and tender embraces, mothers held their babes in their arms for the last time.

"Many attempts – some of them of late years – have been made by historical writers to exculpate Williamson in regard to this terrible butchery," McKnight wrote.

"It cannot be done!," he declared. "The damned blood spot will not out at the bidding of any feeble apologist. The commander of the expedition must be held, not only as particeps criminis, but as its very 'head and front.'" [7]

1. McKnight, Our Western Border, p. 395.

2. Ibid, p. 397.

3. Ibid, p. 406.

4. Booth, Jr., Tuscarawas Valley in Indian Days, p. 292.

5. McKnight, Our Western Border, p. 404.

6. Ibid, p. 403, 409.

7. Ibid, p. 416.

30

Breaking the Heart of God

In Jerusalem at the Holocaust Memorial, Yad Vashem, there is a photo of Jewish women singing to calm their children as they waited in line to be gassed in a Nazi concentration camp during World War II. (I studied Biblical History in 1981 at Jerusalem's Institute of Holy Land Studies, and I imagine that the mothers of Gnadenhutten also sang to their children to soothe their fears as they awaited death.)

The grieving men of Gnadenhutten were held in the small cabin of the cooper, and the weeping women herded with their confused children into another house. They all invoked the Great Spirit, whom Christians call the Holy Spirit. The Christian Indians believed both are the same God, the Name above all names.

Abraham, one of the oldest Indians who had joined the flock at Gnadenhutten, repented at the end of his life for his sins, and recited the Indian translation of the Twenty-Third Palm, as written down years later by Roberta Campbell Lawson of Oklahoma, a granddaughter of Charles Journeycake, who was a grandson of The Buck:

"The Great Father above is Shepherd Chief; I am His, and with Him I want not," said Abraham, the first convert of the Moravians in Pennsylvania. "He throws to me a rope, and the name of the rope is Love, and He draws me to where the grass is green and the water not dangerous, and I eat and lie down satisfied,"

His Name is Wonderful

"Sometimes my heart is very weak and falls down, but He lifts it up again and draws me into a good road. His name is Wonderful. Sometime, it may be very soon, it may be longer, it may be a long, long time, He will draw me into a place between mountains. It is dark there, but I'll draw back not. I'll be afraid not, for it is in there between these mountains that the Shepherd Chief will meet me, and the hunger I have felt in my heart all through this life will be satisfied...." [1]

Rev. David Zeisberger recalled Abraham's repentance: "The Mohican, Abraham, who for some time had been bad in heart, when he saw that his end was near, made an open confession before his brethren, and said: 'Dear brethren, according to appearances we shall all very soon come to the Saviour, for as it seems they have so resolved about us. You know I am a bad man, that I have much troubled the Savior and the brethren, and have not behaved as becomes a believer, yet to him I belong, bad as I am; he will forgive us all and not reject me; to the end I shall hold fast to him and not leave him.'" [2]

The shadow of death hovered over them in the midst of their enemies, but the Indians had no idea how they would die. Perhaps the white men would be merciful and swift with their bullets. But that was not to be.

As the golden orb of the sun resurrected from the darkness of the previous evening--the last sunrise the Christian Indians would see in this life--the captives were bound in groups of two or three with ropes around their necks. Then, as came their turn, each pair was dragged into one of the two slaughter houses, the first for the men, the second for women. With tear-stained faces, mothers carried infants who could not yet walk, holding hands with those who could. More Holy Innocents!

"Sir, spare me my life!" shrieked a woman about to be yanked from her kinsmen. That woman was Little Leaf's great-aunt Maw-We-Ha (Christina), who was given the Christian name of Christina at the Bethlehem Sisters' Home in Pennsylvania, where she spent her youth.

"Christina, the Mohican, who well understood German and English, fell upon her knees before the captain, begging for life, but got for an answer that he could not help her," the Moravian missionary, Rev. Zeisberger, wrote in his diary after he learned of the massacre from the two boys who survived. [3]

Maw-We-Ha, aunt of the wife of Buckongahelas, was dragged away to die, not knowing that her son, Joseph Schebosh, had preceded her in death the previous day.

The militiamen took up the cooper's huge wooden mallet to murder the men, while clubs, hatchets, and tomahawks were used to split open the heads of the women and children. The militiamen ordered their captives to kneel. Their faces still greasy from breakfast, the killers began their grisly task, scalping ninety of my ancestral kinsmen and several of their visiting Indian friends--men, women and children–many of them while they were still alive.

The repentant Abraham, whose long silvery hair was easily grabbed and scalped, would

The Gnadenhutten massacre of nearly 100 peaceful Delaware Christian Indians is portrayed in this sketch by artist William D. Howell.

Courtesy of the Ohio Historical Society

be the first Indian killed. Abraham had recited the English words of the white man's prayers many times, but as the executioner lifted his mallet high above his head, Abraham surely cried *"Kishelemienkw!"* (the Delaware word for "Creator God" in prayer) as the last word of his life.

Also among the men who would be brutally slaughtered was Isaac Glickhikan (Gun Sight), head chief of the Munsee Delaware. A warrior of renown, the Delaware chiefs at Newcomer's Town sent him to the Moravian Christian Indians to convince–probably by strong arm methods–to return to their Delaware villages. Instead, Glickhikan was converted and baptized on Christmas Eve, 1770. Given the Biblical name Isaac, he became a prominent minister in the Moravian village of Salem.

Chief Pakanke, had become enraged when his chief war captain, Glickhikan, left him to join the Moravians. "And even you have gone over from this council to them," Pakanke stormed.

"I suppose you mean to get a white skin! But I tell you not even one of your feet will turn white, much less your body…. Some time or other you will find yourself deceived." [4]

Five other Indian ministers also would be executed at Gnadenhutten, including Captain Johnny, chief of the Turkey clan who had visited George Washington at his New Jersey army headquarters.

The man who murdered Abraham hacked away with demonic fury at thirteen other Indians before his arm grew tired. An elderly widow by the name of Judith was the first woman to die in the women's hut.

Who could forget the screams of the thirty-four terrified Indian children who had sung so sweetly the white man's hymns the night before? Only two boys escaped. Thomas was severely beaten, scalped, and left for dead among the others. At dusk, he crawled over bleeding bodies as he fled from the slaughterhouse into the woods.

Thomas later died of his wounds, but before his death he told of watching a brother, Abel, moving and striving to raise himself off the floor. The militia returned to the house and also observed the movement of Abel. They dispatched him with several blows to the head, while Thomas lay paralyzed with fear.

Another youth, about sixteen, lifted a board used as a trap-door and hid in the cellar of the women's execution house. Blood leaked through the floor onto his head during the killings. A second boy hiding in the cellar could not fit through the narrow window from which the first boy escaped. The heavy-set boy was burned alive the next morning when the militia set fire to the houses to burn all the bodies.

Why didn't the militia quickly shoot their victims instead of savagely cleaving their heads in half and chopping their bodies apart with hatchets? When I read of their modus operandi, I thought of the genocide of the Tutsi by their Hutu neighbors in Rwanda in 1994. The U.N. and the International Committee of the Red Cross estimated that as many as one million Tutsis had died in the carnage: clubbed, drowned, dismembered, and burned to death in church vestries by raging, diabolic Hutus.

"Though the bodies have been removed, almost every mission and parish church in a country that had been among the most Catholic in Africa still bears the traces of the massacres that have occurred within their walls," David Rieff wrote in *Vanity Fair* magazine following the Rwanda tragedy. [5] His article was accompanied by Annie Leibovitz's photos of a mission school that was attacked and a bloody wall where children were slaughtered in the school bathroom.

The Pennsylvania militia would burn the towns of Gnadenhutten, Salem, and Schoenbrunn, but the two surviving boys fled to the village of Schoenbrunn and warned the Indians there. Those Indians escaped with their lives – and the town was deserted when the militia arrived.

Attaching the bloody scalps from the ninety-six people murdered at Gnadenhutten to their hats, their horses, and their belts, the militia returned proudly with their plunder from the Moravian homes to parade them before their Pennsylvania families. They were greeted with hurrahs as heroes.

The second of Little Leaf's diamond teardrops fell to her breast when she learned of the slaughter.

Covered with Blood and Glory

The incident brings to mind the unprovoked attack of Colonel John Chivington and his Third Colorado Regiment of 700 men at Sand Creek, Colorado in 1864, where sleeping Indians were awakened to unexpected death. Eighty-two years after Gnadenhutten, in a Denver parade, soldiers publicly displayed the sexual organs that Colonel John Chivington had allowed them to rip from their victims.

"In a public speech made in Denver not long before this massacre, Colonel Chivington advocated the killing and scalping of all Indians, even infants. 'Nits make lice!' he declared,'" Dee Brown noted in his book *Bury My Heart at Wounded Knee*. [6]

The now defunct *Rocky Mountain News* reported with admiration the attack on the sleeping village at Sand Creek, where between 200 and 400 Indians would be slaughtered, two-thirds of them women and children:

"Among the brilliant feats of arms in Indian warfare, the recent campaign of our Colorado Volunteers will stand in history with few rivals, and none to exceed it in final results.... All acquitted themselves well, and Colorado soldiers have again covered themselves with glory." After learning of the massacre at Sand Creek, Major Edward Wynkoop at Fort Riley "wrote a scathing report to district headquarters, which was forwarded through channels to Washington, in which he called Chivington an 'inhuman monster.'" [7]

The Sand Creek atrocities in 1864 "had not purged Denverites of their bitter animosities toward Native Americans," Father John J. Killoren, a Jesuit priest, declared in his book *Come Blackrobe*.

"Doolittle [Senator James R.] discovered in his 1865 visit to Denver that new residents were calling for the extermination of the Indians." [8]

A French priest in Rwanda who survived the massacres of the spring of 1994 was asked "whether his experiences had shaken his faith in God?" journalist David Rieff wrote. "'Absolutely not,' the priest replied. 'What happened in this country has destroyed my faith in mankind forever.'" (Many Holocaust survivors felt the same way.)

The terrible stories of Gnadenhutten, Sand Creek, Washita, Wounded Knee, and Rwanda remind me of the prayer of Bob Pierce, founder of *World Vision*, an organization that serves suffering children around the world: "Let my heart be broken by the things that break the heart of God."

The Jewish writer Chaim Potok posed this question: "How can you smash a head? There are so many precious and beautiful things in a head. Eyes and a nose and lips …."

Photo by Charlene Scott-Myers

This beautiful expression of grief stands at the Hollywood Cemetery near the James River in Richmond, Virginia. Two U.S. presidents and several Civil War soldiers are buried here.

1. Lawson, *My Oklahoma*, p. 91

2. Booth, Jr., *Tuscarawas Valley in Indian Days,* p. 208.

3. Ibid.

4. Drake, *Indians of North America*, chapter II, p. 15.

5. Rieff, *God and Man in Rwanda*, p. 143

6. Brown, *Bury My Heart at Wounded Knee*, p. 90.

7. Hoig, *Sand Creek Massacre*, p. 162.

8. Killoren, *Come Blackrobe*. P. 281

31

Triumph in Death

Rev. Zeisberger, who had so diligently ministered to American Indians since the age of nineteen, was more than shocked by the death of his followers at Gnadenhutten, Ohio. He was moved to action, and his reaction two weeks after the massacre can be read in *The Tuscarawas Valley in Indian Days, 1750-1797* by Russell Booth Jr.

"Warriors came in, bringing a prisoner, from whom we now get the certain news that all our Indians in Gnadenhutten and Salem were put to death, and that none were spared; he said the militia had 96 scalps, but our Indians numbered only 86, who went away from us. The rest then must have been friends, who did not belong to us...." Zeisberger wrote.

"This news sank deep in our hearts, so that these, our brethren, who, as martyrs, had all at once gone to the Saviour, were always, day and night, before our eyes, and in our thoughts, and we could not forget them ...." [1]

It was the greatest sadness of the aged missionary's long life. His grief further deepened when it fell upon him to gather up all the scattered bones from the burned and mutilated bodies at the Gnadenhutten site to provide them a proper Christian burial.

"Back to the old home the patriarch Zeisberger brought his little company in the year 1798," Archer Butler Hulbert wrote from Marietta College in 1909.

"His first duty amid the scene of the terrible Gnadenhutten Massacre was not forgotten. With a bowed head and heavy heart the old man and one assistant gathered from beneath the dense mass of bush and vine, whither the wild beasts had carried them, the bones of the ninety and more sacrificed Christians, and over their present-resting place one of the proudest of monuments now rises." [2]

The dedication of this marble monument in memory of the ninety-six massacred Christian Delaware Indians was held June 5, 1872 in the state park at Gnadenhutten, Ohio. The Rev. Edmund de Schweinitz spoke, and a great-grandson of Joseph Schebosh, the first victim of the massacre, attended the ceremony. The monument still stands (seventy feet west of the cooper's shop), and the

The Gnadenhutten Monument at the site of the 1782 massacre by a white militia of nearly 100 Delaware Christian Indians in Ohio, who were warned of their danger eleven months earlier by Delaware War Chief Buckongahelas.

inscription reads: "Here, triumphed in death, 96 Christian Indians lie buried."

The bones of the victims had been placed in a cellar two hundred feet south of the monument, covered by a five-foot mound, eighteen feet in diameter. Ten years later, Zeisberger—who had served the Mohawk and Delaware Indians for nearly sixty years--would die and be buried in an obscure plot alongside a dusty country road. His body would rest among his beloved Native People in one of their graveyards in the Black Forest of America at Goshen, near New Philadelphia, Ohio.

The slaughter of the defenseless Christian Indians at Gnadenhutten took place despite the fact that several Delaware chiefs and tribesmen were serving the colonists in the Revolutionary War. Buckongahelas was a dissenter and sided with the British, as he had informed those at the village when he warned them of their peril.

The Gnadenhutten Massacre is one chapter that has been ignored or downplayed in many American history books. At the time that it happened, most whites chose to either applaud it or dismiss it. But one Scots-Irishman, Charles McKnight (1826-1881), did not ignore the slaughter. In a book he wrote in 1876, *Our Western Border, One Hundred Years Ago*, he stated:

"The whole massacre leaves a stain of deepest dye on the pages of American history. It was simply atrocious and execrable – a blistering disgrace to all concerned, utterly without excuse, and incapable of defense. It damns the memory of each participator to the last syllable of recorded time. All down the ages, the Massacre of the Innocents (by King Herod) will be its only parallel...." [3]

Moravian and other Christian denominations would not be welcome again by the Delaware until many years later when the tribe reached Kansas. With sad hearts, the Moravian missionaries literally saw their efforts of so many decades go up in smoke and abandoned their Ohio missions.

Historian Norman B. Wood told the story of Red Jacket, Sa-go-ye-wat-ha, a Seneca chief who never converted, but was buried with a cross due to his Christian wife's influence or insistence:

"He strenuously opposed every effort to introduce Christianity among his people, for he could not understand how it could be so valuable or necessary, when he saw how little it influenced the conduct of white men and the wrongs they inflicted in the name of their God upon the red man."[4]

There is a pithy saying of Red Jacket to a "black-coat, black robe, or black-gown" (various Indian names for priests and ministers): "If you people murdered 'the Savior,' make it up yourselves. We had nothing to do with it. If he had come among us, we would have treated him better." [5]

Red Jacket's saying reminds me of Gandhi's comment: "I like your Christ. I do not like your Christians. They are so unlike your Christ."

The Killers at Gnadenhutten

Who were the killers at Gnadenhutten? They obviously were of the same mind as Union General William Tecumseh Sherman, whom General Ulysses S. Grant placed in charge of all Federal operations in the West.

Sherman scorched Atlanta, made "Georgia howl," and ravaged South Carolina (which had been the first state to leave the union). He didn't have any sympathy for the Natives of this country either. He didn't care whether an Indian was a tomahawk-wielding warrior painted in black with scalps hanging from his belt – or a Pacifist Christian Indian kneeling in fervent prayer.

"The only good Indian is a dead Indian," was Sherman's voiced opinion – and this was an opinion shared by thousands of whites, including those who brought death to the pious people at Gnadenhutten.[6]

The murderers of so many innocents at Gnadenhutten included several high-ranking, well-to-do soldiers and citizens from Pennsylvania. Some of the militiamen had been Paxton Boys.

The Pennsylvania government in 1763 and 1764 had protected many of the dead at Gnadenhutten from attack by the Paxton Boys. Other militiamen at Gnadenhutten would become members of the Whiskey Rebels, participating in the 1794 uprising to protest a federal liquor tax.

According to a partial list published in 1888 in the *Pennsylvania Archives*, the official publication of the State of Pennsylvania, the 160 men in Lieutenant Colonel David Williamson's militia included two captains, Samuel Shearer and John Cotton; two lieutenants, Hugh Forbes and William Wilkins, and one sergeant, Thomas Rankin. Some men who ranked as officers in the Continental Army were named as "privates" in the list.

Most of the killers at the Moravian mission were of Scots-Irish descent, the heritage of my father's side of the family. Many could not speak English. The Irish had suffered much during their long history as victims of British oppression, but they brought great pain and loss to the Delaware people.

"In 1155, the pope [Adrian IV] granted 'ownership' of Ireland to King Henry II of England. Henry landed an army at Waterford in southern Ireland in 1171 and quickly took control of the country. This was the beginning of more than seven centuries of British domination of Ireland." [7]

The British taught the Irish how to hate—and how to pass that hatred from generation to generation. The Irish hated the British more with each passing century. When England broke from the Roman Catholic Church in the 1500s, King Henry VIII established his new "Protestant" church in all the countries under his rule. Irish Catholics did not take kindly to that, and the British responded with strict anti-Catholic Penal Laws for the Irish, barring Catholics from nearly every profession, banning celebration of the Mass and Catholic schools, and ousting most priests.

Wealthy Brits were allowed to seize lands from Irish farmers, a move that turned Irish landowners into poor tenant farmers for centuries.

The Irish also were forced to raise and ship nearly their entire crops and all of their livestock to their British landlords. The lowly potato was the only food the Irish were not required to hand over to the British for hundreds of years. More than one million Irish would die of starvation or hunger-related diseases during the terrible Potato Famine after a fungus rotted and destroyed their principal source of food. Millions more left the country and never returned.

"During the Famine Years of 1845 to 1855, almost one million Irish arrived in the New York port alone," author Sharon Moscinski reported.

"Hundreds of thousands more either anchored at one of the lesser ports in Boston, Baltimore, or New Orleans, or in Canada, and then traveled to the United States. The Irish made up the first large wave of immigrants to America." [8]

While addressing the Kansas Genealogical Society, Inc. in Dodge City, Kansas, Genealogist Dr. Arlene Eakle of Utah told the story of the earlier mass migration from Scotland into Ireland between 1620 and 1640.

"Scotland emptied its debtors' prisons, and those unfortunate prisoners who had been unable to pay their bills were forced with their families into Northern Ireland," she said. "Many of these poor people dreamed of moving on to America, a journey that sometimes took several generations to accomplish."

According to records compiled by the Church of Latter Day Saints, 60,000 Scots-Irish immigrated to America by the 1760s, and then migrated from Pennsylvania through Maryland into Virginia as each area became too crowded, Dr. Eakle revealed.

In the early 1700s, some Irishmen became involved in a flourishing slave trade from Africa in the port city of Liverpool. Later, they took up another prosperous trade as pirates on the high seas. These men may have been ancestors of the murderers at Gnadenhutten in 1782. Many Irishmen joined in the murder of the nearly 100 defenseless Delaware Indians at Gnadenhutten, sixty-one of them women and children. Furious Irish mobs also conducted a four-day riot killing more than 300 innocent blacks after they learned of Lincoln's Emancipation Proclamation in 1863. Approximately 150,000 Irishmen had joined the Union troops, but most of them did not want to fight for freedom of African-Americans.

A list of nearly all of those who died at or near Gnadenhutten was compiled by Rev. Zeisberger in August of 1783. The white Moravian missionaries had stolen their Delaware names from the Indians when they converted, as well as stripping away all vestiges of their culture and separating them from their families. Moravians had the habit of referring to the Delaware as "Indians" if they were Christians, but as "savages" if they were not. It was only the Christian names of the Gnadenhutten victims that Rev. Zeisberger recorded.

Many families were destroyed or nearly wiped out at Gnadenhutten. One man, Joseph Peepy (or Peepi), a Delaware Indian guide and translator for many whites, especially the Moravian ministers, lost several of his family members. His wife, Hannah, the wife of his son, Anton, and several of his grandchildren would perish in the Gnadenhutten Massacre. Joseph died at the age of ninety that same year, probably from his great grief.

In 1876, Historian Charles McKnight wrote: "Many attempts – some of them of late years – have been made by historical writers to exculpate Williamson in regard to this terrible butchery. *It cannot be done!* The damned blood spot will *not* out at the bidding of any feeble apologist. The commander of the expedition must be held, not only as *particeps criminis*, but as its very 'head and front'…. It is a gross abuse of words to call that a *fault* which should be deemed a flagrant *crime*." [9]

Colonel Williamson, the leader of the Gnadenhutten Massacre, escaped unscathed from the Indians' revenge throughout his life, however, and he was not brought to justice by the U.S. military.

The Delaware were one of a multitude of Indian Nations that suffered during the Revolutionary War and the years of pain to follow. The premeditated slaughter of Christian Indians at Gnadenhutten by white "Christians" was similar to the murder and bestial mutilation of the Cheyenne and Arapaho (half of them women and children) at Sand Creek, Colorado, Custer's slaughter of women and children at Washita in Indian Territory (later Oklahoma), and the cold-blooded destruction of unarmed Lakota Sioux men, women, and children at Wounded Knee, South Dakota.

Harry M. Roark, the biographer of Charles Journeycake, grandson of Buckongahelas, called the wholesale slaughter at Gnadenhutten "one of the most shameful massacres recorded in the history of America."

"The soldiers' pretense for this action was that the Indians were Loyalists. The better or more correct reason was the Rangers' hatred of the Indian and their desire for loot." [10]

General Sherman admitted during the Civil War that "War at best is barbarism," [11] but the slaughtering of defenseless non-combatants--whether American Indians or white Americans--was barbarism at its worst.

In hindsight, the great historian C. A. Weslager commented: "Had the villages at Gnadenhutten heeded Buckongahelas's advice, a terrible tragedy might have been averted." [12]

1. Booth, Jr., *Tuscarawas Valley in Indian Days,* p. 209.

2. Zeisberger, *History of Northern American Indians*, p. 4.

3. McKnight, *Our Western Border,* p. 417.

4. Wood, *Lives of Famous Indian Chiefs,* p. 253.

5. Johansen and Grinde, Jr., *Native American Biography*, p. 316.

6. Graybill and Boesen, *Edward Sheriff Curtis*, p. 12.

7. Nardo, *Irish Potato Famine*, p. 12.

8. Moscinski, *Tracing Our Irish Roots*, p. 3.

9. McKnight, *Our Western Border*, p. 416.

10. Roark, *Charles Journeycake*, p. 17.

11. Flato, *Civil War*, p. 89.

12. Weslager, *Delaware Indians*, p. 316.

32

Indiscriminate Slaughter

Members of the Choctaw Nation, not the Cherokee, were the first Indians to traverse the Trail of Tears, suffering terribly and losing more people to death during their three-year removal than the Cherokee, who became forever identified with the bloody trail.

Forced removal of the first group of Choctaw was launched November 1, 1831 from Memphis, Tennesee. When the Choctaw arrived in Little Rock, one of their chiefs told a reporter for the Arkansas Gazette that the route was a "trail of tears and death." The press responded with the phrase "Trail of Tears." Another group of Choctaw was gathered from Vicksburg, Mississippi. The Choctaw left the Mississippi Valley for southern Oklahoma with nearly 19,500 of their people, but at the end of their removal, they numbered only 12,500.

"During the bitter winter of 1831, the migration of the Choctaw began," wrote R. Conrad Stein in his book *The Trail of Tears*. "Many were barefoot, and most had no coats or blankets. Yet they were forced to cross the Mississippi River in zero-degree weather. The federal government had agreed to feed and clothe the Indians during their journey, but money for the provisions was never sent." [1]

As the Choctaw endured floods, blizzards, and starvation, they also were afflicted with dysentery, diphtheria, and typhoid. Watching their children and old ones die first, the tears of grieving relatives froze on their faces as they trudged through ice and snow.

Joseph Kern, who lived beside the trail near Vicksburg, Mississippi, gave a party of starving Choctaw permission to enter his field of pumpkins, where "they ate with great relish. Other Indian nations who walked the trail, including the Creek, also suffered.

"The Creek were driven out of their homes in 1836," author Stein added. "Those who resisted were put in chains and marched double file by United States soldiers. Some thirty-five hundred Creek who started the trek died of hunger and exposure before they reached their new territory."

The Chickasaw were forced to leave their lands in the South in 1837. The Cherokee postponed their journey through recourse to the highest court. The U.S. Supreme Court ruled in 1832 that the federal government must protect the Cherokee nation, but President Jackson had answered:

"John Marshall [Chief Justice of the Supreme Court] has rendered his decision; *now let him enforce it!*"

Sixteen thousand Cherokee left Echota, Georgia in the scorching heat of September, 1838. Four thousand Cherokee would die along the Trail of Tears. Those who perished were among the 20,000 Cherokee who eventually were forced along the 800-mile trail in devastating winter weather. During five-month journeys, their moccasins and boots left footprints all the way from Georgia to Parkhill, near the present town of Tahlequah in The Nations or Indian Territory, now Oklahoma.

Two thousand more Cherokee perished within a couple of years after struggling along the trail. Their deaths were due to illness, lack of food and water, and the bitter weather which they had experienced. Very few elders or children survived the pitiful long walk to Indian Territory. "We lost our past and our future," one Cherokee observed.

The life of President Andrew Jackson, who authorized the Indian Removal Act of 1830, once had been saved due to the assistance of 500 Cherokee allies at the Battle of Horseshoe Bend in 1814. Thomas Jefferson had decided to support Indian Removal as early as 1802, but it was the man known as "the Indian hater," President Jackson, who set it in motion.

The prosperous Cherokee had lived in the Echota Valley for 500 years as a settled, peaceful people who adopted many "civilized" ways. They had their own language, schools, farms, and newspaper. We visited the beautiful Blue Spring in Missouri, where some Cherokee camped for several days waiting for stragglers to catch up with them on their long and painful march on the Trail of Tears. A sign near the clear blue waters of the spring reads: "This portion of the trail will always be held as a memorial to a staunch and valiant people."

Also mourned are the 200 Arapaho and Cheyenne men, women, and children also slaughtered in the Sand Creek Massacre in November 1864 by Colonel John Chivington, a Methodist minister, and his brutal Colorado Third Cavalry. After that debacle, President Lincoln replaced the cruel Colorado Governor John Evans, who on learning the tribes wanted peace, had stated: "But what shall I do with the Third Colorado regiment if I make peace? They have been raised to kill Indians, and they must kill Indians."

My late friend Mary Spurgeon sculpted the magnificent eight-foot-high statue of Wyatt Earp that stands on Wyatt Earp Boulevard in Dodge City, Kansas. Mary lived in the Oklahoma Panhandle until her death in 2009. Also an author, Spurgeon wrote in her book *The Will O' the Wisp,* the story of a young woman who lived in the 1880s with an Indian half-sister. The woman protagonist wonders if their father will allow the half-sister to marry into the Cheyenne Nation from whence the half-sister's mother originated.

"Would he allow her to hazard the possibility of becoming another victim of a massacre such as had happened at Sand Creek when Chivington had led his disreputable drunken company against the unsuspecting Cheyenne? Or of Custer's butchery of Black Kettle's band on the Washita [in 1868] in Indian Territory?" [2]

Concerning the massacres at Sand Creek, Colorado, and Washita, Oklahoma, David Scott Myers wrote in the March 17, 1999 issue of the *Douglas County News-Press* in Castle Rock, Colorado: "In both cases, the fleeing defenseless women and children, along with the old men, were pursued and slaughtered, while the warriors had been caught off guard and unprepared, having been assured by the U.S. government that they were safe in their own designated territory." [3]

We toured the site of the Sand Creek Massacre in Colorado on a lazy, warm summer afternoon. On such a beautiful day, it was difficult to picture the horror of this massacre, which was as ghoulish and ghastly as the 1782 slaughter of Delaware Christian Indians at Gnadenhutten, Ohio. At Sand Creek, Colonel John Chivington and 675 soldiers attacked 120 Cheyenne and Arapaho lodges.

"After hours of brutal and cowardly fighting, the Colorado volunteers lost nine men, and 200 of my ancestors, most of them innocent and unarmed women and children, had been murdered," Ben Nighthorse Campbell told the *Elbert County News* in Colorado. "When the skirmish ended, the volunteers scalped and sexually mutilated many of the bodies of the dead, and proudly displayed their trophies to jeering crowds in the streets of Denver [during a parade]," the *News* reported. [4]

Rancher Robert Bent, one of William Bent's three half-Cheyenne sons, was forced to be a guide for Colonel Chivington. After the attack, he told the story of the massacre, quoted by Dee Brown in his book *Bury My Heart at Wounded Knee*:

"There seemed to be indiscriminate slaughter of men, women, and children. There were some thirty or forty squaws collected in a hole for protection; they sent out a little girl about six years old with a white flag on a stick; she had proceeded but a few steps when she was shot and killed. All the squaws in that hole were afterwards killed, and four or five bucks outside.

"The squaws offered no resistance. Every one I saw dead was scalped. I saw one squaw cut open with an unborn child, as I thought, lying by her side. Captain Soule afterwards told me that such was the fact. I saw the body of White Antelope with the privates cut off, and I heard a soldier say he was going to make a tobacco pouch out of them." [5]

Myers also interviewed Ben Friday, an Arapaho descendant of a woman who escaped the Sand Creek Massacre (Friday's great-grandmother lost a moccasin while fleeing in terror with her sister from the Sand Creek cavalry killers). Ben Friday resided on the Wind River Reservation in central Wyoming, where the U.S. government sent the northern Arapaho tribe to live in the late 1800s. His great-grandfather also miraculously escaped the attack.

"There had been some stories written about him [his great-grandfather]--'Friday the Arapaho Indian,'" Ben Friday said. "Jim Bridger and another trapper, they found this little boy. The camp had moved when this little boy was snaring rabbits. When he came home, nobody was there. Toward the fall, these two trappers found him. They said he was wild as a wild animal. They had to tie him up to keep him in his camp.

"The Indian boy, [Ben] Friday's great-grandfather, was

The Sand Creek Massacre in Colorado on Nov. 29-30, 1864, took the lives of 200 Arapaho and Cheyenne men, women, and children. *Photo by David Scott Myers.*

181

taken to Ft. Lewis, down along the Missouri, to be educated. When he reached 17 or 18, he heard about a boy the Arapaho tribe had been missing for several years. The Arapaho said he had a birth mark. They took off his shirt and sure enough there was a black spot there. He went back to the tribe, and they made him chief." [6]

Medicine Lodge Treaty and the AWOL Custer

An uneasy peace hovered over the plains like a threatening dark cloud in 1867. Black Kettle and his Cheyenne warriors had battled the Delaware in 1853, and ill feelings still persisted between the two Indian Nations. It is not surprising, but disappointing that Delaware men acted as Custer's guides when on April 15, 1867 he was ordered to pursue Cheyenne escaping from their village near Pawnee Fork thirty-one miles from Fort Larned in Kansas.

"With him [Custer] were a number of Delaware Indian scouts and two guides whose special assignment was following the trail," wrote Lawrence A. Frost in his book *The Court-Martial of General George Armstrong Custer*. "None of the [Cheyenne] Indians had been seen by his command, although his Delaware scouts, while in the advance, had seen small numbers watching from the heights at a distance." [7]

The Cheyenne fled in the spring when the bumbling Major General Winfield S. Hancock approached their village, meaning to intimidate them with his entire command of 1,500 men. The Indians felt threatened instead of impressed, remembering the Sand Creek Massacre where so many Natives had been brutalized and murdered. To calm their fears and force them onto two new reservations in Indian Territory, the U.S. government tried another tactic, summoning tribes of the southern plains to Medicine Lodge, Kansas for what was promoted as "the most spectacular meeting ever held between Indians and the U.S. government!"

The Medicine Lodge Treaty Council of October, 1867 certainly was the largest gathering ever of Plains Indians, with some 20,000 Kiowa, Comanche, Arapaho, Apache, and Cheyenne arriving on horseback and slow-moving, creaking wagons. Publicized across the country, the council drew media coverage from *Harpers Weekly*, *The New York Herald*, *The Chicago Tribune*, and *The Missouri Democrat*, among other newspapers. Held in the gypsum hills of south central Kansas, the council's main goal was to protect pioneers traveling to frontier settlements in the West by sending all these Indians far, far away.

Among the famous chiefs who attended was Satanta of the Kiowa Tribe, who murdered a man in the Panhandle, captured his wife and four children and sold them to the army at Fort Dodge, Kansas. Satanta later killed himself by jumping from a window at the Huntsville State Penitentiary in Texas.

Also present at the Medicine Lodge Council were Little Raven of the Arapaho Tribe, who died of old age in Oklahoma, and the peacemaker Black Kettle, head chief of the Cheyenne delegation, who lost his brother White Antelope and narrowly escaped with his own life at Sand Creek.

Other prominent men included George Bent, a half-Cheyenne married to Black Kettle's niece, and the scout Kit Carson. Also in attendance was Carson's boss, the famous Western explorer John Charles Fremont, whose favorite Delaware Indian scout was Chief Solomon Journeycake, one of the four sons of Buckongahelas.

My husband and I were among the thousands who attended the twenty-third Medicine Lodge Treaty Pageant in Kansas in late September, 2011. Only in the hefty pageant brochure on page forty-five could the audience learn that Black Kettle died just a year after signing the Medicine Lodge Peace Treaty in 1868. Not mentioned was the fact that Lieutenant Colonel George Armstrong Custer and his 7th Calvary were the murderers of Black Kettle, his wife, and his people.

The murderous assault on Black Kettle and his band took place at his camp along the Washita River on one of the two new reservations in Indian Territory created by the Medicine Lodge Treaty. (Land referred to as Indian Territory was not established under that name until July 21, 1882.)

Custer had been a no-show at the Medicine Lodge Council, which convened shortly after his court martial for mistreatment of his troops. He had ordered deserters executed without military trial and had been AWOL visiting his wife Libbie at Fort Riley. Custer was suspended from command, rank, and pay for one year, but he was called back into service to lead the slaughter at Washita.

Ironically, Major Joel H. Elliott of Custer's U.S. Seventh Cavalry, who was killed during Custer's attack at Washita, had escorted the Peace Commissioners to the Medicine Lodge Treaty Council in place of the missing Custer. The cowardly Custer would be severely criticized for abandoning Major Elliott and his men to their death in his haste to flee Washita after the assault.

Indian dancers perform at the Medicine Lodge Treaty reenactment in September, 2011. The Medicine Lodge Treaty Council of October, 1867 was the largest gathering ever of Plains Indians, with some 20,000 representatives of different tribes attending.

Photo by Charlene Scott-Myers.

In the fall of 1868, Black Kettle, whose wife also survived the Sand Creek massacre (with nine bullets in her body), led his beleaguered family and weary band of 250 Southern Cheyenne to camp along the Washita River. Black Kettle's camp was composed of 51 lodges, plus four lodges of Arapaho and Lakota who had joined the Cheyenne at their location.

This band of peaceful Indians would be blamed for sporadic attacks of other Plains Indians on wagon trains, settlements, and trading posts. With the Seventh Calvary's band playing "Garry Owen," George A. Custer and his four battalions struck Black Kettle's small camp at dawn on November 27, 1868. Custer avoided the much larger nearby camps of about 6,000 Arapaho, Cheyenne, Comanche, and Kiowa Indians residing along the Upper Washita River.

A historical marker at the camp site is titled "Washita Battle," but it was an unexpected attack and massacre of sleeping, peaceful Indians. A sign states that 103 Indians were killed, but that number is disputed. Three-fourths of the dead were seventy-five women and children, according to the Seventh Calvary's chief of scouts. In his report the day following the attack on the Indian camps, Custer estimated that his Seventh Calvary had wiped out about 100 of Black Kettle's men, but only "some" women and a "few" children.

But Benjamin H. Clark, the chief of scouts, disputed those figures, reporting that seventy-five women and children had been slaughtered. Other witnesses also claimed that three times the number of women had been killed than the mostly elderly men at the camp. The cavalry chased women and children for three miles along the river, shooting down mothers clutching babies as they galloped past. The bodies of Black Kettle, his wife, and many women and children were found in the Washita riverbed four days later.

"The soldiers rode right over Black Kettle and his wife and their horses as they lay dead on the ground, and their bodies were all splashed with mud by the charging soldiers," Alvin M. Josephy, Jr. wrote in *500 Nations*. [8] Pioneers one day would be baptized in the once bloodied waters of the Washita.

Thomas Berger described the valley and the Native People who gathered there in his book *Little Big Man,* from which was created the movie by the same name. (The young man who portrayed the Indian Little Horse in the film was Robert Little Star, a friend of mine from our college days in Oklahoma.) Dustin Hoffman portrayed Little Big Man, a 121-year-old survivor of Custer's attacks at Washita and at the Little Bighorn in Montana.

"We joined Black Kettle at the end of the big summer buffalo hunt in which all the tribes in the area come together, and then moved on down into the Nations [Indian Territory], across the Canadian River, past the Antelope Hills, and onto the Washita ….," Little Big Man recalled.

"There was [sic] several camps there, strung along the river for about ten mile [sic], more Cheyenne below us and Arapaho, Kiowa, Comanche, and some Apache too. The Indians figured to winter in that valley, which was well timbered with cottonwood." [9]

Instead the Cheyenne, Arapaho, and Lakota tribes bled and died in that valley. Describing the impending attack, writer Carl Waldman revealed, "Unknown to Custer, and probably irrelevant to him if he had known, opposite him were the people of Black Kettle's band. Even after witnessing the Sand Creek Massacre at Chivington's hands, Black Kettle had never gone to war with the white man. In fact, he had led his people south into the Indian Territory to avoid the subsequent fighting in Colorado and Kansas." [10]

Custer captured fifty-three Cheyenne women and children and took them as hostages so that the Indians would not fire upon him and his retreating troops. The hostages were marched 100 miles to Fort Supply in Indian Territory and another ninety miles to Fort Dodge in southwestern Kansas.

The Washita Indian camp was razed and set afire. Describing Black Kettle's horses killed at Washita, author Muriel H. Wright noted that "900 Indian ponies [were] shot on the spot by order of Colonel Custer." [11] Their wails of pain and those of human survivors could be heard for hours.

Both Custer and Sheridan claimed the attack at Washita was "a great victory," but Black Kettle was well known as a peace chief who had signed the Medicine Lodge Peace Treaty in Kansas only a year earlier. "Custer grossly exaggerated the magnitude of his victory over the Cheyennes [at Washita]," claimed Donald J. Berthrong in his book *Southern Cheyennes*. [12]

And Nathaniel Philbrick pointed out: "Instead of striking a blow against the hostiles, Custer had unwittingly killed one of the few Cheyenne leaders who were for peace." [13]

Eight years later, Custer would make the fatal mistake of attacking a multitude of 2,000 Indians who were professionals at war—including Crazy Horse and Sitting Bull--at the Battle of the Little Bighorn in Montana. Custer believed that this battle would be as easily won as his attack on women and children at Washita, but the arrogant Custer became known in history as one of the military's biggest losers, even more incompetent than the clumsy General St. Clair.

In South Dakota, we visited the enormous sculpture of the daring Crazy Horse, Custer's nemesis. Since 1948, gigantic heads of the famous chief and his stallion have been blasted out of a mountain in the Black Hills, only eight miles from the four presidents' faces chiseled into Mount Rushmore. Sculptor Korczak Ziolkowski, now deceased, began the Crazy Horse sculpture at the request of Lakota Chief Henry Standing Bear. Ziolkowski's family continues his work on the monument, which will be larger than Mt. Rushmore's presidents when completed.

Crazy Horse of the Ogallala Sioux, fair-skinned and known as "Curly" because of his sandy-colored, curly hair, was the son-in-law of Red Cloud. His father had given him his name, and Crazy Horse had a vision as a young man that he would not be killed by bullets in battle. It was true. He never was shot or seriously wounded in battle. Taking bold risks at the Battle of the Little Bighorn, he led the defeat of Custer and his troops.

In the book *Indians*, William Brandon called Custer's last stand "the sensational moment of truth in the wars of the plains, at least for the Americans."

"It was the kind of humiliating defeat that simply could not be handed to a modern nation of

40,000,000 people by a few scarecrow savages.... The Custer defeat was, in effect, the end of the wars of the plains, and Crazy Horse and Sitting Bull lost by winning." [14]

The victory of Sitting Bull and Crazy Horse against Custer led to terrible revenge from white troops: the slaughter of 100 Sioux warriors and 200 Sioux women and children at Wounded Knee, South Dakota on an icy Dec. 28, 1890.

Author Elaine Landau wrote in her book *The Sioux*, "Close to three hundred Sioux were killed.... Several days after the massacre, a crew was hired to plow the Indians' bodies into a large pit that served as a common grave." [15]

White civilians were paid two dollars for each Indian body they dumped into the long pit dug in the ice and snow. A photograph displays that terrible gash in the earth piled high with frozen bodies, reminiscent of photos of Jewish corpses the Nazis stacked on top of each other in World War II communal pits.

Crazy Horse had been inconsolable when he lost his young daughter, named "They Are Afraid of Her." His friend, the Army scout Frank Grouard, recorded these words: "Crazy Horse had but one child – a little girl about four years of age – whom ....he idolized. While the village was

This is a model of the mountain statue in the background of Crazy Horse, the Ogallala Sioux who with Sitting Bull defeated Custer at the Battle of the Little Big Horn in Montana. The enormous statue, located 17 miles from Mount Rushmore in South Dakota, has been under construction since 1948.

Photo by
Charlene Scott-Myers

located between the Little Big Horn and the Rosebud, in 1873, the chief went out with a war party against the Crows. In his absence the little girl was taken sick and died. "His grief was pathetic."

Crazy Horse asked Grouard to accompany him to visit the child's body that was placed upon a platform seventy miles from the Sioux camp. It took them two days of hard riding to reach the site.

"He [Crazy Horse] went alone to the raised bier, crawled up beside the little girl's remains, and there stayed for three days and nights mourning for the departed one," Grouard recalled.

"Not a mouthful of food or drop of water had passed that father's lips during those three awful days and nights of mourning, and he rode back to his people and desolate tepee with a heavy heart but stolid face." [16]

The Moravian missionary Zeisberger recounted how the Delaware reacted to the death of a chief's son or daughter: "Should a chief have lost a child or near relative, no complaint may be brought before him, nor may his advice be asked on any affairs of state," Zeisberger had observed. And when a chief dies, sympathy is expressed for the whole nation. [17]

Crazy Horse was only thirty-five years old when he was murdered on September, 5, 1877. Soldiers arrested him at the Spotted Tail agency, where he was assured of his safety and promised that he would not be imprisoned. He was taken to Fort Robinson to meet with General Crook, but instead was shown to a building guarded by a soldier.

The author Dee Brown explained what happened next: "The windows were barred with iron, and he could see men behind the bars with chains on their legs. It was a trap for an animal, and Crazy Horse lunged away like a trapped animal, with Little Big Man holding on to his arm. The scuffling went on for only a few seconds. Someone shouted a command, and then the soldier guard, Private William Gentles, thrust his bayonet deep into Crazy Horse's abdomen.

"At dawn the next day the soldiers presented the dead chief to his father and mother.... And then in the Moon of Falling Leaves came the heartbreaking news: the reservation Sioux must leave Nebraska and go to a new reservation on the Missouri."

In the autumn of 1877, soldiers marched the Indians toward their new destination, but several bands turned northwest to escape to Canada to join Sitting Bull.

"With them went the father and mother of Crazy Horse, carrying the heart and bones of their son. At a place known only to them, they buried Crazy Horse somewhere near Chankpe Opi Wakpala, the creek called Wounded Knee." [18]

Writer Frank Huston, a contributor to Adventure Magazine in the early 1920's, summed up the feelings of many Americans regarding George Armstrong Custer:

"Although somewhat addicted to snobbishness, yet I hate pretense, and George Custer has always been anathema to me. His massacre of Kettle's band on the Washita was a fitting supplement to Sand Creek, where Kettle's first abuse by whites occurred." [19]

1. Stein, *Trail of Tears*, pp. 20, 21.

2. Spurgeon, *Will O' the Wisp*, p. 17.

3. Myers, *Sand Creek Purchase Possible*, p. 1.

4. Ibid.

5. Brown, *Bury My Heart at Wounded Knee*, p. 90.

6. Myers, *People of the Plains*, Section C, p. 1.

7. Frost, *Court-Martial of General George Armstrong Custer*, p. 20.

8. Josephy, Jr., *500 Nations,* p. 366, 367.

9. Berger, *Little Big Man,* p. 236.

10. Waldman, *Atlas of the North American Indian*, p. 149.

11. Wright, *Guide to Indian Tribes of Oklahoma*, p. 17.

12. Berthrong, *Southern Chcyennes*, p. 327.

13. Philbrick, *Last Stand*, p. 12.

14. Brandon, *Indians*, p. 347.

15. Landau, *Sioux,* pp. 51, 53.

16. Hanson, *Frank Grouard, Army Scout*, pp. 155, 156.

17. Zeisberger, *History of Northern American Indians*, p. 95.

18. Brown, *Bury My Heart at Wounded Knee*, pp. 312, 313.

19. Graham, *Custer Myth*, p. 80.

33

A Call to Arms

Buckongahelas would have been painfully stunned, then in a fearsome fury when Delaware runners brought him news of the tragedy at Gnadenhutten. The militiamen who murdered the helpless Christians would have been terrified had they glimpsed the look of fury on his face.

The Delaware and other tribes were outraged by the slaughter at Gnadenhutten. The Delaware nation had several chiefs--three "peace" chiefs, one for each of the three clans or phratries, and one or more war chiefs for each clan. In time of war, the war chief assumed leadership of his people over the peace chief. Buckongahelas now took in his hands the reins of authority for the Wolf clan, calling together his warriors and elders of the village to meet for a council of war in the lodge house.

Eventually, most of the warriors from all three clans would fall in line behind the leadership of Buckongahelas in war.

It was time to teach the white man a lesson he never would forget, as the Delaware would never forget their murdered dead at Gnadenhutten. The War Council lasted many long hours. (Women entered the long lodge house only to bring food to their men, unless they were among the few of their gender who had accompanied warriors onto battlefields. Those exalted women were given a place of honor in the lodge house.)

The Delaware finally reached a consensus to join the Wyandot Indians to march against the Pennsylvania militia, who were on their way to attack Sandusky villages. In battle after battle, the Delaware would take an eye for an eye, a scalp for a scalp. Many Indians took only a piece of scalp as large as a dollar, "somewhat like the tonsure of a priest," according to Charles Preuss, the German cartographer of explorer John Charles Fremont. White men took the entire scalp.

James Fenimore Cooper explained in his book *The Last of the Mohicans* why it was so meaningful to Indians to lift a man's scalp: "The scalp was the only admissible trophy of victory. Thus, it was deemed more important to obtain the scalp than to kill the man."

Cooper also claimed that Indians wore scalp locks on the top of their heads "in order that the enemy might avail himself of it, wrenching off the scalp in the event of his fall." [1] Hawkeye, the hero of Cooper's book, explains, "Tis their scalps or ours!—and God, who made us, has put into our natures the craving to keep the skin on the head!" [2]

The tragedy at Gnadenhutten became as much of a rallying call to arms for Indians of northeastern tribes as did the Battle of the Alamo for those who would be Texans: "Remember the Alamo!"

"His [Buckonghelas'] predictions in regard to the fate of the Christian Delawares, were but too speedily accomplished," historian Thatcher wrote in 1832.

"But it was no fault of his; and indeed, in 1783 [the year following the Gnadenhutten massacre], when Captain Pipe sent word to him not to suffer any of them to leave his territory, he [Buckongahelas] returned answer, with his usual spirit, that he never would prevent them from going to their teachers.

Gnadenhutten, scene of a terrible tragedy.

"'Did I not tell you beforehand, that if you drove the teachers off, the believing Indians would follow them? But you would not listen to me, and now we lose both!" The Buck scolded Captain Pipe, who had encouraged the arrests and trial of the Moravian ministers prior to the attack at Gnadenhutten.

"'Who, think you, is the cause of all the disasters, which have befallen these people! *I say you! – You!* Who threatened them with destruction!" Thatcher wrote. [3]

"In 1792, ten years after the massacre, the Christian Indians led by the Rev. Zeisberger, the Moravian preacher, broke away from the main body in the United States and started up their own town on the north side of the Thames in Canada," historian Weslager noted. "Americans destroyed that town too – in the War of 1812." [4]

The Indians never captured Colonel Williamson, the leader of the Gnadenhutten Massacre, but they finally caught up with the Pennsylvania militia. The commanding officer at that time was no longer Williamson, but Virginian Colonel William Crawford, the old friend of the murderer of the son of Buckongahelas, Captain White of West Virginia.

Captain Pipe, father-in-law of Buckongahelas, captured Crawford and a Dr. Knight at the end of May, 1782, three months after the slaughter at Gnadenhutten. It was a dire day for Crawford when he fell into Pipe's hands. Pipe at first thought the prisoner *was* the notorious Colonel Williamson who led the slaughter at Gnadenhutten, and that tragedy hit home for Pipe because many of his relatives–including his sister Christine--lost their lives at Gnadenhutten. But not only was Crawford the leader of the notorious Pennsylvania militia, he also had burnt and massacred a whole village of Indians on the Muskingam River. That was reason enough to kill him when Pipe found out who his captive really was.

Pipe and his brother, Joshua, a Moravian Christian, were the sons of Gideon Maw Weher (Captain Pach Got Goen), the chief of Scotacooks when he was baptized February 13, 1743. Gideon did not live to see his relatives slaughtered at Gnadenhutten, but died January 28, 1760.

Pipe's sister, Maw-We-Ha (Christine or Christina) – the great-aunt of my many greats-grandmother, Little Leaf – married Brother Schebosh, a white Quaker known as John Joseph Bull. They both were murdered by Williamson's troops at Gnadenhutten, as was their son, Joseph, and the children of Captain Pipe's brother Joshua, Anna and Bathseba, aunts of my ancestor Little Leaf.

Captain Pipe, the grandfather of Little Leaf, would show no mercy to Colonel Crawford, who was conducted to the Old Wyandot town. (Neither had Pipe shown mercy to his relatives, having instigated their removal from Gnadenhutten to Sandusky in the first place, leading to their later slaughter at Gnadenhutten when they returned.)

Historian Drake told what happened next:

"Here, Capt. Pipe, with his own hands, painted Crawford and Knight black in every part of their bodies. A place called the New Wyandot Town was not far off. To this place they were now ordered, and Pipe told Crawford that when he arrived there, his head should be shaved, of which, it seems, he did not understand the import." [5]

Crawford would be terribly tortured and burned at the stake June 11, 1782. Near death, he was scalped by a baptized Moravian, Joseph. Crawford's frightful death took place five miles west of what now is Upper Sandusky, Ohio in revenge for the Gnadenhutten Massacre.

When the notorious British agent and Indian trader Simon Girty (Katepacomen), an enemy of the Moravians whom Rev. Heckewelder called "the White Savage," interceded on behalf of Crawford, Captain Pipe angrily responded:

"If you say one more word on that subject, I will plant another stake for you, and burn you along side the White Chief!"

The "White Savage," Simon Girty

Girty escaped death by fire, but he still came to a bad end. The historian Charles McKnight described Girty as "a vulgar, violent old curmudgeon ..., said to have been so besotted with liquor as to have turned his wife's love to hate, and to have been killed by her paramour." [6]

No Reconciliation for the Delaware

After the bloody American Revolution ended in 1783, the Delaware still did not reconcile differences among themselves, but they desired to unite with other Indian nations to increase their strength and protect their people.

"Deprived of their British allies, the Indians sought to unify their forces during the postwar period, and in 1783, thirty-five different tribes or nations, including the Delawares, met on the Sandusky River to form an Indian confederacy 'to defend their country against all invaders,'" historian Weslager reported. [7]

By 1800, the Delaware had settled on the West Fork of the White River and started nine Delaware towns. Chief Buckongahelas' Town was near the headwaters.

"In an estimated Indian population of 149,000 east of Missouri a hundred years ago, the great Algonquin group numbered 90,000 – of this group, the Delaware claimed to be the parent stock, and the claim seems to have been conceded by the related tribes," the Rev. S. H. Mitchell, a Baptist minister, wrote in 1895. [8]

War Chief Buckongahelas was present, but not as a signer, at the treaty at Fort McIntosh, Pennsylvania in 1785 that was signed by his arch rival, his father-in-law Captain Pipe. The treacherous Pipe had acted as principal chief of the Delaware Wolf Clan, but was not authorized to speak for all the clans.

"Even as a chief, Pipe could act legitimately only for the Wolf phratry, not for the Delawares as a whole," explained author Richard White.

"The Turtle and Turkey phratries–badly split by the Revolution and migration–were not properly represented at Fort McIntosh, and neither were the now quite powerful warrior villages that followed Buckongahelas," [19]

Captain Pipe and Half King had defeated the Americans on many occasions, but now they "sold their lands and themselves with them" to the Americans. The general council of the Indian Confederacy rejected the treaties as invalid, and considered the chiefs who signed those treaties as traitors.

Chief Buckongahelas also disapproved of the Fort McIntosh treaties and refused to sign them. But after the signing, he approached General George Rogers Clark (the brother of William Clark, whose expedition crossed the continent with Meriwether Lewis). General Clark was six-foot-tall, weighed 200 pounds, and had a head of red hair. Clark and the shorter chief--with his dangling earrings and brightly colored garb--would have made an interesting contrast in appearance.

"It is hard to conceive of a more lofty spirit than possessed by this proud, virtuous chieftain (The Buck)," wrote historian Lucullus McWhorter.

"At the Treaty of Fort McIntosh he wholly ignored the other peace dignitaries, and stepping up to General Clark, took him by the hand and spoke: "'I thank the Great Spirit for having this day brought together two such great warriors as Buckongahelas and General Clark.'" [10]

Nearly a century later in 1865, two Civil War generals would come together with as much mutual respect: Robert E. Lee never forgot the gracious audience he received from Ulysses S. Grant when the Confederate general surrendered his Army of North Virginia after the Battle of Appomattox.

"Grant had shown one sign of firmness with his troops in the evening: When the [Yankee] guns began firing salutes amid wild cheering, he had them stopped. 'The Confederates were now our prisoners, and we did not want to exult over their downfall,' he said." [11]

Buckongahelas also witnessed, but refused to sign the treaty at Fort Finney in 1786 or the treaty at Fort Harmar in 1789. In his eyes, his father-in-law Pipe was a traitor to the confederacy. Pipe's signature on the treaties brought more Delaware villages under Buckongahelas' leadership.

"Buckongahelas confronted Pipe and blamed him for all the ills that had befallen the Delawares after White Eye's death," Weslager noted. [12]

A Kentucky army destroyed the Shawnee towns at the head of the Great Miami River in 1786, but Buckongahelas' town was not attacked. He eventually would move his people and join the Shawnee and other tribes at the head of the Maumee River near present day Fort Wayne, Indiana. There Buckongahelas would be near his good friend Blue Jacket, but for now they soon would join forces with their powerful ally Little Turtle.

"Our next notice of Buokongahelas [sic] is in 1792, when he showed himself no less magnanimous than at Gnadenhutten and Salem," [13] historian Drake recorded.

Colonel Hardin and Major Trueman were dispatched in May with a flag of truce to the Indian nations of the west, particularly the Maumee towns. Near the town of Au Glaize on the southwest branch of the Miami of the Lake, they came upon some Indians who seemed friendly at first, but finally murdered nearly all of the white men.

"The interpreter made his escape, after some time, and gave an account of the transaction," Drake reported. "His name was William Smally…. He was first conducted to Au Glaize, and soon to 'Buokungahela [sic], king of the Delawares, by his captors.

"The chief told those that had committed the murder he was very sorry they had killed the men. That instead of so doing, they should have brought them to the Indian towns; and then, if what they had to say had not been liked, it would have been time enough to have killed them then.

195

Nothing, he said, could justify them for putting them to death, as there was no chance for them to escape. The truth was they killed them for their effects."

Drake reported that Buckongahelas took Smally to his own cabin, "and showed him great kindness, told him to stay there while he could go safely to his former Indian friends (he having been adopted into an Indian family, in place of one who had been killed, in his former captivity).

"While here with Buokongahelas [sic], which was near a month, Mr. Smally said the chief would not permit him to go abroad alone, for fear, he said, that the young Indians would kill him. Thus, though we do not meet often with Buokungahela [sic], but when we do, the interview is no less honorable to him, than in the instances we have given." [14]

1. Cooper, *Last of the Mohicans*, p. 368

2. Ibid, p. 70.

3. Thatcher, *Indian Biography*, p. 177.

4. Weslager, *Delaware Indians*, p. 21.

5. Drake, *Book of Indians of North America*, Chapter IV, p. 47.

6. McKnight, Charles, p. 418.

7. Weslager, *Delaware Indians*, p. 318.

8. Mitchell, *Indian Chief Journeycake*, p. 8.

9. White, *Middle Ground*, p. 437.

10. McWhorter, Lucullus, *Border Settlers of Northwestern Virginia*, p. 165.

11. Davis, *To Appomattox, Nine April Days, 1865*, p. 355.

12. Weslager, *Delaware Indians*, p. 319.

13. Drake, *Indians of North America*, Chapter IV, p. 44.

14. Ibid, p. 45.

34

Blue Jacket, Friend of Buckongahelas

Blue Jacket was born about 1743 and would grow up to be the principal war chief of the Shawnees, just as his friend Buckongahelas became the principal war chief of the Delaware. Although there was a nearly twenty-five-year age difference between them, as adults both of the men became fast friends for the rest of their lives.

If we could visit the 18th century, we would recognize Blue Jacket and other male members of the small Shawnee tribe–their population was approximately 2,500 at that time--by their shaved heads with little tufts of hair or "topknots" sticking up on the middle of their heads, their tattoos, and their pierced ears and noses and dangling earrings (similar to the fashion of some of today's teenagers).

Oliver M. Spencer, who was captured by the Shawnee in 1792 when he was eleven years old, later described Blue Jacket:

Shawnee Chief Blue Jacket

"This chief was the most noble in appearance of any Indian I ever saw. His person, about six feet high, was finely proportioned, stout [strong], and muscular; his eyes large, bright and piercing; his forehead high and broad; his nose aquiline; his mouth rather wide, and his countenance open and intelligent, expressive of firmness and decision.

"He was considered one of the most brave and accomplished of the Indian chiefs, second only to Little Turtle and Buck-on-ge-ha-la [sic]…," Blue Jacket's biographer John Sugden wrote. [1]

Strange stories have been told through the years about the Shawnee Chief Blue Jacket (Weyapiersenwah), sometimes called "Jim Blue Jacket," one of the strongest allies of Buckongahelas and Chief Little Turtle of the Miami Nation.

In 1877, more than sixty-five years after Blue Jacket died, an article was published claiming that the chief's real name was Marmaduke ("Duke") Van Swearingen. Marmaduke supposedly was captured as a white teenager in the woods of western Virginia with Charley, one of his seven younger brothers. Duke and Charley were out hunting rabbits when surrounded by eleven *Kispokothas* (warrior Shawnees).

As the story goes, the seventeen-year-old Duke had learned quite a few Indian words during his young lifetime, and persuaded the Shawnee to allow twelve-year-old Charley to go free. In return, the six-foot-tall, muscular Duke allegedly agreed to accompany the Shawnee to their camp and be adopted by them. (Whites of all ages often were kidnapped and adopted by Indians of various tribes who had lost a relative to death. Rescued white captives often would refuse to return to their former lives, having acclimated themselves to the Native lifestyle.)

According to this legend, Duke joined the Shawnee Tribe and became a *Kispokotha* who relished his new life. That's one story, as related by author Allan W. Eckert in his book *Blue Jacket: War Chief of the Shawnees*, published in 1969.

An outdoor theatrical production about the life of Blue Jacket--performed each summer in Xenia, Ohio for more than twenty-five years--also promoted the legend. The facts are that Blue Jacket was not Marmaduke Van Sweringen, who was a real person. The Shawnee may have captured Van Sweringen during the American Revolution, but according to a family Bible, he was born in 1763. Blue Jacket was born at least twenty years before Van Sweringen.

Blue Jacket first appears as a grown man and a war chief in written historical records in 1773. A British missionary visited the Shawnee villages on the Scioto River and recorded the location of Blue Jacket's Town on Deer Creek in what now is Ross County, Ohio. (Van Sweringen would have been only ten-years-old at the time.) Blue Jacket was engaged as a Shawnee leader during Lord Dunmore's War in 1774, when Van Sweringen would have been only a lad of eleven.

More than 200 years later in the year 2000, a Wright State University biologist, Dan Krane of Ohio would study saliva DNA from five descendants of Blue Jacket and from five Van Swearingen descendants. His findings suggested that Blue Jacket was an American Indian, and that he and Marmaduke Van Swearingen probably could not have been the same person.

Later results of a DNA test using updated equipment and techniques were published in the September 2006 edition of *The Ohio Journal of Science*. The researchers had tested DNA samples from four men descended from Charles Swearingen, Blue Jacket's "supposed brother," and six descendants of one of Blue Jacket's sons, George Blue-Jacket. The DNA from the two families did not match, and the study concluded:

"Barring any questions of the paternity of the chief's single son who lived to produce male heirs, the 'Blue Jacket with-Caucasian-roots' is not based on reality."

One of the men who furnished DNA for the Blue Jacket-Van Swearingen studies was Robert Denton Blue Jacket of Tulsa, Oklahoma, where my brothers and I were born and reared.

When the Shawnee divided and part of the tribe headed west of the Mississippi, Blue Jacket remained with those who stayed in Ohio. Daniel Boone captured him during a horse thievery raid in Kentucky in 1788, but Blue Jacket escaped. Another time, the feisty Blue Jacket returned the favor and captured Boone and frontiersman Simon Kenton. Despite his acquaintance with Blue Jacket--either as a captor or as a prisoner--Boone never mentioned that he thought that Blue Jacket was a white man.

"The Indians took up their war hatchets and scalping knives to attack wagon trains coming west from Fort Pitt, as well as supply boats moving down the Ohio, once more committing atrocities against white families," historian Weslager wrote.

"The United States was forced to take retaliatory action, and an expedition was sent under General Josiah Harmer in 1789, and a second under General St. Clair in 1791. Both suffered crushing defeats as they faced the allied forces of Little Turtle and his Miami braves, Blue Jacket and his Shawnee fighters, and Buckongahelas and his Delaware warriors." [2]

Blue Jacket's Private Life

In his private life, Blue Jacket was smitten by a tall and ravishing beauty named Wabethe (the Swan), who visited the Shawnees. She was the daughter of Wabete the Elk, the younger brother of Moluntha, chief of the Maykujay Shawnees. Blue Jacket and Wabethe were joined in matrimony, and Wabethe gave birth to one son, Little Blue Jacket, and two daughters. The elder Blue Jacket became a chief of the Maykujay band of the Shawnees.

Blue Jacket had a second wife, Margaret (Peggy) Moore, an English girl captured with her sister at age nine by the Shawnee around 1759 during the French and Indian War. During a visit to her childhood home, Margaret gave birth to a daughter, Nancy, in the late 1760s or early 1770s. She never reunited with Blue Jacket, but later gave birth to Joseph Moore, who died in 1813.

"Nancy was Blue Jacket's youngest child by his wife, Margaret Moore," wrote John Sugden in his book *Blue Jacket*. "The chief never saw her grow up because Margaret, a white woman, returned to her people in Virginia while she was pregnant." [3]

A third Blue Jacket wife was Clearwater Baby (pronounced "Baubee"), the daughter of a Shawnee woman and Jacques Duperon Baby, a French Canadian trader in the Detroit River area. Clearwater gave Blue Jacket six children: James, born ca 1765, died ca 1845; Mary, born ca 1775, died 1806; Sally, born ca 1778, died after 1823; George, born ca 1781, died 1829; and two unnamed sons, who died in 1792 and 1813.

In 1853, Clearwater would travel with her grandson, James ("Jim") and his family to the Northeast Kansas Territory, where she died around the turn of the century. Some authors claim she accompanied her son, James, to Kansas in 1853, impossible if he died in 1845.

Blue Jacket was one of the leaders in the Northwest Indian War, participating in wars for Kentucky and for Ohio. In 1776, Blue Jacket and nearly a hundred Shawnee joined Cornstalk, who had committed the Shawnee to peace, to journey to visit American officials in Pittsburg. Along the way, they dropped by Gnadenhutten where 500 other Indians had convened for a peace conference with U. S. Indian agent George Morgan.

When Blue Jacket and other Shawnees joined the discussions Nov. 1, "They saw Delawares under White Eyes, Killbuck, Buckongahelas, and Pipe, and Iroquois led by White Mingo and Flying Crows, but no Wyandots, Mingoes, or western Indians. In short, this was the rump that would try to maintain peace with the American forces." [4]

By 1778, the war in Kentucky was not going well for the Shawnee, whose only allies were the Mingoes and "a breakaway band of Delawares under Wyondochella [the father of Buckongahelas] and Buckongahelas," Sugden noted.

"In 1778 this band left the Walhonding to form a town three miles north of Blue Jacket's. They were certainly important allies. In three years Buckongahelas increased his following to 240 warriors, gaining recruits as the neutral faction of Delawares crumbled. And Buckongahelas formed a close partnership with Blue Jacket. Indeed, in the years ahead it was the prestige, strength, and support of Buckongahelas that lent Blue Jacket much of his power." [5]

War Chief Blue Jacket was a predecessor to the great Indian Tecumseh, Blue Jacket's pupil. Known as "The Shooting Star," Tecumseh was the Shawnee's most famous war chief and organizer of the second great Indian confederacy. (The Cherokee refused to join this alliance, siding with the U.S. government. Cherokee even fought with U.S. soldiers against the Creeks, but the United States ousted the Cherokee from Georgia anyway.)

Blue Jacket was known as a heavy drinker, and following the Battle of St. Clair, he began to imbibe even more excessively, causing his behavior to become unpredictable.

"Antoine Lasselle, a trader from Kekionga, was the son-in-law of the erratic and often drunken Shawnee war leader Blue Jacket," wrote Richard White in his book *The Middle Ground*.

"His success in urging Blue Jacket to open private negotiation with the Americans (following the Indians' defeat of St. Clair) forced McKee (Alexander, a British agent at Detroit) to have Blue Jacket watched," White reported. [6]

Blue Jacket would fight for four years in several battles alongside Little Turtle and Buckongahelas. Their greatest triumph would be against General St. Clair, their saddest battle their defeat at Fallen Timbers after Blue Jacket assumed leadership of the three tribes. But before that battle, Blue Jacket jumped the gun on the advancing troops under "Mad" Anthony Wayne with an unsuccessful attack on Fort Recovery.

"Tired of waiting for Wayne to make a move, some 1,200 allied warriors, led by Blue Jacket, on June 20 attacked Fort Recovery, Wayne's most forward post. After an initial success in ambushing some of the garrison, the Indians were driven off by cannon fire and retreated with heavy losses." [7]

The impetuous Blue Jacket had hoped Buckongahelas would arrive in time to help him capture the fort, but that did not happen.

"Buckongahelas, we know, was supposed to have brought up the rear with a few hundred reinforcements, mainly Delawares, but he was delayed at the Glaize," author Sugden wrote.

"Apparently, a sister of the Wyandot chief Roundhead and the wife of an interpreter,

Francois Duchouquet, brought some rum to Buckongahelas's warriors, and they were useless for a considerable time. The Delaware chief eventually got his force moving, but he would arrive too late for Blue Jacket's attack on Fort Recovery." [8]

When Blue Jacket did meet up with "Mad" Anthony Wayne, it would be disastrous for the Shawnee chief and his allies Buckongahelas and Little Turtle.

"Fourteen hundred Indian warriors under Blue Jacket collected before Fort Miami at a place since known as Fallen Timbers, where tree trunks uprooted by a tornado and a tangle of newer growth made an almost impenetrable thicket," Angie Debo wrote many years later. "In a desperate battle on August 20 [1793], the Indians were defeated." [9]

Blue Jacket and Buckongahelas reluctantly would sign the Treaty of Greenville in 1795 and the Treaty of Fort Industry in 1805, treaties that cost the tribes millions of acres of their land in the vast Ohio Valley. Blue Jacket and his brother, Red Pole (Mio-Qua-Goo-Na-Gaw), met with President Washington on December 2, 1796. A life-size wax sculpture of the two men was displayed in the Charles Wilson Peale Museum until the museum was destroyed by fire. On their return trip from Philadelphia, Red Pole died of pneumonia at Pittsburgh on January 28, 1798. He was buried there with full military honors.

"No contemporary record marked the passing of the veteran war chief [Blue Jacket], but from what was said later, it seems that he died in his village on the Detroit River in the early part of 1808, while Tecumseh and the Prophet were establishing their new town on the Wabash in Indiana Territory," author Sugden wrote. [10]

Despite his personality problems and bouts with alcohol, Blue Jacket is remembered favorably by historians: "Some of the greatest Indian captains, orators and statesmen were Shawnees; among whom were Cornstalk, Paxnous, Blue Jacket, and Tecumseh," Lucullus McWhorter wrote in 1915. [11]

At the age of sixteen, Charles Bluejacket, grandson of the famed Shawnee warrior "Captain Bluejacket," left Ohio and arrived in 1832 in the area that would become the state of Kansas

Charles Bluejacket

in 1861. Shawnee, Kansas is named for their tribe, and the northeastern Oklahoma town of Bluejacket is named for Charles, its first postmaster. Charles remained in Kansas for nearly forty years, serving as an interpreter, a Union Civil War captain, and as a chief of the Shawnees from 1861 to 1865. He was ordained a Methodist minister in 1859, and removed to Oklahoma Territory in 1871.

The Rev. Charles Blue Jacket returned to Kansas from Oklahoma in the 1890s when he was an elderly man. A statue of him, sculpted by former Hallmark artist Charles Goslin, stands in the city park of Shawnee, Kansas. Charles reared a family of twenty-three youngsters, some of them adopted, and the statue portrays him seated and reading to children.

Sculptor Charles Goslin with his statue of Charles Bluejacket.

1. Sugden, *Blue Jacket*, p. 33.

2. Weslager, *Delaware Indians,* p. 321.

3. Sugden, *Blue Jacket*, p. 243.

4. Ibid, p. 51.

5. Ibid, p. 55,

6. White, *Middle Ground*, p. 463.

7. Josephy, Jr., *500 Nations,* p. 300.

8. Sugden, *Blue Jacket*, p. 162.

9. Debo, *History of the Indians*, p. 92.

10. Sugden, *Blue Jacket*, p. 254.

11. McWhorter, Lucullus, *Border Settlers of Northwestern Virginia*, p. 430.

35

Little Turtle, Born Warrior

Little Turtle was an interesting character, born around 1752 along the Miami River just east of Indiana in the vast Northwest Territory, the son of a Miami chief and a Mohegan mother who may have been captured in war and adopted by the tribe.

Little Turtle

Little Turtle was given the Indian name "Michikinikwa." Although kinship was determined through the mother's line among Algonquians, the Miamis chose to ignore this tradition and made Little Turtle a chief at an early age. There was something remarkable about this young man. He appeared more solemn and dignified than his peers.

Sporting a single feather on his scalp, Little Turtle was said to be a fine specimen of a man, a born warrior, and a speaker of such power that he drew thousands to follow him. Always alert, he slept with a white man's gun. As he advanced in age and wisdom, he became one of the greatest Algonquian war chiefs and a favorite negotiator with the Americans. He was a close ally of Buckongahelas.

It was Little Turtle who urged that wild ponies be caught and tamed for the Natives' use. Wild horses had roamed North and South America until 6,000 B.C., when they became extinct. Horses were re-introduced to the Americas by European explorers. When Indians first saw a horse, they were puzzled. The creature was as big as an elk, but it packed like a dog, so they called it an "elk dog."

Little's Turtle's main goal in life was to unite as many tribes as possible to oppose the thrust of the Long Knives into Indian lands. "Each little tribe is no better than my little finger," he would say. "But coming together to form the fist, we can strike!"

The newly-formed United States outrageously claimed control of the entire vast Northwest

Territory after the American Revolutionary War ended in 1783. Thus Chief Little Turtle summoned his friends to stop the U.S. government's plans to drive the Indians from the territory, established in 1787.

George Washington took office as the infant country's first president in 1789, serving until 1797. Washington had negotiated with the Delaware and other tribes in their camps many years previously. When construction of Fort Washington was completed near the mouth of the Little Miami River (present day Cincinnati), the Indians were enraged and viewed the new fort as a dangerous obstacle on the Ohio river.

"In 1790, President George Washington ordered an expedition outfitted with the purpose of pacifying the hostile Indian nations on the northwest frontier. Brigadier General Josiah Harmar was given the command of a large force of about 1,100 Pennsylvania, Virginia, and Kentucky militia, plus 300 or so federal regulars, mustered at Fort Washington (Cincinnati)," Carl Waldman wrote. [1]

"Pacifying" apparently meant "attacking." General Harmar, known to be a heavy drinker, and his troops traveled north into Indian Territory along the Maumee River Valley.

"Yet Harmar, despite the size of his force, was no match for the brilliant and eloquent Indian leader commanding the loose confederacy of tribes – Little Turtle (Michikinikwa), a Miami chief," Waldman pointed out.

"Little Turtle and his warriors, including Miamis, Shawnees, Ojibways, Delawares, Potawatomis, and Ottawas, sniping at their enemy and burning their own villages to feign panic, lured Harmar's men deeper into Indian country. Then, in two surprise September ambushes, the Indians routed the enemy, killing 183 and wounding 31 more." [2]

Harmar had divided his troops and first sent an advance force of 180 men into the forest. These men were trapped and slaughtered at the hands of Little Turtle himself. Harmar then divided his army again to encircle the Indians, but his three hundred and sixty remaining troops were outnumbered, a third of them killed. Harmar's army retreated in disgrace back to Fort Washington.

White settlers along the frontiers found the Indians' success truly alarming. Harmar had lost 108 of his men killed and twenty-eight wounded.

"This dreadful slaughter so reduced the strength and spirits of Harmar's army that he was happy in being permitted to retreat unmolested, … having thrown away the lives of more than half of his regular force," wrote historian Charles McKnight in 1876. [3]

When Washington received news of the defeat, he was disgruntled, but not surprised.

"I expected little from it from the moment I heard he was a drunkard," the president said of Harmar, according to Alvin M. Josephy, Jr. [4]

As a result of Harmar's embarrassing defeat, the first standing army of the United States was organized. The Legion of the United States was established in 1791 for the primary purpose of defeating the Indian enemies of white intruders into Ohio. As the Americans organized themselves for battle, so did the Indians under the able command of the Miami's Little Turtle. President Washington designated General Arthur St. Clair as governor of the Northwest Territories to command the wilderness campaign.

A native of Scotland and a wealthy Pennsylvania veteran of the Revolutionary War, St. Clair was described by Josephy as "enormously heavy, snobbish, and given to bouts of temper tantrums, asthma, and gout." [5]

Two smaller expeditions set out immediately while St. Clair organized his larger campaign. A total of 800 Kentuckians went against Wea towns on the Wabash, while 600 troops destroyed Indian towns on the Eel River.

"The burning of towns, crops, and the captivity of their women and children only made the savages more desperate, and the chiefs, Little Turtle, Miami; Blue Jacket, Shawnee, and Buckongahelas, Delaware, were busy forming a new and strong Indian Confederacy," McKnight wrote. [6]

Another historian, Norman Wood, noted: "Little Turtle, ably assisted by Blue Jacket, head chief of the Shawnees of this period, and Buckongahelas, who led the Delawares, formed a confederation of the Wyandots, Potawatomis, Chippewas, and Ottawas, Shawnees, Delawares and Miamis, and parts of several other tribes.

"These were substantially the same tribes who had thirty years before been united under Pontiac, and formed an exact precedent for the combination of Tecumseh and his brother at Tippecanoe some years after...." [7]

The Indians would clash with General St. Clair and his more than 1,000 troops in a battle whose free-flowing blood would stain the pages of history books with red for years to come.

"The leader of the Indian army in this bloody engagement was a chief of the Missassago tribe, known by the name of the 'Little Turtle,'" McKnight wrote.

"Notwithstanding his name, he was at least six-feet high, strong, muscular, and remarkably dignified in his appearance. He was forty years of age, had seen much service, and had accompanied Burgoyne in his disastrous invasion. His aspect was harsh, sour and forbidding, and his person, during the action, was arrayed in the very extremity of Indian foppery, having at least twenty dollars' worth of silver depending from his nose and ears. [8]

"The plan of attack was conceived by him alone, in opposition to the opinion of almost every other chief. Notwithstanding his ability, however, he was said to have been unpopular among the Indians, probably in consequence of those very abilities, wrote author Sugden. [9]

It was St. Clair, the controversial first governor of the Northwest Territory (who eventually was removed from his post), who had emphasized to Harmar that the Indians "should be made to smart." [10]

But it was the hard-drinking Harmar who had smarted with humiliation when he was defeated by the combined brilliance of Little Turtle, Buckongahelas, and Blue Jacket. General St. Clair would be the next to suffer under their expertise at war.

1. Waldman, *Atlas of the North American Indian*, p. 114.

2. Ibid.

3. McKnight, *Our Western Border*, p. 532.

4. Josephy, Jr., *500 Nations*, p. 292.

5. Ibid, 293.

6. McKnight, *Our Western Border*, p. 537.

7. Wood, *Lives of Famous Indian Chiefs,* p. 284.

8. Sugden, *Blue Jacket*, p. 93.

9. McKnight, *Our Western Border*, p. 546.

10. Josephy, Jr., *500 Nations*, p. 291.

36

The Battle of St. Clair

General Arthur St. Clair

Oddly enough, my brothers and I have a distant relative--the red-headed, Scots-Irish Indian scout William Crum—who participated in the Battle of St. Clair. One of his descendants, H. B. Crum, son of William Pearce Crum (who married our great-great-grandfather's sister Martha Elliott), wrote about his ancestor William.

He was "born somewhere in western New York in 1770," H.B. began.

"He was feared by the Indians for his deadly marksmanship with [a] long, smooth barrel squirrel rifle. Among the Delawares, he was greatly esteemed for his fleetness of feet, and many times they tried to capture him alive so as to induce him to become a member of their tribe, but [they] never succeeded."

Unfortunately for Crum, he didn't join up with the Delaware warriors, but chose instead to scout for St. Clair, a decision he later regretted.

"He served as a scout and guide with St. Clair's ill-fated expedition against the Indians of Indiana and Illinois in 1791," H. B. wrote. "The scouts, some twenty in number, protested to St. Clair against his method of posting single sentries far apart at considerable distance from the army. Their protestations were of no avail.

"Incensed at his neglect of ordinary precautions when in hostile Indian country, the scouts, who were not enlisted soldiers, refused to camp with the army, and on the night of the attack were camped about one and one-half miles to the southwest of the main army, where they had posted their own sentries. Like the army, they camped upon the banks of the Wabash."

The Indians crossed the river for the surprise attack just before daybreak.

"The day the golden-haired Custer fell at the Little Big Horn [also known as the Battle of the Greasy Grass] with about 275 of the cream of the Seventh Cavalry around him has been dramatized as the biggest single victory the Indians ever scored against the army," wrote C. Fayne Porter in his book *The Battle of the 1,000 Slain.*

"But this is far from the truth," Porter declared. "Where Custer lost one man, St. Clair lost almost three, killed on the field of battle or missing and presumed dead, and no one will ever know how many of the seriously wounded died as a result of the battle." [1]

In February of 1789, General Arthur St. Clair, a native of Scotland, had been summoned to Philadelphia, then the nation's capital, to meet with his friend and fellow former warrior George Washington, who had been elected president. Washington gave St. Clair, a veteran of the Revolutionary War, a new assignment: to invade the Ohio country and rid it of the troublesome Little Turtle's confederacy.

St. Clair was the man of the hour. He had been appointed governor of the Northwest Territory, a vast area that eventually would include the states of Ohio, Indiana, Illinois, Michigan, and Wisconsin.

"In taking leave, therefore, of his old military comrade, St. Clair, he [President Washington] wished him success and honor, and added this solemn warning: 'You have your instructions from the Secretary of War. I had a strict eye to them, and will add one word--b*eware of a surprise!*'" historian Wood recorded. [2]

Congress had passed an act to increase the army's numbers, and with the president's warning ringing in his ears, General St. Clair set out to raise a second army, an effort that consumed a year. St. Clair found it difficult to locate suitable recruits for his new army.

"St. Clair was not only old and infirm, but weak and sick with an attack of gout, and at times almost helpless," Wood noted.

"Moreover, he had been very unfortunate in his military career in the Revolutionary War. Neither he nor the second in command, Maj.-Gen. Richard Butler, possessed any of the qualities of leadership save courage,"

"The troops were, for the most part, of wretched stuff. St. Clair was particularly unpopular in Kentucky, and no volunteers could be found to serve under him. The militia of Kentucky had been called on, and about 1,000 reluctantly furnished by draft; but as they were all unfavorable to the commander-in-chief, many desertions took place daily. They seemed to think that the only possible outcome of his expedition was defeat." [3]

By late summer of 1791, 2,000 men had joined ranks with St. Clair and were billeted in hundreds of tents in the border town of Marietta. At least 600 of those men deserted the cause before the army advanced into Native territory.

"About a quarter of the men deserted in route, and to keep the others happy, St. Clair permitted about two hundred soldiers' wives to travel with the army [Fifty-six of the wives would lose their lives in the battle that was to come.]" [4]

As they limped along, marching north, the 1,400 soldiers took their time, pausing to build Fort Hamilton and Fort Jefferson along the way as a defense against the Indians. As brilliant as the American generals thought themselves to be, they failed to realize that Indians often avoided the forts and chose their battle sites on more advantageous locales.

Buckongahelas, whose standing by this time was the highest of any leader or chief in the Delaware nation, brought 500 men to join with 700 other warriors led by Chiefs Little Turtle and Blue Jacket. Buckongahelas started up a town for the Delaware near his friends. The trio of great Indian leaders met in Ohio and calmly mapped their military strategies to defeat the Northwest Territory general, Arthur St. Clair.

The Delaware, Shawnee and Miami numbered 1,200 warriors, but they were joined in the battle by Wyandots, Mingoes, Ottawas, Potawatomis, and Ojibwes Indians. They camped on the Wabash River on the chilly November evening of Nov. 3, 1791, hidden in dense woods where they erected a barricade that would shield them against their enemies. The breath of the Natives and their ponies--like puffs of smoke--sat upon the silent night air. The horses, painted in different designs, shuffled with restless energy as if sensing the bloody battle that would be upon them come the dawn.

St. Clair was a tired and weak old man. He and his men were so exhausted after their long trek over boggy lands that they didn't bother to erect fortifications to protect their camp that night. The army of regulars and rough woodsmen who were volunteers were at odds, the latter not wishing to take orders from the former. The regulars camped in one area--the volunteers in another. And as Crum pointed out, the scouts were in still a third area. St. Clair's gross errors in judgment were the cause of his army's dreadful downfall.

An Army of Deer Led by a Deer

"Napoleon is quoted as saying, 'Better an army of deer led on by a lion than an army of lions led by a deer,'" the author Wood noted. "In the light of subsequent events, this [the battle of St. Clair] was much like an army of deer led on by a deer." [5]

This gibe became one of General Washington's favorite quotes, and it seems aptly descriptive of his feeble military leaders at that time.

A light snow began to fall during the night, and by crack of dawn, the air was frigid and frosty with ice. The battle between St. Clair and the Indians would begin in piercing cold. Blue Jacket softly sang an Indian hymn as the sun sliced into the bitter morning's fog.

Blue Jacket's biographer John Sugden described the approaching Indian Confederation: "St. Clair's camp lay less than a mile upstream of Blue Jacket's, and the warriors soon covered the distance. They marched in files that made a half-moon formation. The Wyandots and Mingoes were on the right flank, and the Ottawas, Potawatomis, and Ojibwes guarded the left, both wings ready to sweep around the enemy force or to check any flanking movements against the Indians.

"In the center strode the warriors of the triumvirate, Shawnees, Delawares, and Miamis under Blue Jacket, Buckongahelas, and Little Turtle. As they closed in, they extended their front to prevent the Americans from gaining their rear." [6]

While most of the American soldiers still snored, the Indian warriors crept near to the white men and encircled their encampment. The horses of those who followed quietly behind now were as excited and eager to begin battle as their riders. The Indian scouts crawled undetected to within inches of the sentries before they were spotted.

"At dawn the next morning, with piercing yells, the Indian force, led by the thirty-nine-year-old veteran war strategist Little Turtle, launched an attack on St. Clair's men," Alvin Josephy Jr. wrote in his book *500 Nations*.

"Emerging from the forest and coming at the Americans from three sides, the Indians charged first into the camp of the militiamen, taking them by surprise and killing many of them with hatchets and knives as they tried to fight back. Fleeing in panic, the survivors raced across the stream to St. Clair's main camp on a small plateau, spreading fear among the troops that were gathered there. A moment later, the Indians charged onto the plateau, engaging the Americans again in furious hand-to-hand fighting." [7]

By then it was too late for St. Clair and his men, as hundreds of shouting Indians poured out of the woods and awakened many soldiers who were still sleeping – and soon would sleep forever.

In the space of only a few minutes, the first skirmish had turned into a slaughter. The white men who had sprung from their pallets – some without time to grab their weapons--were forced to retreat. Before their startled eyes, they saw large masses of painted Indians advancing toward them from three directions.

The Indians were led by three men on horseback—terrifying in appearance--Little Turtle, Buckongahelas, and Blue Jacket, all seated tall on their mounts, their blackened faces set strong against their enemy.

Perhaps Chief Buckongahelas wore a breastplate made of bone that his daughters, Little Leaf and her sister, had labored on for many days. Breastplates were decorated with abalone shell, ermine, turkey beard, and horsehair, the bones laced together with rawhide. The Buck's daughters would have prayed that their handiwork would protect their father's life. Little Turtle's single feather was in his hair, and many scalp locks hung from his buckskin shirt. The neck of Blue Jacket would have been encased in a heavy bone choker to protect his jugular vein.

Blue Jacket, his dark eyes blazing, seemed to be everywhere in the battle, and quickly lifted fourteen scalps. A tale circulated for many years that a white Army captain thrust a bayonet into Blue Jacket, who in turn sent his tomahawk into the captain's stomach. According to the legend, when Blue Jacket knelt over the captain to remove his scalp, the man opened his eyes and cried, "Duke, I'm your brother Charley!"

Then supposedly, the captain died, and Blue Jacket looked with sorrow at his long-lost little brother, whose life he had saved long ago in the forest when the Shawnee took them captive. Then, as folklore goes, Blue Jacket scalped his brother. It was said that this action haunted Blue Jacket and accounted for his heavy drinking and erratic behavior. But Blue Jacket was not the dead captain's brother.

St. Clair, with his huge size a very large target, lost five horses shot or knocked from underneath him during the three-hour battle. He was unwounded, however, although his uniform was torn by eight bullets. Wearing only his hat and a greatcoat over his underwear, St. Clair tried to climb back onto a horse, but gave it up when both his horse and his orderly were killed.

"St. Clair, who at that time was worn down by a fever and unable to mount his horse, nevertheless, as is universally admitted, exerted himself with a courage and presence of mind worthy of a better fate," Charles McKnight wrote in the book *Our Western Border* in 1876.

"He instantly directed his litter to the right of the rear line, where the great weight of fire fell, and where the slaughter, particularly of the officers, was terrible." [8]

Battle of a Thousand Slain by Peter Dennis.

With soldiers dropping to his right and left, and as far as he could see, St. Clair screamed orders into the wind. But his orders went unheard. A lock of St. Clair's hair was shorn off by a bullet, but it did not issue from the weapons of Buckongahelas, who was renowned as a marksman with both musket and rifle. The great chief would not have missed his mark. Some white artillerymen fired into the melee, but their shots went wildly high.

"A moment later, Blue Jacket and a group of Shawnees and Delawares, the latter fighting under the war chief, Buckongahelas, swarmed over the battery and killed the gunners," Josephy Jr. recorded. [9]

The Indians chose the officers and gunners as their special targets; the only regular regiment in St. Clair's army suffered every officer killed or wounded. His voice hoarse from yelling, St. Clair watched in horror as his men began to scatter. He tried in vain to rally the bloodied soldiers, but finally, he too gave up the fight.

Realizing his crushing defeat, the general mounted a pack horse, one of his few horses left alive, and joined the remnants of his army who were abandoning their wounded, stampeding down the road from whence they came. For thirty miles, the white troops and their wives ran for their lives, breathless and fearful--flinging their weapons away as they went.

"One fleeing woman, whose flashing red hair served as a beacon, sped ahead of the troops," Glenn Tucker reported in *Tecumseh*. [10]

"The flight continued … until sunset, when the routed troops reached Fort Jefferson, some thirty miles distant, completely exhausted…. Leaving their wounded at Fort Jefferson, the retreat was continued until the half-armed rabble reached Fort Washington and the log huts of the infant city of Cincinnati," added Wood. [11]

The "rabble" had covered in five days the same distance it had taken them five weeks to reach the battlefield, and their defeat has been called "one of the most lopsided in U. S. military annals."

The Battle of St. Clair had raged for three hours, and by day's end, the three Indian war chiefs and their warriors had killed a total of 636 of St. Clair's original 1,400 troops (including thirty-eight officers). Other troops numbering 242 were wounded, and many later died. Only twenty-one Indians lost their lives in the melee, with forty wounded.

These casualties definitely dwarf in number the 275 men under Custer's command who died at the Little Bighorn in 1876 (Custer's two brothers, Tom and Boston, and Custer's brother-in-law James Calhoun, as well as Custer's eighteen-year-old nephew, Harry Reed, were among the dead.) [12]

"In January, 1792, Brigadier General Wilkinson conducted a party to the scene of St. Clair's defeat and buried the bodies of the slain in great pits dug through the snow into the frozen ground," Tucker wrote. [13]

"St. Clair's Shame"

The commander's crushing defeat became known as 'St. Clair's Shame." It was exactly the disaster the president had warned against. President George Washington's reaction to news of the disaster was one of rage.

"In the agony of his emotion, he (Washington) struck his clenched hands with fearful force against his forehead, and in a paroxysm of anguish exclaimed: 'It's all over! St. Clair's defeated – routed; the officers nearly all killed – the men by wholesale – that brave army cut to pieces – the rout complete! Too shocking to think of – and a *surprise* in the bargain!'" historian Wood recorded.

"He uttered all this with great vehemence. Then he paused and walked about the room several times, agitated, but saying nothing…. Then turning to the secretary, who stood amazed at the spectacle of Washington in all his wrath, he again broke forth: "*Yes, sir. Here, in this very room, on this very spot*, I took leave of him (St. Clair). I wished him success and honor. 'You have your instructions,' I said, 'from the Secretary of War; I had a strict eye to them, and will add but one word – beware of a surprise! I repeat it – beware of a surprise! You know how the Indians fight us.'

"He went off with that as my last solemn warning thrown into his ears," Washington wailed. "And yet to suffer that army to be cut to pieces, hacked by a surprise – the very thing I guarded him against! O, God! O, God! He's worse than a murderer! How can he answer it to his country? The blood of the slain is upon him – the curse of widows and orphans – the curse of Heaven!" [14]

Washington's intimate advisers revealed that the only other time they had witnessed him so angry was the day he met with General Charles Lee, who had ordered his troops to retreat without firing a single shot at the British during the Revolutionary War Battle of Monmouth in 1778.

"St. Clair's defeat, with the possible exception of that of Braddock, was the most complete and overwhelming in the annals of Indian warfare," added Wood.

"Little Turtle deserves to rank among the four greatest Indians, the other three being Pontiac, Tecumseh and Chief Joseph. Indeed, when it is remembered that 'nothing succeeds like success,' and that he alone of all the Indian commanders had three victories to his credit (for the defeat of the whites at Blue Lick, Kentucky is also conceded to him), he might be regarded as in some respects the greatest American Indian." [15]

My relative Crum offered his own summation of the battle: "St. Clair, scarcely waiting to feel out the strength of the enemy, ordered a retreat which in the dense forest gave the Indians an immense advantage. Out of 1,400 effective troops, St. Clair lost in killed and wounded more than half his army."

1. Porter, *Battle of 1,000 Slain*, p. 38.

2. Wood, *Lives of Famous Indian Chiefs*, pp. 287, 288.

3. Ibid, 288.

4. Johansen and Grinde, Jr., *Native American Biography*, p. 216.

5. Wood, *Lives of Famous Indian Chiefs*, p. 288.

6. Sugden, *Blue Jacket*, p. 122,

7. Josephy, Jr., *500 Nations*, p. 293

8. McKnight, *Our Western Border*, p. 539.

9. Josephy, Jr., *500 Nations*, p. 294.

10. Tucker, *Tecumseh*, p. 59.

11. Wood, *Lives of Famous Indian Chiefs*, p. 296.

12. Philbrick, *Last Stand*, p. 20.

13. Tucker, *Tecumseh*, p.61.

14. Wood, pp. 297, 298.

15. Ibid, pp. 296, 283.

37

"Mad Anthony's" Revenge

"Mad Anthony" Wayne

Congress was just as enraged by the disastrous Battle of St. Clair as was the president, and appropriated more than $1,000,000 to raise still another army, this one under the command of General "Mad Anthony" Wayne, 47, who had served at Valley Forge and Yorktown.

"Indians universally called him (Wayne) the 'Black Snake,' from the superior cunning which they ascribed to him; and even allowed him the credit of being a fair match for Buckongahelas, Blue Jacket or the Turtle himself," historian Wood reported.[1]

General Wayne's opinion of the Native confederation wasn't as complimentary. He described his foes as a "victorious, haughty and insidious enemy--stimulated by British emissaries to a continuance of war...."[2]

Between 1791 and 1792, Buckongahelas re-established his town on the Au Glaize River in Ohio near villages of his allies, the Shawnee and the Miami. Other tribes had migrated to Ohio, including the Mingo, Kickapoo, Wyandot, Ottawa, Potawatomie, and Mascouten. A census counted 11,403 Indians in the area from Detroit and Saint Joseph south to the Ohio and from Detroit west to the Wabash country.

"The Glaize, as it was called, was a fascinating place in 1792, a rendezvous for powerful Indian war chiefs and British and French traders," according to writer Sugden.[3]

Buckongahelas was by now the most influential Delaware leader, as Weslager recorded: "In 1791, the Mahican chief Hendrick Aupaumut, sent by the United States to negotiate peace with the western tribes, refers in his journal to 'Puckonchehluh' (Pachgantschilas) [Buckongahelas] as the 'Head Heroe' of the Delawares."[4]

Chief Pipe's followers from the Sandusky finally joined the Indian confederacy after its great victory against St. Clair. The Buck favored peace, if that peace would include Shawnee demands for an Indian boundary along the Ohio. Buckongahelas spoke out at an inter-tribal congress in 1792, and "crushed any prospect of a wedge being driven between him and the Shawnees.

"'Don't think ... that it was their [the Shawnees'] sentiments alone," explained Buckongahelas. "All of us are animated by one mind, one head, and one heart, and we are resolved to stick close by each other and defend ourselves to the last." [5]

Buckongahelas was among the chiefs and head men from twelve tribes chosen to negotiate for peace and settle boundaries with the Americans on the Detroit River in July and August of 1793. The Ohio River previously had been established as the boundary separating whites and their families from Indian lands west of the mountains, but Americans still lusted after the vast Ohio Territory. Now the whites offered to grease the hands of the Indians with money to gain their lands, but at the 1793 council, the Indians proposed that the white man's funds be handed over instead to the settlers who were so rudely and rapidly encroaching upon Delaware lands. The Indian nations themselves were divided, however.

An Irritating Foe of Buckongahelas

Captain Joseph Brant (Thayendanega), a fierce Mohawk and member of the Iroquois, was an irritating foe of Buckongahelas, although Brant also was an avid ally of the British in the American Revolution.

Brant's grandfather, Sa- Ga-ean-Qua-Prah-Ton, was one of four "American kings" who visited Queen Anne's court in London in 1710. Brant also visited England in 1776, and became a popular celebrity for the British. He wished to lord it over all the tribal leaders.

Leading a delegation of confederation chiefs, Brant also conversed with the Americans, but neglected to inform them that the Indian

218

confederation still demanded the Ohio boundary as the line separating the Indians from the Americans. Brant favored the Muskingum as the boundary – and incurred the wrath of Buckongahelas.

The Delaware and other confederate tribes had another reason for hating their ancient enemy, the Iroquois: they had refused to lend a hand in the battles against Harmar and St. Clair.

"To agitate the Delawares, Captain Joseph Brant revived the whole question of the Delawares' wearing petticoats, and he conducted a gratuitous ceremony of making men of them again. During the ceremony, an Indian was dressed like a warrior of old, his head shaved, face painted, wearing only a breechclout and carrying a war club," historian Weslager wrote. [6]

The reaction of Buckongahelas to his comments was not quite what the fierce Mohawk Indian Captain Brant expected.

"'What shall we do with this murderous club, except to use it against you our uncles who have so often and so richly deserved such treatment at our hands?'" [7] Buckongahelas angrily responded.

Breaking with ritual and interrupting "in a very abrupt manner" a speech that Brant was delivering, The Buck implied that Brant was a liar.

"His flagrant break with council ritual in interrupting a speaker sounded louder than anything he [Buckongahelas] said," White, author of *The Middle Ground*, declared. "The old forms, the old symbols, could not hold the tensions within the confederation." [8]

After Blue Jacket's "botched and unsuccessful" attack on Fort Recovery, Little Turtle met with Lieutenant Colonel England at Detroit, who later described the Miami chief as "the most decent, modest, sensible Indian I ever conversed with." [9]

Negotiations between the Indians and Americans through intermediaries continued for two weeks, but were unsuccessful, and the Indian confederation was falling apart under the strain.

"There is evidence that the Americans knew all along that the peace effort would fail and pursued it only to convince public opinion in the United States and abroad that, as [George Washington's] Secretary of State Thomas Jefferson put it, 'Peace was unattainable on terms which any of them would admit.'" [10]

Buckongahelas was called "a powerful supporter" of the Ohio boundary of 1768, but the Americans wanted the Ohio Valley, and they wanted it all to themselves. If the Indians would not hand it over to them meekly, they would take it by force. "Mad Anthony" would have his revenge.

1. Wood, *Lives of Famous Indian Chiefs,* p. 301.

2. White, *Middle Ground,* p. 458.

3. Sugden, *Blue Jacket*, p. 132.

4. Weslager, *Delaware Indians*, p. 355.

5. Sugden, *Blue Jacket*, p. 135.

6. Weslager, *Delaware Indians*, p. 321.

7. Ibid, p. 322.

8. White, *Middle Ground,* p. 462.

9. Ibid, p. 467.

10. Josephy, Jr., *500 Nations,* p. 297

38

Fallen Timbers, Fallen Indians

The new army raised by Congress began to train under the "Black Snake," General "Mad Anthony" Wayne, who ironically also was crippled with gout as General St. Clair had been. Wayne devoted two years to preparing his force, the Legion of the United States. By 1794, he and his men were ready to march the northern trail, the same path taken by the humiliated St. Clair.

General Wayne and his new army had been shocked when they visited the scene of St. Clair's defeat. There they found 500 skull bones within 350 yards. Five miles further, the woods still were strewn with skeletons, knapsacks, guns, and other debris.

"A stern disciplinarian, Wayne bullied the army into shape and led it into the field so effectively that Little Turtle, assessing the man he was now up against, advised the Indians to seek peace," the book *Indian Wars* reported. [1]

The Battle of Fallen Timbers, called by some the Battle of Presque Isle, would take place north of Fort Meigs about a mile from the Maumee River floodplain (near the present location of Toledo, Ohio). Warriors would include the Shawnee, Miami, Mingo, Wyandot, Three Fires, and Delaware from the lower Maumee, the Sandusky, and the Detroit.

The Indians would form a mile-long line along the river, and fight to the death on a knoll littered with trees ripped from the ground by a recent tornado, thus the battle's name "Fallen Timbers." The night before the battle, the Indian war chiefs—Little Turtle, Buckongahelas, Blue Jacket, and the Ottawa chiefs Egushaway and Little Otter—met once again in council. Some Indians urged an immediate attack on the white men's encampment, but Blue Jacket, who commanded 1,400 warriors, favored a plan to attack the next day at a site of their choosing.

Little Turtle, the six-foot-tall expert at battle strategy, had an uncanny premonition of the disaster that awaited them. He announced that he wished to sue for peace. Little Turtle knew "Mad Anthony" Wayne to be anything but mad. When Wayne pitched camp, it was during the middle of the day when his soldiers were rested and could erect a protective wall of logs that surrounded their camp. "Mad Anthony" Wayne would not be surprised in his bed at dawn as St. Clair had been.

The Battle of Fallen Timbers

"We have beaten the enemy twice, under separate commanders," Little Turtle told his fellow warriors, including Buckongahelas and Blue Jacket. "We cannot expect the same good fortune to always attend us.

"The Americans now are led by 'The Chief Who Never Sleeps,'" Little Turtle warned. "The night and the day are alike to him; and during all the time that he has been marching upon our villages, notwithstanding the watchfulness of our young men, we have never been able to surprise him.

"Think well of it," the Miami chief warned. "There is something whispers me (sic), it would be prudent to listen to his offers of peace." [2]

Accused of a cowardice that he never exhibited, Little Turtle finally withdrew his objections, but relinquished leadership of the battle to the Shawnee Chief Blue Jacket and Turkey Foot, another Miami chief. Both men favored war with "Mad Anthony" Wayne.

"Although Little Turtle resigned from his position of leadership, he nevertheless announced that he would not leave the coalition, but would take the Miamis into battle with the other tribes," [3] historian Josephy, Jr. wrote.

Blue Jacket must have had his own premonition of disaster.

"Blue Jacket ordered the Shawnee villages along the Maumee River evacuated," Thomas Flaherty wrote in his book *The Mighty Chieftains*.

"He sent the women and children to safety in present day Michigan and decided to make a stand in a clearing along the river in northwestern Ohio. The site was only five miles upstream from Fort Miami, a redoubt newly built by the British. Blue Jacket hoped to seek help there should the need arise." [4]

The Battle of Fallen Timbers, fought on August 20, 1794, was often called "the last battle of the American Revolution," even though the war ended in 1783. The Natives went into battle outnumbered more than three to one.

Fourteen hundred Indian warriors formed themselves into three lines extendeing for two miles and close in distance to one another: the Miami and Delaware to the left, the Ottawas, Potawatomis and smaller Great Lakes tribes in the center, and to the right, the Shawnee, Wyandots, "and a seventy-member contingent of white militiamen [British] painted and dressed like Indians, who had come from Canada to help the tribes." [5]

The tribes would face 4,000 whites – 2,200 infantry and 1,500 militia cavalry--all of them embittered by the defeat of St. Clair and emboldened to produce a victory in this battle.

The battle began on a damp and dreary morning near the western shore of Lake Erie with an ambush by 1,000 Indians of 150 Kentucky volunteers leading the way for Wayne's troops. Within an hour of the first attack, the Indians were pushed several miles through the woods to the walls of the British fort of Maumee five miles away from the battle.

"When the Americans had arrived at proper distance, a body was sent out to begin the attack, 'with orders to rouse the enemy from their covert with the bayonet; and when up, to deliver a close fire upon their backs, and press them so hard as not to give them time to reload,'" historian Drake reported.

"This order was so well executed, and the battle at the point of attack so short, that only about nine hundred Americans participated in it. But they pursued the Indians with great slaughter through the woods to Fort Maumee, where the carnage ended. The Indians were so unexpectedly driven from their strong hold, that their numbers only increased their distress and confusion. And the cavalry made horrible havoc among them with their long sabers." [6]

The Indians fled in panic toward the British stockade, but the British refused to open the fort's gates to them, although indicating earlier they would do so. Many Native warriors were shot while trying to cross back over the Maumee River.

"After the fight with Wayne's army, Buckongahelas collected the remnant of his band, and embarked with them in canoes, and passed up the river, to send a flag of truce to Fort Wayne," wrote Drake.

"When the chief [Buckongahelas] arrived against the British fort, he was requested to land, which he did. When he had approached the sentinel, he demanded, '*What have you to say to me?*' He was answered that the commandant desired to speak with him.

"'Then he may come HERE,'" The Buck replied.

"The sentry then said the officer could not do that, and that he would not be allowed to pass the fort if he did not comply with its rules.

"'What shall prevent me?' said the intrepid chief. Pointing to the cannon of the fort, the sentry said, 'Those.' The chief replied indignantly, 'I fear not your cannon: after suffering the Americans to defile your spring, without daring to fire on them, you cannot expect to frighten Buckongehelas!' He re-embarked and passed the fort, without molestation," Drake reported.

"By 'defiling their spring,' he (Buckongahelas) meant an ironical reproach to the British garrison for their treachery to the Indians." [7]

Buckongahelas and Blue Jacket both had fought valiantly with the British in the Revolutionary War. The British commander had promised to open the gates of the fort to the battling Indians at Fallen Timbers, but the gates remained locked that day. Many Indian warriors were slaughtered pounding at the fort's gates. Forgotten were the lives the Delaware had forfeited for the British little more than ten years previously. The British betrayed the Delaware and the other Indians who fought with them.

The dead Indians on the Fallen Timbers battlefield were scalped and mutilated by the "civilized" Americans. To further destroy the spirit of the Indians, the soldiers burned all the cornfields and towns of the tribes for miles around.

In a letter to the Secretary of War in August, 1794, General Wayne referred to the Indian property he and his men destroyed: "The very extensive and highly cultivated fields and gardens show the work of many hands. The margins of those beautiful rivers – the Miamis of the Lake and Au Glaize – appear like one continued village for a number of miles, both above and below this place.

"Nor have I ever before beheld such immense fields of corn in any part of America, from Canada to Florida," wrote the man who had ordered the wanton destruction of that "one continued village" and of all of that corn. [8]

At the end of the Battle of Fallen Timbers, Wayne counted thirty-one soldiers killed and approximately 100 wounded. The British were among the last to retreat, and they suffered a greater percentage of death than either Wayne's army or the Indian Confederacy. Only forty Indians perished or were severely wounded in the attack, but the surrender of the tribes insured that their confederation was crushed forever.

A Psychological Blow to the Tribes

The defeat of the Indian Confederation was a psychological blow to the tribal members, who had died in large numbers for the British. Cowardly British hid behind the walls of Fort Maumee in the tribes' hour of greatest need at the Battle of Fallen Timbers.

The Delaware abandoned their villages along the Au Glaize and moved to the mouth of the Maumee River, where the British offered provisions to Buckongahelas and more than 1,000 of his people. Other Indians retreated to the western shore of Lake Erie.

Later that winter, Britain withdrew much of its support of the Indians, and Buckongahelas saw the handwriting on the wall. His people were hungry, destitute, and in danger of annihilation. It was a message he could not ignore, and he joined his Shawnee friend Blue Jacket in reaching out for peace. Brought to their knees, as Little Turtle had foretold, the tribes were given a choice: sign away your lands in the Old Northwest or be exterminated.

Although Buckongahelas, Little Turtle, and Blue Jacket had surrendered to "Mad Anthony" Wayne at the Battle of Fallen Timbers, Buckongahelas was called by one writer of the day "the most

225

distinguished warrior of the Indian confederation." The U. S. government allowed the Delaware to return to their villages and plant corn along the Au Glaize in May, 1795.

General Wayne's campaign for the Battle of Fallen Timbers had been equipped with a force of 2,000 regulars, plus an additional 1,600 militia from Kentucky, mostly cavalry armed with long swords. Among his officers was twenty-one-year-old William Henry Harrison, later promoted to general, then governor of Indiana Territory, and Superintendent of Indian Affairs.

Wayne had been determined to defeat the Indian confederation, which included the mighty Shawnee Tecumseh, only in his twenties, and his brother. Tecumseh would emerge unscathed from the Battle of Fallen Timbers, and would live to form a new confederation of Indian tribes east of the Mississippi. Attempting to regain lost Indian lands, Tecumseh and his confederation would be defeated in a battle in 1811 with General Harrison and his troops near Tippecanoe Creek in Indiana Territory. Tecumseh died in this battle.

Harrison, who would become the ninth president of the United States in 1841, was cited for bravery at Fallen Timbers and witnessed and signed the Greenville Treaty. He greatly admired the Delaware War Chief he had fought against, Buckongahelas Journeycake, and had the following to say about him:

"This man possessed all the qualifications of a hero; no Christian knight was ever more scrupulous in performing all his engagements than the renowned Buckongahelas." [9]

1. Utley and Washburn, *Indian Wars*, p. 114.

2. Wood, *Lives of Famous Indian Chiefs*, p. 303.

3. Josephy, Jr., *500 Nations,* p. 301.

4. Flaherty, *Mighty Chieftains*, p. 58.

5. Josephy, Jr., *500 Nations,* p. 302.

6. Drake, *Indians of North America,* Book 5, Chapter 5, p. 58.

7. Ibid, Chapter 4, p. 45.

8. Viola, *After Columbus*, p. 123.

9. McWhorter, Lucullus, *Border Settlers of Northwestern Virginia*, p. 165.

39

The Treaty of Greenville

One year after the Battle of Fallen Timbers, leaders of the defeated Indian confederation, including Buckongahelas, were forced to sign the Treaty of Greenville, ceding most of the Ohio Territory (an immensely larger area than the present state of Ohio) to the United States.

"…Buckongahelas resisted white expansion into the Ohio country, but did so with a human demeanor that sometimes won the admiration of even his enemies," states the *Encyclopedia of Native American Biography*. [1]

"Mad" Anthony Wayne "negotiated an important treaty with twelve vanquished tribes at Greenville, Ohio on August 3, 1795," historian C. A. Weslager wrote in his book *Delaware Indian Westward Migration*.

"There were 1,130 Indians present representing the participating tribes, including a contingent of 381 Delaware men, women, and children, the largest of any of the tribal delegations." [2]

The chiefs and warriors were gathered at Fort Greenville to witness their give-away of two-thirds of the Ohio Valley (except the northwestern corner) and a large part of Indiana. Chief Buckongahelas, accompanied by Chief William Anderson, arrived at Greenville on June 21 and remained there until the treaty was finalized August 3, 1795.

"Fourteen chiefs and great men represented the Delawares at the signing of the Greenville Treaty, including the warrior Buckongahelas, Kikthawenund ("creaking boughs"), who was better known as Chief William Anderson, and Tetabokshke (Tetepachksit), referred to in the document as the 'Grand Glaize King,' but who had now become the nominal head of the Delaware Nation," Rev. Weslager wrote. [3]

Other Delaware who signed the treaty included: Lemantanquis (aka Black King); Wabatthoe, Maghpiway (aka Red Feather); Peekeelund; Wellebawkeelund; Peekeetelemund (aka Thomas Adams); Kishkopekund (aka Captain Buffalo); Amenahehan (aka Captain Crow); Queshawksey (aka George Washington); Weywinquis (aka Billy Siscomb), and a Delaware named Moses. (It seems that whites gave the hard-to-pronouce Indians' names new English names.)

Still others who signed the treaty–and one prominent Indian who didn't--are written about by author Glenn Tucker in his book *Tecumseh, Vision of Glory.* "The treaty bore the names of the leaders of the race: Little Turtle, the Crane, New Corn, Leatherlips [I love this name!], Buckongahelos [sic], Red Pole, Black Hoof, and many others."

Historian Norman B. Wood also recorded: "The name of one Indian who had become outstanding in the battles against the whites was missing. Tecumseh stood apart. He would not attend the Greenville Council. He scorned all treaties that gave Indian lands to the encroachers." [4] (Tecumseh was much like the great Lakota Sioux Crazy Horse, who refused to sign any treaty with the government of whites, who were known to break every treaty they signed.)

With his wrinkled and shaking hand, the great sachem and sorrowing War Chief Buckongahelas, now about 75 years old, placed his X on the Treaty of Greenville. Buckongahelas' name was recorded as "Bukongahelas." (No one ever seemed able to spell The Buck's name the same way twice.)

Blue Jacket brought 143 Shawnee to Greenville, Ohio, where the treaty reluctantly was signed by the chiefs of twelve nations. The dozen chiefs were from "the following vanquished tribes: Delawares, Wyandot, Shawane, Ottawa, Chippewa, Potawatomi, Miamis, Eel River, Wea, Kickapoo, Piankeshaw, and Kaskaskia," Weslager reported. [5]

Chief Buckongahelas was an unhappy signer of the treaty at Greenville, but he pledged his allegiance to the fledgling Union by scratching his X onto the treaty document.

"After the treaty was signed, Buckongahelas in his role as a hero war captain was quoted as saying, 'All who know me, know me to be a man and a warrior, and I now declare that I will for the future be a true and steady friend of the United States, as I have heretofore been an active enemy,'" Rev. Weslager recorded.

"These words did not mean that Buckongahelas now loved the white man – only that he would not again take up arms against the Americans, a promise he never broke." [6]

The old chief and his countrymen were losing most of their hunting grounds west of the Ohio River. They also forfeited huge tracts of land as a result of their defeat at Fallen Timbers and the Treaty of Greenville. The states of Ohio, Indiana, Illinois, Pennsylvania, and Michigan would be

carved out of the vast territory gained by the whites.

"At the end of the treaty, Red Pole (a Shawnee), Buckongahelas, and Mashipinnashiwish, a Chippewa chief, all acknowledged the Americans as their father," wrote author Richard White in *The Middle Ground.* [7]

Little Turtle was so reluctant to sign the hateful treaty that he waited until all of his allies had scratched their Xs onto the document. Then he stood up and proudly strode forward to sign his Indian name.

"I am the last to sign it," he said, "and I will be the last to break it." Like Buckongahelas, Little Turtle kept his word.

"The war for Ohio seemed to be over," author John Sugden observed. "On 28 September, the secretary of war informed the president that 'the chiefs who signed the treaty are not numerous, but I observe among them the names of Blue Jacket, the great warrior of the Shawanoes [sic], Misquacoonacaw [Red Pole], their great speaker, and Buckongelas [sic], the great warrior of the Delawares, and of Augooshaway the Ottawa.' In his view, they had the signatures that mattered.'" [8]

229

Little Turtle Sits for a Portrait

Two years later, Little Turtle was invited to Philadelphia to meet the Great White Father, George Washington, and sat for a portrait by the painter Gilbert Stuart.

Little Turtle addressed the legislatures of Ohio and Kentucky in 1802, seeking new laws prohibiting the sale of whiskey to Indians. He charged that whiskey traders had "stripped the poor Indian of skins, guns, blankets, everything--while his squaw and the children dependent on him lay starving and shivering in his wigwam." The states ignored his plea, and whiskey continued to flow in great quantity into Indian hands, destroying their health and the harmony of their families. Hundreds of Indians died in drunken fights, and thousands died from the effects of alcoholism.

After the Battle of Fallen Timbers, Little Turtle assumed the role of peacemaker between Indians and whites, and became "a celebrated hero among the people he had fought so masterfully. He died of a complication from gout – a white man's disease – in 1812." [9] The great Miami chief drew his last breath on July 14 of that year at his home near the junction of St. Joseph River and St. Mary Creek. Seventeen years after he signed the Treaty of Greenville, he was buried with full military honors by U.S. army officers.

To nearly the end of his life, Blue Jacket held in vain the hope that Little Turtle's once powerful Indian confederacy might be restored with British help, but it didn't happen. A disillusioned Blue Jacket would die of a fever in the spring of 1810.

After the Treaty of Greenville, "Buckongahelas, the most prominent war leader among the Delawares of the White River, remained a more influential figure than the *phratry* chiefs, and he acted as a chief to the Americans," wrote White. [10]

Following the Greenville Council, Buckongahelas joined his Shawnee friend Blue Jacket in the region of Fort Wayne, Indiana. The Piankashaw, a division of the Miami Tribe, ceded a large tract of land that included most of the southeast quarter of the present state of Indiana to the Delaware, Munsees, and Mohicans in 1770. The Buck and his people received the first Delaware annuities from the Greenville Treaty in 1796.

Chief Buckongahelas and Delaware Principal Chief Tetepachsit (aka Tetapachxit or Tetapuska) of the Turtle Clan left the Maumee, leading about sixty of their people to the West Fork of the White River in 1797 or 1798.

Buckongahelas had hunted in the area while living on Rush Creek in what is now Logan County, Ohio. The Buck was the leader of a town of log huts known as Chief Buckongahelas Town. By the 1800s, the Delaware occupied from nine to eleven villages along the West Branch of the White River in Indiana, stretching from present day Indianapolis to southeast of Muncie.

"The most easterly town was located on the south bank of the West Fork about three miles southeast of the present city of Muncie, Indiana," Weslager wrote.

"It was called Woapicamikunk or Wapicomekoke from a Delaware word meaning 'At the white place.' This was the largest town on the river, and the headquarters of the aging Buckongahelas of the Wolf group, 'an old warrior of renown but a hardened pagan and an enemy of the conversions of his people to Christianity.' The settlement was sometimes called Buckongahelas's Town." [11]

The Delaware pronounced the town's name as if it were spelled "Woapikamiki." The river became the "Wapahani" or "Wapihani." The village of Chief Tetepachsit was four miles below Buckongahelas's town.

1. Johansen and Grinde, Jr., *Native American Biography*, p. 55, 56.

2. Weslager, *Delaware Indian Westward Migration, p. 49.*

3. Weslager, *Delaware Indians,* p. 329.

4. Tucker, *Tecumseh,* pp. 72, 73.

5. Weslager, *Delaware Indians,* p. 322.

6. Ibid, p. 330.

7. White, *Middle Ground,* p. 472.

8. Sugden, *Blue Jacket,* p. 208.

9. Waldman, *Atlas of North American Indian,* p. 115

10. White, *Middle Ground,* p. 495.

11. Weslager, *Delaware Indian Westward Migration,* p. 57.

40

The Buck's "Foot Ball" Game

Toward the end of the 1790s, Buckongahelas hosted a day-long Indian "foot ball" game for 100 men and women participants. The game truly was "foot ball," since the players wore no shoes. Each team faced 100 players!

As early as 1656, the colonist Daniel Denton described the Delaware Indians he met after emigrating from England to America in the 1640s: "Their recreations are chiefly foot-ball and cards, at which they will play away all they have, excepting a flap to cover their nakedness."

Delaware men and women often played foot ball together, but women were excluded from the game when their men opposed other clans. Women also were excluded from games during their menstruation, when they hid away in huts designed exclusively for them.

Lenape foot ball or "Pahsah" or "Pahsaheman," was an Algonquian game, not one copied from whites. The game was found among Lenape living along the east coast, but not among other tribes, except for the Creeks in the Southeast. An oval ball about nine inches in diameter was formed of deer skin and stuffed with hair. The men fasted and prayed prior to a serious game with other villagers, while the women (the New World's first cheerleaders) yelled for their men on the sidelines and screamed out wild curses at the opposing team. Heavy bets often were placed upon the outcome of such games.

If the women were losing, they could insert an elderly woman into the game, knowing that no man would dare knock the ball from her frail hands. Such was the great respect for their elders among the Delaware and other tribes of North America. Sometimes an elderly woman would hide the ball in her apron pocket and saunter over the goal.

Jacob Burnet, (1770-1853), author of *Notes on the Early Settlement of the North-Western Territory*, witnessed the Delaware "foot ball" game that Chief Buckongahelas hosted near the River Auglaise to entertain white visitors.

Jacob Burnet

Burnett, an associate justice on the Ohio Supreme Court from 1821 to 1828 and U.S. senator from 1828 to 1831, recorded that the visitors were received "very kindly by the venerable old Delaware chief Bu-kon-ge-he-las [sic], whose name has been given to a fine mill-stream in Logan County. He was one of the chiefs who negotiated the treaty at the mouth of the Big Miami, with General George R. Clark, in 1786, in which his name is written Bo-hon-ghe-lass."

"In the course of the afternoon he got up a game of football, for the amusement of his guests, in the true aboriginal style. He selected two young men to get a purse of trinkets made up, to be the reward of the successful party. That matter was soon accomplished, and the whole village, male and female, in their best attire, were on the lawn, which was a beautiful plain of four or five acres, in the center of the village, thickly set in blue grass. At each of the opposite extremes of this lawn, two stakes were set up, about six feet apart.

"The men played against the women; and to countervail the superiority of their strength, it was a rule of the game, that they were not to touch the ball with their hands on the penalty of forfeiting the purse; while the females had the privilege of using their hands as well as their feet; they were allowed to pick up the ball and run and throw it as far as their strength and activity would permit. When a squaw succeeded in getting the ball, the men were allowed to seize —whirl her round, and if necessary, throw her on the grass for the purpose of disengaging the ball—taking care not to touch it except with their feet.

"The contending parties arranged themselves in the center of the lawn—the men on one side and the women on the other—each party facing the goal of their opponents. The side which succeeded in driving the ball through the stakes, at the goal of their adversaries, were [sic] proclaimed victors, and received the purse, to be divided among them.

"All things being ready, the old chief [Buckongahelas] came on the lawn, and saying something in the Indian language not understood by his guests, threw up the ball between the lines of the combatants and retired; when the contest began. The parties were pretty fairly matched as to numbers, having about a hundred on a side, and for a long time the game appeared to be doubtful.

"The young squaws were the most active of their party, and most frequently caught the ball; when it was amusing to see the struggle between them and the young men, which generally terminated

233

in the prostration of the squaw upon the grass, before the ball could be forced from her hand.

"The contest continued about an hour, with great animation and various prospects of success; but was finally decided in favor of the fair sex, by the Herculean strength of a mammoth squaw, who got the ball and held it, in spite of the efforts of the men to shake it from the grasp of her uplifted hand, till she approached the goal, near enough to throw it through the stakes." [1]

Jefferson Disappoints Buckongahelas

"By 1801 the main body of Delawares was well established in a series of villages, variously estimated from nine to eleven, on the West Fork of the White River between the present cities of Muncie and Indianapolis," historian Weslager noted in his book *The Delaware Indians*.

"The most easterly town, situated about three miles south of present Muncie on the left bank of the river, was called Buckongahelas's Town, but it was also referred to as Wapicomemoke or Wapekommekoke, a variant of the Delaware name Wapeksippu, which means White River. The gallant war captain Buckongahelas lived here, as did the well-known white trader and interpreter John Conner, who had an Indian wife." [2]

In November, 1801, Buckongahelas and Principal Chief Tetepachksit of the Turtle Clan accepted an invitation to visit the U.S. capitol and meet with Thomas Jefferson, the newly-elected third president of the United States whose inauguration was March 4, 1801.

The two elderly Delaware chiefs were joined by Captain William Wells, the son-in-law of The Buck's friend Little Turtle and the U.S. Indian agent at Fort Wayne. While in Washington, the chiefs met with President Thomas Jefferson, members of his cabinet, senators, and representatives. Perhaps on this visit they shared some of Jefferson's fond French food like Blancmange, a pudding made with almond milk and gelatin, and fine French wine, for Jefferson was known as the greatest connoisseur of wines in the country.

Thomas Jefferson

Music Touches His Soul

Jefferson may have dismissed his native guests with fuller stomachs, but he sent them away them with empty hands and hearts. But the heart of Buckongahelas received healing on the way home however, when for the first time in his life he heard the music of a reed organ during services in the United Brethren Church in Lititz, Pennsylvania. Moravians missionaries had founded Lititz in 1756.

"So moved was Buckongahelas that tears welled in his eyes, until he reminded himself that a warrior must not give way to his emotions in public," Tetepachksit reported to missionaries at Goshen upon their return. Music touches the soul and allows release of the pain of past sorrows. It was one of Scripture's "tender mercies" that The Buck heard the organ's lovely chords that day and was able to unleash a portion of his deep grief.

At the first presidential inaugural held in the new capital of Washington, D.C.--Jefferson had called for "Freedom of Religion, Freedom of the Press, and Freedom of Person."

"Jeffersonian Indian policy originally sought the coexistence of Indians and whites…. Jefferson sought to make the Indians one with the Americans and culturally indistinguishable from them. The key was labor and property," wrote author White.

"As he told the Delawares: 'When once you have property, you will want laws and magistrates to protect your property and persons, and to punish those among you who commit crimes. You will find that our laws are good for this purpose. You will wish to live under them….'" [3]

Jefferson admitted his answer to the "Indian problem" was the removal of all Indian nations to the West, but he also stated that if they resisted, "We would never stop pursuing them with war, while one remained on the face of the earth."

As a result of a conference that General Harrison held at Vincennes, Indiana on September 17, 1802, with chiefs of the Potawatomi Kickapoo, Eel River, Kaskaskia, Wea, and Piankashaw, "a wave of resentment against the United States government spread through the tribes," Weslager explained.

In December of 1802, the year he resigned as war chief, Buckongahelas was aware of the growing tribal resentment against the president. He returned to Washington to meet with Jefferson a second time, accompanied again by Principal Chief Tetepachsit of the Miami tribe. For years, Buckongahelas had hoped to reunite his people who had scattered like seeds in the wind, some living beyond the Mississippi, others north and west of the treaty line in Ohio or in Canada.

"The Delawares and Miami decided to take their complaints directly to President Jefferson, and in December, Tetepachsit, Buckongahelas, and other Delaware chiefs appeared before the President in Washington. Their principal grievance was that white settlers were encroaching on land that belonged to the Indians. The Indians said they had not signed any treaties permitting white families to settle on their territories." [4] (Tetepachksit later would be denounced by the half-crazed Prophet, the one-eyed Shawnee preacher and brother of the great Tecumseh. Tetepachksit's own son would strike him in the head with a tomahawk and throw him alive into an open fire, where he burned to death)

Once again, the chiefs exited their meeting with the president as disappointed men. Buckongahelas would be forced to ratify the cessions of huge amounts of Delaware land in additional treaties. The Buck signed his second treaty at Fort Wayne, Indiana on Miami of the Lake in Indiana Territory June 7, 1803. This treaty ratified a negotiation for land proposed at Vincennes, forcing the Algonquian tribes of Delaware, Shawnee, Potawatomie, Miami, Kickapoo, Piankashaw, Eel River, Wea, and Kaskaskia to cede additional large tracts to the United States.

In his book, *Indian Biography*, Benjamin B. Thatcher quotes from Dawson's *Memoirs of Harrison*: "When the transaction at the council of Vincennes was mentioned [at Fort Wayne], it called forth all the wrath of the Delawares and the Shawanese.

"The respected Buckongehelos [sic] so far forgot himself that he interrupted the Governor, and declared with vehemence, that nothing that was done at Vincennes was binding upon the Indians; that the land which was there decided to be the property of the United States belonged to the Delawares; and that he had then with him a chief who had been present at the transfer made by the Piankishaws to the Delawares of all the country between the Ohio and White rivers, more than thirty years before.

"The Shawanese went still further, and behaved with so much insolence, that the Governor was obliged to tell them that they were undutiful and rebellious children, and that he would withdraw his protection from them until they had learnt to behave themselves with more propriety." [5]

The chiefs immediately left the council house in a body. Subsequently the Shawnee reluctantly submitted, "though it does not appear that Buckongahelas set them the example," Thatcher reported.

"...the Governor overcame all opposition, and carried his point. But he did not gain the good will, or subdue the haughty independence of the War-Chief of the Delawares [Buckongahelas], who, as long as he lived, was at least consistent with himself in his feelings towards the American people. Nor yet was he in the slightest degree servile in his attachment to the British. He was not their instrument or subject, but their ally; and no longer their ally, than they treated him in a manner suitable to that capacity and to his own character."

Buckongahelas signed the Treaty of Vincennes in 1804, and Thatcher called him "the most distinguished warrior in the Indian confederacy, and as it was the British interest which had induced the Indians to commence, as well as to continue the war. Buckongahelas relied on their support and protection.... But the gates of Fort Mimms [Miami] being shut against the retreating and wounded Indians, after the battle [Fallen Timbers], opened the eyes of Buckongahelas, and he determined upon an immediate peace with the United States, and a total abandonment of the British." [6]

The Delaware lost the great salt spring on the Saline Creek which runs into the Ohio, and thus were deprived of a vital source of salt. The government agreed to deliver 150 bushels of salt to the tribes each year--thirty bushels to the Delaware--but reneged on the promised shipment because of the expense. The Delaware received only $100 per year instead.

Thatcher called The Buck "a great hero," and praised "his perfect Indian independence--the independence of a noble nature, unperceived to itself, and unaffected to others." Other historians have described Buckongahelas as "a wise statesman exercising a moderating influence on his own and other tribes."

The Great Buck Gathered to His Fathers

Now Buckongahelas was dying. Some history accounts report that the notorious war chief fell ill and died in May of 1805, but did he? According to five-time Pulitizer Prize nominee Allan W. Eckert, author of *A Sorrow in Our Heart, the Life of Tecumseh*, Brigadier General William Henry Harison invited several tribes to join Americans as offensive allies. On July 5, 1813 Harrison held council with neutral Shawnees, Delawares, Senecas, and Wyandots.

"The assembled chiefs, Tecumseh's spies reported, had included Buckongehela of the Delawares and Chiuxca... and they had quickly held a private council and then reconvened with

237

Harrison, and it was Tarhe, principal chief of the Tyabdots, who gave their reply. 'We have been waiting many moons,' Tarhe had told Harrison gravely, 'for an invitation to fight for the Americans.'" [7]

Buckongahelas had joined the British in the Revolutionary War because a white American had murdered his son, but he lost faith in the British when he and other Delaware warriors were turned away from a British fort after they lost the Battle of Fallen Timbers. The Buck would have been 93 years old in 1813, and it is unlikely that he would have been chosen to represent the Delaware at the 1813 council.

Historian Samuel G. Drake in 1833 placed The Buck at an even later date at the signing of the Treaty of St. Mary's in 1818 when Buckongahelas would have been 98. Perhaps a younger chief had taken his name in order to honor him.

"A chief, called Pachgantschihilas [Buckongahelas], distinguished himself upon the frontiers, immediately upon the retreat of Colonel Broadhead's army; not as many others have, but by magnanimity and address. He was, according to Mr. Heckewelder [the Moravian minister], the head war chief of the Delaware nation. And subsequently his name was set to many treaties between his nation and the United States, from that of Gen. Wayne at Greenville *to that of St. Mary's in 1818*: if, indeed, Bokongehelas [sic], and several other variations stand for the same person." [8]

The Treaty of St. Mary's was signed Oct. 64, 1818 at St. Mary's, Ohio. The Delaware Nation agreed to relinquish its occupancy rights to all lands in Indiana. Historians Thatcher and Weslager agree with Drake's interpretation of the name "Petchenanalas" or "Pachgantschihilas" as variations of the names Buckongahelas used.

"The Delaware chiefs, captains, and elders who made their marks as signers of the treaty were, 'Kithteeleland or Anderson, Lapahnihe or Big Bear, James Nanticoke, Apacahund or White Eyes, Captain Killbuck, The Beaver, Netahopuna, Captain Tunis, Captain Ketchum, The Cat, Ben Beaver, The War Mellet, Captain Caghkoo, *The Buck, Petchenanalas*....'" C. A. Weslager wrote. [9]

Did Buckongahelas live to sign the 1818 treaty? The old chief was humming to put himself to sleep for the last time, his salt and pepper long hair damp from his feverish forehead. He could barely see his sons and daughters. His blood pressure was falling fast, which causes blindness in persons near death. He had survived the loss of his beloved teenage boy, so many terrible battles, so many betrayals by the British, and vicious attacks, and now he was dying of the infirmities and diseases of old age. He surely would have preferred a quick death upon a bloody battlefield.

Perhaps a short time before his last breath, barely lifting his head, Buckongahelas whispered, "Lapich Knewel (I will see you again!)."

"Nuxati! (Dear Father!)" his daughter Little Leaf, my many greats-grandmother, would have responded.

"Mexumsati! (Grandfather!)," his granddaughter, Mary, another of my grandmothers, would have cried.

The Delaware believed that when this greatest of my grandfathers passed from this earth, he found peace at last. His spirit entered the house of *Kishelamukonk*, where he enjoyed the healing embraces of the Great Spirit and the Son of *Kishelamukonk*. The great Buck had died on the White River near the present-day site of Muncie, Indiana. (My Great-Grandfather Greenstreet, the Buck's descendent, also died there many years later.)

The West Virginia historian Lucullus Virgil McWhorter (whose Scots-Irish ancestor, Henry McWhorter, journeyed early to the territory in 1790), penned these words describing Chief Buckongahelas: "It is hard to conceive of a more lofty spirit than possessed by this proud, virtuous chieftain." [10]

John C. McWhorter, brother of historian Lucullus McWhorter and author of *The Scout of the Buckongehanon*, described him thusly: "… one of the proudest, noblest and greatest of the primitive warrior-statesmen of the world–Buckongahelas, mighty sachem of the Delawares." [11]

Thatcher published this statement in his *Indian Biography* in 1836: "A more noted personage in his own time than even Logan [a Mingo chief] was Buckongahelas, who rose from the station of a private warrior to be … head war-chief of his nation." [12]

And in a letter dated April 27, 1849, former Indian agent John Johnston of Fort Wayne, Ind. wrote to Dr. L. C. Draper: "Buckingehelas (sic), a very distinguished war chief of the Delawares, lived some years subsequent to my agency for that nation, died on White River, Indiana prior to the final removal of the tribe to the southwest of Missouri .... He probably had no superior as a warrior and orator. I first remember to have seen this chief about the year 1800 when on a visit to the

President of the United States." [13]

In a subsequent note to Dr. Draper on Dec. 1, 1850, Johnston observed, "As we had but one Washington, so the Delawares had but one Buckingehelas [sic], a great warrior, chief and councilor, whose prowess in war and wisdom and actions in peace overshadowed that of all others, his name descended to no other." [13] In another missive to Dr. Draper in June, 1843, Johnston described Chief Buckongahelas as "universally esteemed and greatly lamented."

Many Delaware believed Buckongahelas' death to have been the work of witchcraft. The Shawnee prophet Tenskwatawa (the crazed brother of Tecumseh) led a witch hunt in 1806 that brought about the murder of several Delaware accused of being witches, among them Tetepachsit.

Soon after the Treaty of Greenville in 1795, many chiefs who had signed the treaty mysteriously died. The Potawatomis lost sixty people, including several chiefs, to death shortly after the council. The Shawnee chief, Red Pole, also died. The tribes accused the United States of poisoning their people, but others were convinced that tribal members had executed headmen with whom they disagreed.

1. Burnett, *Notes on Early Settlement of Northwestern Territory*, pp. 68-69.

2. Weslager, *Delaware Indians, p. 333.*

3. White, *Middle Ground*, pp. 473-474.

4. Weslager, *Delaware Indians,* pp. 338-339.

5. Thatcher, *Indian Biography*, p. 178.

6. Ibid, pp. 178, 179.

7. Drake, *Indians of North America*, Chapter IV, p. 43.

8. Weslager, *Delaware Indian Westward Migration*, p. 72.

9. McWhorter, *Border Settlers of Northwestern Virginia*, p. 165.

10. McWhorter, John C., *Scout of Buckongehanon*, p. 273.

11. Thatcher, *Indian Biography*, p. 172.

12. McWhorter, *Border Settlers of Northwestern Virginia*, p. 165.

13. Ibid.

41

Goodbye to Indiana

War broke out again between the Americans and the English in 1812, but the Delaware in Indiana remained neutral. Indiana became a state in 1816, and once more, the Delaware and descendants of Buckongahelas were not welcome in the land that they called home.

The St. Mary's, Ohio Treaty of October 3, 1818 forced the Delaware tribe to relinquish all of their remaining lands in Indiana and Ohio. In return, they were promised new lands west of the Mississippi, and granted perpetual annuities that amounted to nearly $5,000 for the entire tribe.

More than 20,000 Lenape people had resided on the east coast of the continent 200 years previously, but only 2,000 Delaware–remnants of a once great nation–would participate in the removal from Indiana to Missouri. Some 200 tribal members, calling themselves "Absentees," split from the Delaware Nation in Indiana in 1795. They moved to Cape Girardeau, and eventually to Texas.

The followers of Roasting Ear, a chief of this Absentee group who died in Texas, ended up in Anadarko, Oklahoma some 200 miles from Bartlesville, Oklahoma where the main body of the Delaware settled after their eviction from Kansas. The Absentees took as their name as The Delaware Tribe of Western Oklahoma, and now are known as the Delaware Nation.

The Delaware were given three years to move from Indiana. (Chief Buckongahelas would not go with them, having died in Indiana.) Chief Solomon, son of Buckongahelas, and Chief William Anderson, whose father was a white man, would lead their people to Missouri. Chief Anderson was described as "a man of large size and light complexion, well made with a Roman nose, and about 65 years old" by David Berdan, a scout for land speculation for the New York Emigration Society, who met with Anderson Dec. 1, 1819. [1]

Chief William Anderson and his wife, Dancing Feather, who died in June, 1805, had three sons: Capt. Suwaunock, Secondyan, and Sarcoxie, and a daughter, Mekinges or Ma-cun-chis (last born), known to whites as "Elizabeth." Mekinges was the wife of William Conner, a white trader and interpreter. Her family origin has been disputed, however, by historian C. A. Weslager, who asserted that she possibly was a member of the Ketchum family.

Annette Ketchum of Bartlesville, Oklahoma, wife of former Delaware Chief Dee Ketchum, is a direct descendant of Sarcoxie, the older brother of Mekinges. There are descendants of the children of Mekinges alive today too. The oldest son of Mekinges, John Conner, succeeded Captain Ketchum as chief of the Delaware Tribe.

"Mekinges is my favorite ancestor because the tribal family and community were more important to her than anything," said Annette.

Mekinges and her husband, William Conner (whose father and family had traveled with the Moravian Christians), lived with their six children on lands reserved to the Delaware along the White River in Indiana. They had moved from Anderson Town to four miles south of present Noblesville, where Conner opened a trading post.

Chief Anderson was opposed to a proposed treaty that would take away Delaware lands in Indiana, but the Conner brothers set about to change his mind, reported Weslager. The U.S. government was kept informed by William Conner and his brother, John, who also had a Delaware wife. Both of the Conner brothers were engaged in trade with the Delaware.

"Jonathan Jennings later reported to the United States Senate, 'I have no hesitation in stating, that those two individuals (John and William Conner) had it in their power to have prevented any purchase of Indian title to lands on the waters of the White River, unless, if it had been required, a large reserve had been made in their favor, owing to the connexion [sic] made with the titles of the Delawares and Miamis tribes by the treaty of 1809, at Fort Wayne.'[2]

"Because he (William) had been faithful in rendering service to the United States, and particularly in persuading the Indians to agree to sign the agreement, he was secretly promised title to the lands occupied by himself and his Indian family. After the Delawares left Indiana, he continued to occupy the lands, and eventually was given a deed for 640 acres."[3]

The Delaware Nation was forced to cede the lands it occupied in Indiana to the United States in a treaty signed at St. Mary's in Ohio October 3, 1818. The Delaware leaders included "The Buck,

Petchenanalas," who signed the treaty with an X. (It is because of this signature that some historians believe that Buckongahelas lived until 1818.)

William Conner, acting as interpreter, and his brother John were among the witnesses to the signing of the St. Mary's treaty. That same year William Conner had petitioned to secure legal rights to his wife's Delaware land, which was included in the territory the Indians were supposed to vacate under terms of the treaty. It appeared that the government handed over the property to William Conner in return for him exerting his influence on the Delaware to leave their Indiana lands.

Unknown to the Delaware Mekinges, her white husband Conner had decided to remain in Indiana. She was "very anxious and much worried" when he did not prepare for the trip, and heartbroken when she finally learned that he would abandon his family. She would move west with her fatherless six children, four young sons and two daughters. She planted six sprigs of the fast-growing shrub "Live Forever" around the homestead – one for each of her six children – to remind Conner of his offspring and in hopes that no one else would move into their home to take their place.

But within three months after his family's departure from Indiana to Missouri in 1820, Conner wed a white woman, Elizabeth Chapman, whom he moved into the house he formerly occupied with Mekinges. Elizabeth delivered him ten children, and Conner later built a large brick home on his property overlooking the White River in 1823. (The Delaware sons and daughters of Conner attempted unsuccessfully in the 1860s to gain title to their father's land.)

Chief Anderson had invited Stockbridge-Munsees living among the Oneida Iroquois in New York and 100 Brotherton Delaware from New Jersey to join him along the White River in Indiana. Upon their arrival, however, the Indians learned that the lands promised them had been sold, and they headed north to Wisconsin rather than join the Delaware. Other Delaware went to live with kinfolk in Muncy, Ontario, Canada.

With heavy hearts, the remaining Delaware left their lands in Indiana to move west of the Mississippi. Their first stop was Missouri, where they would be miserable, suffering from lack of food, flooding, the theft of their horses, the hostility of the Osage Indians, and the murder of several of their people, including Chief Anderson's youngest son.

A ferry boat carried 1,346 Delaware from Indiana and their 1,500 horses across the

Mississippi River at Kaskaskia, Illinois in November, 1820. The *Arkansas Gazette* noted in the Dec. 2, 1820 issue that 800 members of the tribe had passed Fort Kaskaskia and appeared to be in destitute condition. Many Delaware camped on the Current River in Missouri during the winter of 1820. In the spring, they planted 100 acres of corn, but an early frost destroyed the crops.

Several hundred Delaware migrated elsewhere in Missouri or in Arkansas. Some Delaware did not begin the painful trek to the Missouri Territory until 1821. Many Delaware settled in the Ozarks of Missouri in 1822 on swampy lands along the James Fork of another White River on land claimed by the Osage. The Delaware started up a town known as Anderson's Village, named for Chief Anderson. The Osage, Shawnee, and Miami nations did not welcome the Delaware or other displaced eastern tribes, and often undertook violent forays against their new neighbors. In the Delaware's favor, however, was the fact that they were well experienced in war.

"Eastern Delawares and Shawnees and Potawatomis and many others, driven across the Mississippi, were fearful adversaries, expert with firearms at a time when the plains people had few guns...," historian Josephy Jr. wrote in his book *Indians* [2]

Further suffering came from James Fork River flooding in spring and summer and the scarcity of bear, elk, deer, and beaver, whose pelts the Indians desperately needed to sell or use for themselves. Delaware hunters had to travel long distances to find game for their people, who were starving.

Chief William Anderson, Black Beaver, and Natcoming, a former captain with the Cape Girardeau Delaware, "addressed a pathetic letter to General [George Rogers] Clark in February, 1824," author Weslager recorded.

"Last summer, a number of our people died just for want of something to live on ... We have got in a country where we do not find all as stated to us when we was asked to swap lands with you, and we do not get as much as was promised us at the treaty of St. Mary's neither ...

"Father," the letter continued, "We did not think that big man would tell us things that was [sic] not true. We have found a poor hilly stony country and the worst of all, no game to be found on it to live on. Last summer our corn looked very well until a heavy rain come [sic] on for three or four days and raised the waters so high that we could just see the tops of our corn in some of the fields, and it destroyed the greatest part of our corn, punkins [sic] and beans ...

"Father – You know it's hard to be hungry. If you do not know it, we poor Indians know it." [3]

The Bureau of Indian Affairs (BIA), the oldest bureau of the U.S. Department of the Interior, was established that same year and still exists. It now serves some 1.7 million American Indians and Alaska Natives and manages sixty-six million acres of land held in trust by the United States for American Indians and Alaska Natives. But in its infancy, the bureau didn't contribute much to the destitute Delaware in Missouri.

In autumn of 1824, Delaware Chief Anderson suffered another blow: the murder of his youngest son by Osage tribal members who had stolen Delaware horses. By May of 1826, Anderson and his people were in desperate condition. Once again, the chief contacted Major Clark in St. Louis, asking for the tribal annuity to be increased by $3,000, noting that what was received was "barely enough to clothe half our people with one article of clothing."

The United States government negotiated the Treaty of Council Camp with the Delaware September 24, 1829, forcing them to forfeit the rights to the land on which they had settled in Missouri.

A delegation of six chiefs and warriors traveled to the lands they would be occupying "forever." One of the six, the guide Black Beaver, was not impressed, calling the lands between the Kaw and the Missouri Rivers "too much like a pair of white man's pants," in other words, flat as a pair of slacks resting on a bed. Not only did Kansas flatten more the further west you traveled, its daily high winds and wild tornadoes were not great selling points. The Sioux name "Kansas" means "People of the South Wind." The strong winds and flat landscape were not attractive to the Delaware, but at this point in their history they had little choice in their destiny.

Chief Anderson, who by now was 73, was eager to leave Missouri, but anxious about the trip. The Delaware would have to abandon their homes on the James Fork of the White River in southwestern Missouri, slowly moving their cattle and horses with them.

"Throughout September a surveying party headed by Isaac McCoy … was at work in present eastern Kansas north of the Kansas river," author Louise Barry reported. "By October 2 these surveyors had run the lines of the Delaware Indians' general reserve, and marked out the bounds of Cantonment Leavenworth." [4]

The Delaware had lived in Missouri for eight years, but now they were on the road again, this time headed to the center of the country that would be designated Kansas Territory in 1854 and become the State of Kansas in 1861. The Delaware first settled around Lawrence in Wyandotte County near the Kansas River, and later moved north to what became Leavenworth County. The first contingent of about sixty Delaware men, women, and children left Missouri in October, 1829 and arrived in Kansas in November of that year, historian Weslager reported.

"In the fall of 1830, Anderson arrived at the new home with a large group, and herds of horses and cattle. Others followed soon thereafter. Practically all of the families traveled on horseback.... The distance of the entire journey was upwards of 200 miles." [5]

In her book *Kik Tha We Nund, the Delaware Chief William Anderson and His Descendants*, Ruby Cranor described the terrible conditions of that journey:

"Chief Anderson and his family, including Sacoxie [his son], his wife and his three children were in the first vanguard. There were about 100 souls in this first group. Sarcoxie was one of the leaders. They left the James Fork area during the fall of 1830, but due to government red tape, supplies and horses which had been promised to them was [sic] slow in being made available.

"This group arrived in Kansas on November 1 [1830], starving and had no provisions. Chief Anderson was sick and disheartened. The government which he had always befriended had been so slow in responding to his people's needs and many had died. Sarcoxie was greaving [sic]. He had lost his wife, leaving him with four motherless children to raise.... That first winter was severe and the Delaware people suffered much.... They had lost so many soldiers to the white renegades and the government was so slow in getting supplies to them that they were destitute," Ruby Cranor wrote. [6]

The Delaware had arrived in "the promised land" west of the Missouri and north of the Kansas River, also north of the Shawnee. By December, their numbers had swelled to some 400 starving Delaware. The majority of the Delaware Nation was old men, women and children, Agent Richard W. Cummins wrote on December 3, 1830.

The Baptist minister Isaac McCoy and his sons, Rice and John C., also had surveyed the north land of the Delaware "outlet," a ten-mile strip of land north of the Kansas reserve, which, by terms of the 1829 treaty, was to provide the Delawares access to western hunting grounds.

McCoy reported that it was a "remarkably dry" season – "an uncommon drought had prevailed throughout that whole region…." And after October 14, when a prairie fire "swept away the grass on both prairies and woodlands…the journey was made with some difficulty. Grass for the horses could rarely be found and the animals failed rapidly. Winds carrying dust and sand, as well as smoke and ashes from the burned prairies, added to the travelers' discomfort." [7]

The outlet did not sound all that attractive to Delaware hunters.

"As soon as they began to hunt in that part of the reserve called the outlet, they ran into trouble with the Pawnee, a resident tribe angered by the appearance of strange Indians whose language and customs differed from their own," Weslager reported.

"In an effort to repulse the strangers, the Pawnees organized war parties and ambushed the Delaware hunters. According to their custom, the Delawares were forced to retaliate to save their honor, and injury and death resulted on both sides, a repetition of the same kind of trouble the Delawares had experienced with the Osage in Missouri." [8]

Chief Anderson had hoped to gather all of the scattered Delaware from the Red River and in the Spanish country (Texas) to join his people in Kansas, but he didn't live to see that hope fulfilled. He would die in his seventies at his home on the Delaware reserve in Wyandotte, Kansas after September 22, 1831. According to the Moravian missionary Heckewelder, pneumonia and consumption were "exceedingly common among the Indians," but Anderson may have died of smallpox.

Baptist Missionary Johnston Lykins observed of Chief Anderson that although he had some white blood (like Crazy Horse), he was reluctant to embrace the white man's manners and customs. Like his forefathers before him, including his ancestor Netawatwees, Chief Anderson was known as a great and honorable chief.

In March of 1832, only six months following Chief Anderson's death, the Pawnee attacked and murdered his son, Chief Pooshkies Anderson, and two other Delaware (one a woman). Thus two of Chief William Anderson's sons were lost to death by violence. Chief Shawanuk and twenty-two other warriors sought blood revenge on June 24, 1833, but they found the Grand Pawnees' village deserted. The last claims of the Delaware and Shawnee to lands in Missouri in the Cape Girardeau area would be relinquished in a treaty on October 26, 1832. The artist George Catlin was a witness.

Louise Barry wrote in her book *The Beginning of the West*: "On February 5 [1833] Agent R.

247

W. Cummins wrote Sup't [sic] William Clark about property lost by Delaware chief Captain Pipe, William Montue, Isaac Hill, and Solomon Jonnicake [sic] while their party (about 30 persons) was en route from the Little Sandusky river, Ohio, to present Kansas. These men—all influential in their nation—were among the last of the Delawares to emigrate to the West." [9]

Unsuccessful Mormon efforts were made to proselytize the Delaware following Chief Anderson's death, but a Delaware Methodist Mission was established near Anderson Town on the Kanzas River early in 1832. Baptists Johnston Lykins and Daniel French visited the Delaware in February of 1833, and "Shawnanoe" Baptist missionaries began preaching trips to the Delaware.

"In this way Delaware Baptist Mission got its start," Barry wrote. "(Ira D. Blandard of Ohio--a young, self-appointed missionary--had been living among the Delwares for more than a year, learning their language. On April 21 he was baptized at 'Shawanoe' Baptist Mission.) [10]

The Delaware obtained the first saw and grist mill in Kansas in 1833. In October the first permits were issued for trade on Delaware and Kickapoo lands. The "immigrant nations"–the Delaware, Shawnee, Peoria, Ottawa, Kickapoo, Potawatomie, Wea, and Kaskaskia--met the Pawnee, Otoe and Omaha for a peace council at Fort Leavenworth on November 8, 1833. A spectacular meteor shower occurred four nights later, captivating all the Indians as a good omen.

1. Weslager, *Delaware Indian Westward Migration*, p. 77.

2. Josephy, Jr. *Indians*, p. 340.

3. Weslager, *Delaware Indians*, pp. 363, 364.

4. Barry, *Beginning of West*, p. 176.

5. Weslager, *Delaware Indian Westward Migration*, p. 217.

6. Cranor, *Kik Tha We Nund*, p. 70.

7. Barry, *Beginning of West*, p. 177.

8. Weslager, *Delaware Indians*, p. 377.

9. Barry, *Beginning of West*, p. 225.

10. Ibid

42

As Long as the Rivers Flow

In Washington the politicians also were rejoicing. In 1833, President Andrew Jackson's Secretary of War Lewis Cass congratulated the country on the fact that "the country north of the Ohio, east of the Mississippi, including the States of Ohio, Indiana, Illinois, and the Territory of Michigan as far as the Fox and Wisconsin rivers, has been practically 'cleared of the embarrassments of Indian relations,' as there are not more than five thousand Indians, all told, left in this whole region." [11]

Cass was wrong. By 1836, 30,000 American Indians had been removed west of the Mississippi, but 72,000 were yet to be removed, according to *Senate Report 288* of the 24th Congress, first session. The report's *Census of Indian Tribes* revealed that a total of 826 Indians were living on the Delaware Reserve in Kansas. The following year, the Rev. Isaac McCoy of the Baptist mission reported the Delaware population as 921. After eight years in Missouri, the Delaware chief Captain William Anderson and about 100 of his people had set out for their new reservation near Fort Leavenworth, Kansas, but they were not the first Delaware to do so, as some writers have asserted.

"The first contingent of about sixty men, women, and children left Missouri in 1829 and arrived in Kansas in November of that year," Weslager reported.

"In the fall of 1830, Anderson arrived at the new home with a larger group, and herds of horses and cattle. Others followed soon thereafter. Practically all of the families traveled on horseback." [1]

Sixty-two more Delaware arrived north of the Kansas River between Lawrence and Leavenworth, Kansas on December 1, 1830 to view for the first time the two million acres of land promised to them by the U.S. government for "*as long as the rivers flow, the birds fly, and the flowers burst into bloom.*"

"At the chief's [Anderson] insistence, the government [had] consented to give forty horses to the poor and destitute members of the tribe, and to loan the Indians six wagons, and teams of oxen to assist in moving them to Kansas." [2]

Instead of settling in Kansas, which was named for Kanza Indians (People of the South Wind), some Delaware moved down into the northeastern part of territory that would become Oklahoma, although the United States had assured that "the country in the forks of the Kansas and Missouri rivers, selected for their home, shall be conveyed and *forever secured* to the Delaware Nation as their 'permanent home.'"

The Delaware came in small groups of 100 or so over a three-year period into Kansas Territory. Shawnee, Ottawa, Pottawatomie, and Wyandotte Indians were among the other immigrant tribes in Kansas.

"In the early part of 1828, the [Delaware] tribe started their long journey through Indiana where they sojourned awhile, then on to Southwest Missouri where they spent the winter; and in the spring of 1829, they concluded their journey to their reservation in Kansas," Henry Roark wrote.

"In the early spring of 1829, the Delawares arrived at the village of their friends the Shawnees where they sojourned for some time before they renewed their journey to their reservation in Kansas." [3]

Chief Anderson was one of many Delaware who were seriously ill by the time their ragged moccasins touched their new land. Chief Anderson did not die in 1830, as some historians have reported. He was still alive in January of 1831 when three Mormon missionaries visited the Shawnee and Delaware in Kansas, and recorded that Anderson showed interest in their teachings. And the following year on September 22, 1831, Chief Anderson wrote to the Secretary of War regarding the Delaware Kansas reserve, "The land is good, and also the wood and water, but the game is very scarce."

According to Cranor's book about Chief Anderson, he did not die until October.

"In the last part of October in 1831 the beloved Chief Anderson died and the entire nation went into mourning," she wrote. "After a while Me shay quo whak, known as Capt. Patterson of the turtle clan was chosen as head Chief and Sa cox ie [one of Anderson's sons] was approved as the Chief of the turtle clan." [4]

"Chief Anderson died in 1836, after having had the satisfaction of living long enough to see his people settled in their new homes." [5]

The old chief perished, possible from smallpox, sometime after writing a letter on Sept.

22, 1836. The *Kansas Historical Quarterly* reported the following: "Died: William Anderson, aged head chief of the Delaware nation, in the later part of September, at his home on the Delaware reserve, present Wyandotte county. He had been a 'Kansas' resident less than one year. Though Anderson had some white blood, according to Missionary Johnston Lykins, he had 'shewed but little disposition to embrace…[white man's] manners and customs…." [6]

The population of the Delaware nation in Kansas reached 1,000, but eventually dwindled to 800 due to disease and attacks by other tribes. The Delaware Reservation originally extended from the mouth of the Kansas River westward to the Kaw Reservation, an area of hilly lands that emptied into a vast prairie scourged by high winds.

On his way to an expedition in the Rocky Mountains, Prince Paul Wilhelm of Wuerttemberg, Germany journeyed with American Fur Company representatives, passing through Shawnee land in what today is Wyandotte County, Kansas in January, 1830. Noting his observations of the border between Missouri and Kansas, he wrote:

"… the country presented to me a few wooded hills and small prairies … clusters of lofty trees intermingled with a few sumac and dwarf oak bushes. The land includes that section of the country lately ceded to the Delawares, Peorias, and Shawnee Indians…. Traces of cultivated ground, and the possession of cattle, and even of a few black slaves, already indicate the change which may be wrought in the course of time, and under a free, mild, and pacific government …." [7]

The beginning of the eventual end of Delaware residence in Kansas occurred on October 21, 1836 when the Delaware and other tribes met with Agent Richard W. Cummins (head of the Northern Agency, Western Territory). The Indians signed an agreement giving consent to the United States to open roads and establish military posts on their lands. The Delaware reservation near Fort Leavenworth would be coveted by railroads as a freight route.

Chiefs of the Delaware, Shawnee, Piankeshaw, Wea, Peoria, and Kaskaskia tribes gave "our full consent that the United States open and establish a road through each of our countries, and establish therein such military posts as the Government of the United States may think proper…." [8]

Signers from the Delaware Nation included Nah-comin (Nah-ko-min), who became principal chief following the death of Captain Patterson in 1835, Captain Ketchum, who would follow Nah-comin as chief, Captain Swanock, Sackindeattun, (Secondine), Nonon-da-gomin, and four others.

By 1838, the Delaware in Kansas Territory had cultivated 1,500 acres of land in grain and vegetables, raised numerous cattle, and were living in relative peace with their neighbors. Delaware hunters often sojourned to the Rocky Mountains to bring back beaver. What seemed to be an idyllic existence was marred, however, by the introduction of whiskey onto the reservation.

"The only hindrance now in the way of the Delawares, Shawnees, and Kickapoos, is 'ardent spirits,'" an Indian agent wrote after several instances of whisky traffickers robbing the Indians of their horses, guns, and even the blankets from their backs. Many Indians were murdered outright or left to freeze to death on the prairie.

Chief Nah-ko-min, principal chief since 1835 and leader of the Delaware who fought the Seminole, died about the first of March, 1848, and Captain Ketchum succeeded him. Following Ketchum in rank were Sakendiathen (Secondine) and Sah-coc-sa (Sarcoxie).

Half-way through the nineteenth century, the "free, mild, and pacific government …." observed by Prince Paul of Wuerttemberg in Kansas Territory had changed into a national clamor for the property of America's Indian peoples living in Kansas and beyond.

Gold was discovered at Sutter's Hill in California on January 24, 1848, and the rush to the gold fields began. The rapid influx of whites through their land was another nail in the coffin for the Delaware and other tribes who had been promised their reservations in Kansas for *"as long as the rivers flow, the birds fly, and the flowers burst into bloom."*

1. Jackson, *Century of Dishonor*, p. 49.

2. Weslager, *Delaware Indian Westward Migration*, p. 216.

3. Roark, *Charles Journeycake*, p. 24.

3. Cranor, *Kik Tha We Nund*, p. 70.

4. Weslager, *Delaware Indians*, p. 374.

5. Cranor, *Kik Tha We Nund*, p. 16.

6. Barry, *Beginning of West*, p. 168.

7. Ibid, p. 316.

43

Weather and Indian Attacks

In the early and mid-1800s, many grave dangers besides disease threatened Indians and whites. Prairie fires, heavy rains, flooding, and attacks by other Indians contributed as many woes to the Delaware and neighboring tribes in Kansas as did the white man.

The artist George Catlin visited the Fort Leavenworth area in the fall of 1832, and executed a painting, *Prairie Meadows Burning*, showing Indians fleeing on horseback from a terrifying prairie fire that Catlin himself witnessed near the Delaware homesteads.

In 1853, during the fifth expedition of Colonel John C. Fremont, the most renowned Western explorer of the mid-19th century, his party was caught in the midst of an enormous prairie wildfire. His scout Delaware Chief Solomon (son of Chief Buckongahelas), was accompanying Fremont

"Prairie Meadows Burning" by George Catlin.

from St. Louis to join the expedition, and led Fremont through the fire. (Fremont had been recuperating from an illness in St. Louis.)

Heavy rains also plagued the plains during the mid-1800s in the country's mid-section that became Kansas Territory.

"Never saw such a time of rain," wrote the Ottawa Indians' missionary Jotham Meeker on May 30, 1844, nine months after a smallpox scare. "It has fallen almost every day in the last three weeks. The river has overflown its banks, and the bottoms in many places have been inundated more or less for three weeks….," Louise Barry reported in her book *Beginning of the West*.[1]

The flooding continued into June, and the swollen Kanzas River rose at least twenty feet. A small steamboat sunk below the Falls of the Platte in Missouri, and sixty Santa Fe trade wagons were delayed by high water at Pawnee Fork, over which the traders finally threw up a bridge.

"At Pottawatomie Catholic Mission on (Big) Sugar creek—a Marais de Cygnes tributary-- Father Christian Hoecken recorded that it had been raining for 'forty days in succession,' and that 'great floods covered the country …' [but] damage … was not great 'in the mission area.'" [2]

Missionary Ira D. Blanchard of the Delaware Baptist Mission in present Wyandotte County recorded on June 30, 1844: "The first days of June were … fine …; but to the surprise of all, the rain again commenced, and for two weeks fell in perfect torrents. The Kansas River rose at least twenty feet above what had been supposed to be high 'water mark,' carrying with it houses, farms, cattle, horses, etc., and sweeping the whole bottom country.

"The [Delaware] village near us is all destroyed," Rev. Blanchard added. "There is not even a stalk of corn left in all their fields; and their old stock [of grain] all carried away by the flood…." [3]

Thousands of Indian families along the water courses were without shelter from the storms, and many of them had lost their last bit of food. One woman wrote in July that "The rains commenced falling in such torrents as to remind us of Noah's day."

The weather was not the only thing worrisome to the Delaware in northeastern Kansas. Attacks by other tribes were numerous –and deadly-- decimating the already dangerously reduced numbers of the remnants of the once powerful Delaware Nation and other tribes friendly to them.

The memory of the slaughter of Moravian Christians at Gnadenhutten was burned deeply into Delaware minds and hearts, but in 1837 they had allowed the Munsee Moravians to transfer their mission from Canada to Kansas. John Killbuck and seventy-two Moravian Christian Indians settled in December in Wyandotte County in the village of Westfield within the Delaware reservation.

In September of 1837, a distraught missionary, the Rev. William H. Gray, and two men arrived at Fort Leavenworth in a canoe en route from Oregon to St. Louis.

"The third Flathead delegation, headed once more by Old Ignace, departed from the rendezvous with William Gray," Father Killoren wrote. "On their way to St. Louis, however, the entire delegation was killed by a party of Sioux at Ash Hollow," [4]

The small party had included four whites and five or six Indians. In October of 1841, the Sioux attacked a fall hunting party of sixteen Delaware, and fourteen Delaware died. But the Delaware took with them twenty-eight Sioux to the heavenly hunting grounds!

A year later – in June, 1844, the Sioux struck again, attacking a hunting party of fifteen Delaware on the Smoky Hill River and killing them all, including the great Delaware War Chief Capt. Shawanock or Swanac.

The Pawnee were another thorn in the sides of the Delaware, from whom the Pawnee often stole horses--and in bands as large as 400 to 500 men, Pawnee attacked wagon trains on their way west, robbing them of mules, horses, clothing, and guns – and often their lives. Despite the peace treaty they had signed, 400 Delaware and Shawnee finally set out to fight the Pawnee.

Indians Having Fun With Flour

There is an amusing story about one Pawnee attack in October of 1846 in an area of Kansas in which 300 sacks of flour were among the loot retrieved from nineteen wagons. The Pawnee allowed the wagoneers to walk away unharmed, but ripped open their sacks – and scattered the flour to the winds.

"The prairie for miles around the spot was … as white as if covered with snow," according to an account rendered by two of the teamsters. The Indians covered their hair and bodies with flour, and danced about, pretending to be 'white men.'

"The Pawnee frolicked in the flour – powdered themselves, snow-balled each other; then made use of the flour sacks," the teamsters said. "One wound his as a turban; some devised other garb." [5]

The Pawnee admired the letters on the sacks, and designed some unusual breech-cloths from the sacks, with the letters "U.S." displayed in a prominent spot on the front.

Indian Agent R. W. Cummins recorded on January 6, 1845 that 240 Delaware, 171 Shawnee, and 80 Munsee were deprived of bread stuffs by the floods of the previous spring. Most of the families lost their homes, as well as their crops and fences, and many hogs, cattle, and horses. Relief efforts were not forthcoming until six months after the flooding, when Superintendent Thomas H.

Harvey of St. Louis authorized the purchase and distribution of nearly 14,000 bushels of corn to Indians whose crops were ruined by the previous rains and floodwaters. The Delaware received 342 bushels, the Shawnee 480, the Osage 5,000, and the Munsee 178, a total of 6,000 bushels. It is not known who received the remaining corn.

In May of 1845, the Indian population in the area that would become Kansas Territory ten years later included: 4,100 Osage, 1,059 Delaware, 887 Shawnee, and only 278 Munsee. These small numbers compared to nearly 28,000 Creek and Seminole, 26,000 Cherokee, and 16,500 Choctaw and Chickasaw in Oklahoma Territory.

In 1846 when Francis Parkman passed through Westport (ten miles west of Independence), he found that town booming: "… full of Indians whose little shaggy ponies were tied by the dozens along the houses and fences. Sacs and Foxes with shaved heads and painted faces, Shawnees and Delawares in calico frocks and turbans, Wyandots dressed like white men, and a few wretched Kanzas wrapped in old blankets, were strolling along the streets or lounging in and out of the shops and houses." [6]

But in May of 1847, a band of Comanche warriors attacked two parties from Santa Fe two days in a row, robbing them of fifty mules and horses. The Comanche were notorious for accosting parties of whites and Indians, whether headed east or west. Both the Comanche and the Sioux brought great sorrow to the Journeycake family: the Comanche by burning to death the grandparents of Watomika (Father James Bouchard, S.J.), and the Sioux by murdering Kistalwa and Whapakong, two of the four sons of Buckongahelas.

Despite or perhaps because of the growing threat of Indian attacks and white invaders, the Delaware Nation called a "Great Council," inviting tribes residing in the Kansas area to meet on October 10-17, 1848 near Fort Leavenworth on the Delaware reserve. In attendance were the Shawnee, Wyandot, Pottawatomie, Ottawa, Miami, Chippewa, Wea, Peoria, Kickapoo, Kansa, and the Sac & Fox tribes. The unfriendly Osage—enemies of many of the tribes--were absent and probably not invited.

A visitor to the council, Richard Hewitt, later described the "grandeur of Indian costume … the social and friendly feeling exhibited amongst the people there congregated, the enjoyment of the dance, and the great numbers engaged in them, contrasted with the sober and staid countenances of the older chiefs, the harmless countenance and the musical voice of the females present ....''[7]

The tribes at the council decided that the Wyandot Nation would continue as "keepers of the Council-fire of the Northwestern Confederacy." The tribes also had considered "the best measures for promoting peace and good neighborhood among themselves ...," according to Bishop James O. Andrew of the M. E. Church, South, who conversed October 18 with Kickapoo returning home from the council.[8]

Bishop Andrew spent five days in Kansas, visiting and preaching at the Delaware Methodist Mission and Delaware Church. He found the Kansas River ferry to be jointly owned by the Delaware and the Shawnee, and for two days, he toured the Shawnee Mission, which he described as having "the air of a clever, thriving village." He also was impressed by the Shawnee 500-acre farm, which he called "one of the most extensive and well-managed" he had ever seen.

All was not well on the Great Plains, however, according to Father Pierre-Jean De Smet, the beloved Jesuit who so tenderly tended the Indians throughout his lifetime. He wrote a warning note to his benefactors in Europe June 10, 1849: "The facts ... reveal clearly the melancholy future which at no very remote epoch awaits these nations, if efficient means are not employed for preventing the woes with which they are threatened... In the plains, war and famine lend their aid; on the frontier of civilization, liquors, vices and maladies carry them off by thousands." [9]

Father De Smet, whom Jesuit author Father Killoren described as "more than a witness to, and a reporter of, the invasions of the Great Plains," had foreseen the inevitable. Writing again three years later, De Smet warned:

"Already, even (in 1851), it is perceptible that the whites look with a covetous eye on the fertile lands of the Delawares, Potawatomies, Shawnees, and others on our frontiers, and project the organization of a new Territory – Nebraska." [10]

Nebraska Territory and Kansas Territory were created May 30, 1854. The numbers of white and black settlers galloping into Kansas Territory and across Indian lands increased at a rapid rate after that. More than 1,000 white settlers barged onto Delaware lands between 1854 and 1860, destroying the dream of Kansas as "the home of the Delaware forever." Kansas became a state January 29, 1861, further drawing white settlers. And both the white and African American population in Kansas exploded after the Civil War's end in 1865.

The year after the Delaware vacated their lands in Kansas and left for Oklahoma in 1868, the beloved Indian church building at White Church in west Kansas City was converted into a school. The pupils of the White Church School had no desks, but sat on logs. (We visited the White Church graveyard where Delaware Chief Solomon Journeycake is said to be buried.)

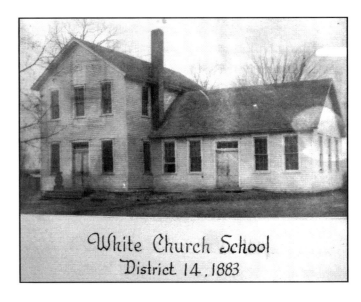

White Church School
District 14, 1883

"The first floor was reserved for white children, the second floor for Negroes," wrote Lewis D. Wiard, County Superintendent of School Offices, in *History and Growth of Wyandotte County Educational System* on Sept. 9, 1963.

Congress finally called for an investigation of *The Negro Exodus from the Southern States*, where the Ku Klux Klan had escalated its violence following the Confederate defeat, murdering more than 4,000, mostly blacks, but a few whites. In 1860 there had been 625 African Americans living in Kansas, the Kansas Historical Society reported. Twenty years later, that number was more than 43,000. Nearly 20,000 African Americans settled in Kansas in 1879 and 1880.

1. Barry, *Beginning of West*, pp. 513, 514.

2. Ibid, p. 515.

3. Ibid, pp. 516, 517.

4. Killoren, *Come Blackrobe,* p.56.

5. Barry, *Beginning of West*, p. 652.

6. Garraghan, *Jesuits of the Middle United States*, p. 256.

7. Barry, *Beginning of West*, p. 781.

8. Ibid.

9. Killoren, *Come Blackrobe*, p. 127.

10. Ibid, pp.126, 127.

44

Life and Death in Kansas

In 1832 and again 1833 St. Louis was visited by the Asiatic cholera, the Jesuit historian Gilbert J. Garraghan reported in his book *Jesuits of the Middle United States.*

"'The cholera is still at St. Louis,' [Father Peter] Verhaegen wrote to the East, June 23, 1833. 'Almost four or five persons die of it every day....'

In August of the same year, Father Verhaegen wrote again: 'We have a great deal of sickness at St. Louis. The cholera left the city but the bilious fever sweeps our citizens off as fast as the cholera could do. We have had as many as twenty burials a day, and regularly almost twelve die of the fever every twenty-four hours.'" [1]

Unfortunately, when cholera left the city of St. Louis, it spread to Kansas and other nearby states.

Smallpox broke out among several tribes in 1839, and in September of that year, Dr. James De Prefontaine of Westport, Missouri vaccinated 517 Delaware, 809 Shawnee, and 237 Kickapoo in Kansas. But despite the large numbers of people vaccinated, Kennekuk (the Kickapoo Prophet) would die of smallpox in February, 1852 on the Kickapoo reserve in present Leavenworth County.

In her book *The Beginning of the West*, Louise Barry reported that in the spring of 1849 another cholera epidemic broke out in St. Louis, Missouri, killing a tenth of the population within five months. In a letter April 15, 1849 from Independence, Missouri, emigrant John A. Johnson noted: "Every boat that now arrives from St. Louis has cholera on board and more or less die on every one of them.... [2]

Father De Smet, the famed Belgian Jesuit missionary to Indians, wrote on June 28 that cholera was "dreadfully ravaging St. Louis," and thousands had died of it "within the past fifty days." Hundreds of families were leaving the city. The virulent disease returned to Kansas City, Missouri late in June.

Many families fleeing cholera poured into Kansas in 1849, bringing the disease and another dreaded illness--smallpox--with them. As early as May, 1849, the steamboat *Mary*, which departed

Father Pierre Jean De Smet, S.J., top row center, a close friend of Father James Bouchard, S.J., met with Indians from several tribes in 1859.

from St. Louis and sailed up the Missouri, suffered the death of forty-eight crew and passengers from cholera. Many passengers were Mormons on their way to Omaha, Nebraska.

During his journeys in the 1840s, Father De Smet visited the Delaware and the other border tribes of the Shawnee, Kansa, Pawnee, Iowa, Omaha, Otoe, Kickapoo, and Sauk tribes. Many of these Indians had been stricken by cholera as whites carried the disease into their territories during what Jesuit Father John Killoren called "the immigrant invasion of 1849."

"Formerly the Iowas, the Omahas and the Otoes subsisted principally on the product of their buffalo hunts; at present they are reduced to the most pitiful condition, having nothing more for food but a small quantity of deer, birds and roots .… . "The Pawnees and the Omahas are in a state of nearly absolute destitution.," Father De Smet reported at the end of the 1840s. [3]

"De Smet and [Father John] Elet learned that even before the close of May, cholera deaths had occurred among the Miamis, Shawnees, Delawares, and Wyandottes.… Later in the year Indian agent John Barrow reported that over 1,200 Pawnees, nearly one-fourth of the tribe, had died of cholera in the summer of 1849," Father Killoren recorded. [4]

On one of Father De Smet's begging tours (he had crossed the ocean nineteen times on behalf of American Indians), he raised funds for a mission school for Indian girls in eastern Kansas.

"A few days after returning from his 1840 journey, De Smet had met with Mother Duchesne, who from the mid-1820s, shared with the Jesuits a special concern for educating Indian children," Jesuit Father Killoren wrote in his book *Come Blackrobe*.

Mother Rose Philippine Duchesne

"In New Orleans De Smet met with Mother Duchene's superior and presented their joint request: that the Sisters of the Sacred Heart open an Indian girls' school in conjunction with the Jesuits' Potawatomi mission at Sugar Creek in Kansas." [5]

Before the end of 1841, Mother Duchesne and three other sisters from her order opened the Sugar Creek School. Mother Duchesne had been born to the wealthy Duchesne family in Grenoble, France in 1769. She received the name Rose Philippine in honor of her mother, Rose, and St. Rose of Lima, the first woman canonized a saint in the Americas. Philippine's father, Pierre, was a prominent lawyer and her mother, an ancestor of Casimir, the president of France in 1894. Philippine entered the Visitation Convent of St. Marie at age 18. During the Reign of Terror, the convent was taken over and used as a prison for enemies of the French Revolution.

Sister Duchesne petitioned the Sisters of the Society of the Sacred Heart to receive her and her nuns into their community in 1804.

Gifts of Human Scalps

On February 8, 1818, at the age of forty-eight, Mother Duchesne left Paris for America with four other sisters on the ship *Rebecca*. When the Sacred Heart Sisters arrived in New Orleans May 29 (the Feast of the Sacred Heart), Mother Duchesne knelt with gratitude to kiss the blessed earth of her New World.

The sisters established the first convent west of the Mississippi and the first free school for girls in the United States. Mother Duchesne retired in 1834 at age sixty-five to Florissant, Missouri, where Belgium Jesuits had settled in 1823 to work among the Indians. She became a friend and supporter of Father De Smet, a founder of the Missouri Province of the Society of Jesuits.

At age seventy-two in July, 1841, she joined the colony for native girls at Sugar Creek, where the Indians greeted her with gifts of human scalps!

She was undeterred, and earned their admiration due to her deep religious devotion, rumored to be spending whole nights in prayer. (A curious native sprinkled leaves on the edge of her skirt one evening as she prayed, and in the morning, he returned to find her still praying, the leaves undisturbed.)

"….The Potawatomi Indians called her 'the woman who always prays.'" [6] She died at age eighty-three on November 18, 1852 at St. Charles, Missouri.

Of his dear departed friend, Father De Smet wrote foretelling her future status in the church: "No greater saint ever died in Missouri or perhaps in the whole Union." Pope John Paul II canonized Mother Duchesne a saint on July 3, 1988.

Another saintly Catholic who devoted himself to the Native Peoples in Kansas, especially the Potawatomie, was Bishop John Baptiste Miege, another Jesuit priest. Father De Smet had recruited and rescued Miege from Europe in 1848 when so many countries were in dangerous disarray.

"Rome in revolution, Italy upside-down, France aflame, Belgium threatened, Germany in a storm, princes and kings driven out, taking to flight, tottering on their thrones, the peoples of Germany constituting themselves at Frankfort into a national assembly and decreeing the exclusion of the Jesuits from all the Germany states…. America alone seemed to offer an assured asylum." [7]

Bishop Miege was consecrated a bishop in St. Louis on March 25, 1851, and established his See at St. Mary's Mission for Potawatomie Catholics in northeastern Kansas. The Potawatomie tribe included 3,500 Indians living in small villages on thirty square miles of land.

On January 1, 1852, describing the dire state of the Indians in his care, Bishop Miege wrote: "Cholera, fevers of every kind, and small-pox … have made great ravages among our Indians this year…. The Indian families who surround us have each their log house…. These [number] 600 or 700 simple and truly pious savages." [8] The bishop counted among his flock 1,500 converted Indians distributed between three villages.

Disease also struck the Delaware on their reserve near Leavenworth in May and August of

1853, when a severe outbreak of cholera occurred among them and the Shawnee and Miami Indian Nations. The Rev. John G. Pratt of the Delaware Baptist Mission recorded that eight Delaware died in August and many others were ill.

In a letter written February 16, 1853, the Rev. S. M. Irvin from the Ioway & Sac Mission in Kansas reported that the Iowa nation had diminished by half since their mission commenced fifteen years previously. By the 1850s, only 400 were still living from a total of 830. Of the six chiefs alive in 1838, only one had survived. (Former Iowa Chief White Cloud and the Iowa's second chief, Ne-u-mon-ya or Rain Walker, were among the chiefs who died.)

Kansas's first bishop, John Baptist Miege

There were nearly 25,000 Indians of several tribes in what now is Kansas when Bishop John Baptist Miege ministered there as the first bishop of the Territory of Kansas. That number dwindled by disease, death, and forced migration to approximately 500 by the year 2000.

The jovial and saintly Catholic Bishop Miege was more welcomed by the Potawatomie and Osage than the Delaware, who were wary of Catholics. Ironically, five years later in 1855, a Delaware--Watomika, son of Kistalwa and grandson of Buckongahelas--would become the first American Indian ordained a Catholic priest, a Jesuit, in the United States. He took the name "Father James Chrysotom Bouchard."

The twelfth of fourteen children, Miege was born in 1815 in a village in Savoy, a French-speaking area southwest of Switzerland. Ordained a Jesuit priest in Rome, he requested to be a missionary to Indians in North America, but was assigned to a small church at St. Charles, Missouri.

Father Miege thought it was a prank when he received a letter of appointment as vicar apostolate of Indian Territory, dated July 23, 1850. He responded to Rome, writing that he enjoyed their practical joke, but the joke was on him. The "tall and dignified" priest would serve as bishop of a vast vicariate that Pope Pius IX erected July 19, 1850. He would live at the Indian mission the Jesuit Order had opened at Sugar Creek, Indian Territory (now Kansas).

His initial dismay turned to joy upon his arrival at his new appointment.

"I do not think that I have experienced such delightful emotions as those which made my heart beat when for the first time I heard, in our wilderness, these natives sing so loudly and with such heartfelt devotion the praises of our Mother [Mary, mother of Jesus]," [9] wrote Bishop Miege.

Sister Virginia Pearl, CSJ, of the Catholic Diocese of Dodge City, which was established 100 years later, recalls: "Bishop Miege chose my great-grandfather, who came to this country from Ireland, to be the driver of his carriage. My great-grandmother, his wife, was Potawatomie."

Her great-grandfather drove the bishop and his carriage extremely long distances. The territory of the vicariate extended 1,250 miles north to south and 600 miles from east to west.

The "diocese" then was known as The Apostolic Vicariate of Indian Territory east of the Rocky Mountains. It included a huge area that later would become Kansas, Nebraska, Oklahoma, Montana, and Wyoming. Parts of North and South Dakota west of the Missouri River and a large portion of Colorado also were in the vicariate.

Sister Virginia Pearl   "Mother Rose Philippine Duchesne taught my great-grandmother her prayers at Sugar Creek," recalled Sister Pearl, one of thirty-three women featured in the book *A Passion of Her Own, Life-Path Journeys with Women of Kansas.* In the book published in 2004, she tells the story of her ancestors' "Trail of Death."

A total of 859 Potawatomie were involved from September to November of 1838 in a U.S. forced removal from St. Joseph, Michigan to Sugar Creek, Kansas beside the Osage settlement, Sister Pearl related.

"The Potawatomie people walked for sixty days at gunpoint. It was such a deep injustice. Only 650 of the 859 Indians made it to Kansas. Many of them (mostly the elderly and children) died along the way, and some ran away at night."

Bishop Miege, who ministered to the Potawatomie, built the first cathedral in Kansas from logs at St. Mary's Mission.   When he returned from a visit to Rome in April, 1853, he brought with him an organ for the church. The Indians were enchanted by what they thought was its "magical music." The bishop also carried from Rome a painting of the Immaculate Conception by Italian artist Benito that still hangs at the Church of St. Mary's, the former Potawatomie Mission.

As devoted to American Indians as Miege was, he still did not bring many Delaware into the Catholic fold, even when assisted by the Delaware priest, Father James Bouchard (Watomika.)

"Jesuit missionaries found native women—whom they called 'firebrands of hell'—much more difficult to convert than the men," author Donna Lucey observed.[11]

1. Garraghan, *Jesuits of the Middle United States*, p. 296.

2. Barry, *Beginning of West*, p. 807.

3. Killoren, *Come Blackrobe*, p. 126.

4. Ibid, p. 124.

5. Ibid, p. 68.

6. Crews, *American & Catholic*, p. 69.

7. Garraghan, *Jesuits of the Middle United States*, p.526.

8. Barry, *Beginning of West*, p. 1060.

9. Strecker, *Church in Kansas*, pp. 61, 62.

10. Wenzl, *Legacy of Faith*, p. 13.

11. Lucey, *I Dwell in Possibility*, p. 20.

45

Chief Solomon "Joneycake"

Chief Solomon "Joneycake" (aka "Everett", Jonnicake or Johnnycake, the name later changed to "Journeycake" by his son, Charles) was the youngest son of Buckongahelas, born circa 1790 in the Tuscarawas River area of northeastern Ohio.

By the end of the 1700s, most Lenape had been forced from the Delaware River areas of Pennsylvania, New Jersey, and New York. The tribe was known as the Delaware Nation and was composed of many bands that had resisted the colonial government. The Delaware had lived in western Pennsylvania, and Chief Buckongahelas had hunted in the deep forests of West Virginia before moving to the vast Ohio area that now includes several states.

"Before the removal across the Mississippi, there were probably about 2,000 persons in the main body of Delawares living at Piqua and along the White River, but this figure by no means constituted the total Delaware Indian population in the United States and Canada," historian Weslager wrote.

Weslager listed the Moravian Delaware on the Thames in Ontario, the Munsies living at Muncy Town on the Thames *above* the Moravians, and a third Canadian group of mixed Delaware, Mahican, and Munsies settled at the mouth of the Grand River under the protection of the Cayuga. Weslager estimated the total population of the three groups to be 1,000 to 1,200 men, women, and children. Some 100 Delaware were living with the Stockbridge Indians in Wisconsin.

"Along the Sandusky River in Ohio, there still remained another small enclave of less than 100 Delawares clinging to lands allotted them by the Wyandot, which the United States permitted them to occupy after the main body moved from Ohio," Weslager wrote. "In 1829, the government signed a treaty paying them to abandon these lands and move west to join the main body.

"Among these Sandusky Delawares was a chief named Solomon Joneycake [sic], whose descendants under the name Journeycake were later to become prominent leaders of the tribe in Kansas and Oklahoma." [1]

Chief Solomon was renowned as a hunter in Crawford County, Ohio. One story that circulated among Indians and whites concerned his presence at an Ohio bear feast, where he probably provided the bear. The huge animal reportedly was roasted whole, except for its feet and head, which were boiled into a soup.

With nearly 100 followers, Solomon refused for years to leave his land and small house near the John Stewart Wyandotte Mission in Upper Sandusky, Ohio. He had begun a family of his own. The six-foot, 200-pound Chief Solomon had fallen in love with the petite Sally Castleman. Sally was born in 1797 near Sandusky, daughter of the famous Indian captive Mary Castleman of Virginia, who was born in Pennsylvania in 1777.

The beautiful, red-haired Mary Castleman and her younger sister Margaret were tapping maple trees for sugar when Wyandotte Indians captured them on the Ohio frontier around the time of Mary's fourteenth birthday on April 1, 1791. The two petrified sisters were forced to run the gauntlet (a long line of Indians who taunted and sometimes struck their captives), but the two girls, like nearly all children taken captive, emerged unharmed. Their father, William, headed west from the panhandle of West Virginia, searching for his kidnapped daughters.

Angus McIntosh, a trader from Detroit and father of fifteen children, purchased Margaret for twenty-five dollars. Her sister Mary was sold for thirty dollars worth of food to Elizabeth Kuhn Williams Sr., also a Wyandot captive who lived with her captive husband, Isaac Williams Sr., on the Lower Sandusky.

Mary later married Isaac's son, Abraham, a half-blood Indian born at White Woman Creek Ohio Territory. (Abraham was the son of Isaac's former Indian wife, daughter of a Wyandotte chief.)

At the age of twenty, Mary gave birth to her first child, Sally, in 1797 near Sandusky, Ohio. Mary's husband Abraham was thirty-eight years older than Mary. He had two sons by another woman before he met and married the ravishing young captive, Mary. (As a trader, Abraham brought Wyandotte tribesmen together with Colonel "Mad" Anthony Wayne for the Greenville Treaty in 1795, following the Indian Confederation's disastrous defeat at the Battle of Fallen Timbers.)

The Greenville Treaty specified that white captives were to be returned to their families of origin. When William, the father of the two Castleman girls, learned of the treaty, he located in

Detroit his daughter Margaret, who was more than happy to be rescued from her hectic life with a family of fifteen children. But Mary did not wish to separate from her husband, although he treated her with cruelty. Her dad had traveled to Lower Sandusky to find her, but she refused to leave with him. When she discovered that she was pregnant, she was secluded from her husband until she gave birth to Sally. A brother for Sally, Isaac George, was born a year later in 1798.

"Sally ... became one of the direct descendants of those who had witnessed the horrible massacre of 1782 [at the Moravian Christian village at Gnadenhutten, Ohio]," wrote the Rev. Harry M. Roark, a Baptist pastor in Blackwell, Oklahoma and Gainesville, Texas, author of *Charles Journeycake, Indian Statesman and Christian Leader..* [2]

Mary's gorgeous flaming-red hair caught the eyes of many men--both Indian and white-- who did business with her husband at the Lower Sandusky trading post. Abraham was excessively jealous. He took to drinking rum and abusing his wife while in his cups. After he threw a hatchet that barely missed her head, she decided to leave him.

In agony, Mary pondered her decision. Her husband's next bout with alcohol could mean her death. And if she took the children with her, she feared he would hunt them all down, murder her and maybe the children too. Sorrowfully, she slipped away with the help of a friend, and never saw her children, Sally and Isaac George, again. Mary re-joined her parents in 1802, and later married John Wells, a border scout in Jefferson County. They lived on Yellow Creek until John's death in 1812. When Sally was grown, her mother Mary tried to contact her, but Sally refused to see her. Abraham had poisoned his two children against the woman who had escaped his threats and tyranny. Mary went blind before her death on August 12, 1874 at the age of ninety-seven. She was buried in Atwater Cemetery in Portage County, Ohio, where the grave's tombstone reads: *"Asleep in Jesus."*

Sally Marries the Delaware Solomon

Sally married the Delaware Indian Solomon "Joneycake," son of Buckongahelas, in the backwoods cabin of Justice of the Peace Peter Kinney in Erie, Ohio. Solomon and Sally became the parents of four children in Ohio: Charles, born December 16, 1817 in the Upper Sandusky in Huron; Isaac, born 1819; Nancy, born 1821; and John, born 1828.

The St. Mary's Treaty of 1818 stipulated that the Delaware must cede all of their lands east of the Mississippi River--their remaining property in Ohio, Indiana, and Michigan--and move west. Solomon put off leaving as long as possible, but by the late 1820s, he realized the futility of further resistance to white demands and began preparing his people to journey west. (Those Delaware who had settled in the Cape Girardeau vicinity of the Mississippi River had been forced into Kansas after Missouri became a state in 1821.)

Northeastern Kansas wasn't exactly the friendliest spot on the continent where Indians might settle, as the Rev. Isaac McCoy discovered in 1830 when he traveled there to survey the area on which the Delaware would take up residence.

"McCoy, a Baptist missionary charged with surveying the official boundary of the Delaware Indian Reservation, opened, on October 4, 1830, several burial mounds located about one mile west of Fort Leavenworth," wrote the author of *The Kansa Indians*, William E. Unrau.

"Composed of stones and earth, they yielded fragmentary bones of partially burned adults and children."

The mounds later were ascertained to be Doniphan, a village of the Kansa Indians in the early eighteenth century that had been visited by the French explorer Erienne Veniard de Bourgmont in 1724, "and where Lewis and Clark observed some village ruins at a later date," reported Unrau. [3]

There were other problems. The site of the new Delaware reservation was near the present-day town of Lawrence, "believed to be on one of the allotments awarded to the Kansa half-bloods in 1825, but ... actually situated on the western edge of the Delaware Reservation as determined by the supplementary Delaware treaty of 1829, a situation which precipitated chronic difficulties between the two tribes." [4]

In the fall of 1831, Delaware Chief Solomon, Captain Pipe, William Monture, and Isaac Hill--all influential leaders of their nation--left the Pipe Town Reserve for Kansas. Solomon and relatives decided not to accompany other Delaware who were boarding a steamboat to leave their homeland.

"Some of the Indians, like the contingent of fifty-eight Delawares who had been living on reserved land along the Sandusky River (and a large party of Seneca who accompanied them), were afraid of boarding a steamboat," historian Weslager noted.

"This group, which included a Delaware named Solomon Joneycake, as his name was spelled in the government records, rode overland all the way to St. Louis on horseback." [5]

They were among the last of the Delaware to migrate west, having been delayed by a fatal disease that killed most of their horses, excepting two that belonged to Solomon that ran away. The Delaware saw this as a providential sign to put off their departure. They also may have received word that several Shawnee in Kansas had been stricken with smallpox in mid-summer, and by October 1, the disease had spread to the Delaware living north of the Kansas River. Solomon moved his family some fifty miles to spend the winter with the Shawnee at White River, Indiana, where his father Buckongahelas had died in 1805.

Solomon's family probably camped in southwest Missouri before they arrived in Kansas, and learned to their dismay that nine Shawnee and fifteen Delaware had perished from the pox.

Charles Journeycake was a boy when his family finally left Sandusky, Ohio and eventually crossed the Kansas River, swollen by recent rains.

"The young brave, then less than twelve years old, mounted the leader and fearlessly plunged into the swollen river," Rev. Roark, wrote.[6]

It was necessary for several of his relatives' horses to swim the rushing waters, and the boy Charles had exhibited great bravery by leaping upon the lead horse to ford the river. Reaching the other side safely, he let out a whoop of joy and motioned to the Delaware to follow.

The American painter Henry F. Farny, born in France in 1847, immortalized the courage of young Indian men chosen to test the safety of rivers in his painting *Fording the Stream* in 1905. This piece is among more than 10,000 paintings, drawings, and sculptures--many of them by American Indian artists–on display at Gilcrease Museum of the Americas in Tulsa, Oklahoma.

"Mrs. Sally Journeycake [mother of Charles], in 1831, became the first interpreter for missionaries in the

Sally Journeycake, mother of Charles

Copyright 1895 by Judson Press, used by permission of Judson Press

Territory of Kansas.... With gladness she rendered into the language of her people the wonderful words of the gospel which had been so blessed to her." [7]

Sally was respected by whites and Indians alike. While Chief Solomon was absent on a hunting trip, she fell violently ill and following her recovery, reported a vision of Jesus Christ. The Delaware and other tribes take very seriously their dreams and visions, and both Sally and Solomon and their offspring would convert to Christianity in later years. Their son, Charles or Ne-sha-pa-na-cumin ("He who stands twice at daylight"), would become a Baptist minister.

Solomon's two oldest sons would become prominent in the Delaware Tribe in Kansas Territory and in Indian Territory (Oklahoma). The brilliant Charles had a plain face when he was a youth (distinguished and handsome in his old age), but his younger brother Isaac with his trim moustache and dark looks reminded me of my dad and five brothers. Charles would be in the limelight of the U.S. Supreme Court, and his brother Isaac would serve as the U. S. interpreter for the Treaty of Fort Leavenworth (Kansas) on July 2, 1861, and be a signer as a delegate of the April 8, 1867 treaty between the United States and the Delaware in Washington.

Solomon's daughter, Nancy, would marry Gorge Ketchum, ancestors of former Delaware Chief Dee Ketchum of Bartlesville, Oklahoma (the husband of Annette Ketchum). George and Nancy had two sons who were ministers at White Church in Wyandotte County, Kansas. Chief Dee Ketchum's great-great-grandfather was Charles (aka Lewis Charles Ketchum).

1. Weslager, *Delaware Indians*, pp. 352, 353.

2. Roark, *Charles Journeycake*, p. 20.

3. Unrau, *Kansa Indians*, p. 17.

4. Ibid, p. 114.

5. Weslager, *Delaware Indians*, p. 360.

6. Roark, *Charles Journeycake*, p. 25.

7. Mitchell, *Indian Chief Journeycake (1895)*, p. 26.

46

Solomon Joins Explorer Fremont

Among the steamboat *Antelope* passengers in 1839 was Lt. John Charles Fremont, an officer of the Army Corps of Topographical Engineers, a man who would be a powerful influence on the life of Solomon and the exploration of the country.

In his book *Jesuits of the Middle United States*, Volume 1, Jesuit historian Gilbert J. Garraghan recorded that Jesuit missionary Father De Smet also traveled with Fremont on the steamboat *St. Peter's* on its annual trip to the Yellowstone, carrying supplies to Indians on April 29 of 1839.

"During the 1840s and 1850s, American explorer and map-maker John Charles Fremont (credited as the father of the Oregon Trail), led five expeditions throughout the West," explained Arlene Hirschfelder in her book *Native Americans*.

"Relying on Delaware Indians as hunters and scouts, Fremont explored thousands of miles of Indian country." [1]

Solomon Journeycake was listed in the book *Kik Tha We Nund, Delaware Chief William Anderson and His Descendants* by Ruby Cranor. She mentioned the number of Delaware chosen for Fremont's third expedition in 1845 as twelve, including Solomon, whom she lists as "Sol Everett," his Anglicized name. [2]

Before his 1853 expedition, "The messenger Col. Fremont sent to the Delaware camp returned with a number of braves, some of whom had accompanied Colonel Fremont on a former expedition—he selected ten, among whom was a chief named Solomon, who had been with him before, and for whom Col. Fremont felt a great friendship," Solomon Nunes Carvalho, recorded. [3]

Solomon Carvelho, Self-Portrait, 1848, Library of Congress

"Today we met our Delawares, who were awaiting our arrival," noted Carvalho, the first official photographer appointed to the staff of an exploring party.

"A more noble set of Indians I never saw, the most of them six feet high, all mounted and armed *cap-a-pie* [head to foot], under command of Captain Wolff, a 'Big Indian,' as he called himself.

"Most of them spoke English, and all understood it. 'Washington,' 'Welluchas,' 'Solomon,' 'Moses' (John) were the names of some of the principal chiefs. They became very much attached to Col. Fremont, and every one of them would have ventured his life for him." [4]

Col. John Charles Fremont

On his third expedition in June, 1845, the "Pathfinder" Fremont was accompanied by Kit Carson and several Delaware hunters who were all distinguished for bravery, among them Solomon Joneycake, Jim Shawanock, Jim Secondine (aka Sagundai or Secondeye), and Jim Connor.

It was important "that parties making expeditions through unexplored country should secure the services of the best guides and hunters, and I know of none who are superior to the Delaware and Shawnee Indians," H. Allen Anderson wrote.

"Jim Sagundai (Secondeye) gained national notice after serving as a scout and hunter on John C. Fremont's third expedition, particularly after saving the life of Fremont's right-hand-man, Kit Carson, during a skirmish with hostile Klamath Indians in the Oregon Country in the spring of 1846." [5]

In May of 1847, Kit Carson was on his way from California carrying dispatches and letters to Washington, DC, when his party was attacked by the Pawnee. The Delaware, Shawnee, Kickapoo, and Wyandot had entered into a treaty of peace with the Pawnee only days earlier. Kit Carson was an old friend of the Delaware, but in 1863, he would betray his Indian friendships by laying siege to 8,000 Navaho in Arizona, killing their livestock and scorching their crops to bring them to the point of starvation and surrender in 1864.

The Navaho would be forced to walk 300 miles from their lands to Fort Sumner, New

Mexico, where they were kept in pitiful squalor.

John C. Fremont's fifth and last expedition to the west began on September 22, 1853. He took ill the next day, but his party of twelve persons continued through the Kansas Valley, and was joined on September 27 by Captain Wolff and nine other Delaware chiefs, including Solomon Joneycake.

The photographer Carvalho experienced his first buffalo hunt Oct. 25, 1853 during the fifth expedition. Later he recalled that at one time on the divide between Walnut Creek and the Arkansas River, they traveled through immense herds of buffalo, as many as 200,000. Of the Indian buffalo hunters who accompanied him, Carvalho had this to say:

"A Delaware Indian, in hunting buffaloes, when near enough to shoot, rests his rifle on his saddle, balances himself in his stirrup on one leg; the other is thrown over the rifle to steady it. He

then leans on one side, until his eye is on a level with the object, takes a quick sight, and fires while riding at full speed, rarely missing his mark, and seldom chasing one animal further than a mile." [6]

Five days after Carvalho's first buffalo hunt, as the expedition was looking forward to Fremont's return from St. Louis following his illness, the party encountered dense, suffocating smoke as a wildfire swept across the prairie and came dangerously close to their encampment on the Saline fork of the Kansas River.

According to Carvalho, "The whole horizon now seemed bounded by fire. As far as the eye could see, a belt of fire was visible…. The whole horizon now seemed bounded by fire. The fire gradually increased, yet we dared not change our ground; first, because we saw no point where there was not more danger, and secondly, if we moved away, 'Solomon,' the Indian chief, who after conducting us to the camp ground we now occupied, had returned to guide Col. Fremont, [and] would not know exactly where to find us again.

"After breakfast, one of our Delawares gave a loud whoop, and pointing to the open space beyond in the direction of Solomon's Fork, where to our great joy, we saw Col. Fremont on horseback, followed by 'an immense man' on 'an immense mule,' (who afterwards proved to be our good and kind-hearted Doctor Ober); Col Fremont's 'cook,' and the Indian 'Solomon,' galloping through the blazing element in the direction of our camp. Instantly and impulsively, we all discharged our rifles in a volley." [7]

Photo by Charlene Scott-Myers

The White Church cemetery near Leavenworth, Kansas.

After Delaware Chief Solomon's exciting life of tromping through the Rockies, braving an enormous prairie wildfire with Fremont, and seeing his children settled in Kansas, the son of Buckongahelas and father of Charles Journeycake would die at the fairly young age of sixty-five in 1855.

Solomon was buried at White Church Delaware Indian Cemetery on what then was part of the Delaware Reserve near Leavenworth, Kansas, according to his descendant, Delaware author Helen York Rose. She wrote that she hoped to erect a headstone over his grave before her own death. Unfortunately, that did not happen. Born February 6, 1916, Rose died June 29, 1995. Annette Ketchum's husband, former Delaware Chief Dee Ketchum, conducted Rose's burial service. (Annette painted the traditional rouge spots high on Rose's cheeks, so the heavenly host would know that she was a Delaware.) It is not certain, however, where Solomon is buried at White Church.

More than 100 grave sites, most of them Indian and eight of them unmarked, can be found at the cemetery. The church and cemetery were founded in 1831 by Thomas and William Johnson of the Methodist Mission to the Delaware Indians, and is now a Kansas City, Kansas historical site. Several members of the Ketchum family are buried there, including the beloved Captain John Ketchum, chief of the Delaware Nation in Kansas for twenty-eight years. A tall obelisk engraved with a lamb resting in the sun's rays marks Ketchum's grave.

According to Jerry Brotherson, eighty-six, who lived across from the church and has been a member for more than eighty years, the church has no record concerning the Indian graves, just the ancient head stones that mark some of their graves.

"These have been preserved with new headstones that the church purchased," he said. "There is no known record of any of the burials of the unmarked burial sites. It is generally accepted that there are many Indians buried there who have no marker."

Brotherson found a small sack of tobacco on Jacob Ketchum's grave years ago, and a woman descendant of Ketchum told him that Indians often left tobacco as sacred gifts at gravesites. Brotherson asked her about Solomon's possible burial at the White Church Cemetery, and she responded:

"Yes, I have heard that he was buried there, too. I think it was written in one of the books on the Journeycakes written by Helen York Rose. She was a member of the family. However, to my knowledge she had no information on where he was buried in the cemetery, and we found no records of his burial there. I am assuming she must have gotten the information from family members and perhaps the family Bible."

In May of 2010, we visited the small cemetery west of White Church, which has the distinction of being the oldest established church in Kansas still in use. The first of the three "White Churches" built at the site was a log structure constructed "near a spring and walnut grove that were much used by the Indians," Brotherson said.

Three ministers arrived in 1832 to establish the Delaware Indian Mission at White Church.

Thomas Johnson, his brother William, and Thomas Markham established the Methodist Episcopal Church mission among the Indians at the present site. Sally Journeycake, the wife of Delaware Chief Solomon and mother of Charles and Isaac Journeycake, was their interpreter. Isaac later also became an interpreter.

Photo by David Scott Myers

The wooden church was whitewashed inside, and the Indians named it "White Church." By 1834, White Church had forty Delaware Indian members and twenty-four of their children in the mission school. One of the earliest settlements in Wyandotte County, White Church is located fourteen miles west of Kansas City, Kansas, and now is inside the city limits. The original church was destroyed by fire in 1844.

The black walnut trees near the property came in handy. The second White Church was a walnut frame structure about forty by sixty feet, erected facing in an easterly direction by the nearby

spring. When the Delaware moved to their reservation in Kansas in 1829-1830, they brought with them a saw mill, which was useful in building both churches. Disaster struck the church and nearby school for the second time on May 11, 1886, when a tornado destroyed both buildings. The third and present church was dedicated July 29, 1906, and now houses the White Church Christian Church.

Behind the church in the White Church Cemetery, we photographed the grave marker of

Captain James "Jack" Ketchum, born in 1780 of the Turtle Clan and principal chief of the Delaware for twenty-eight years. A member of White Church for twenty-two years, he died in 1857 at age seventy-seven, two years after Solomon's death. Nearby are graves of the Rev. James Ketchum, first ordained Protestant minister of the Delaware nation, and his brother, the Rev. Charles Lewis Ketchum, sons of George Ketchum and Nancy Journeycake, daughter of Solomon, granddaughter of The Buck.

James Ketchum was an eloquent preacher and Charles his skilled interpreter at White Church. But in 1845, when a split occurred in the Methodist Church over slavery, the two brothers parted. Charles withdrew from White Church and aligned himself with the northern branch of the denomination, while James remained at White Church affiliated with the southern branch. Charles died at age forty-nine in 1860, his younger brother James at age forty-seven in 1866. Once estranged because of slavery, the two Ketchum brothers now rest peacefully side by side in the White Church Cemetery.

1. Hirschfelder, *Native Americans*, p. 43.

2. Cranor, *Kik Tha We Nund*, p. 45

3. Carvalho, *Incidents of Travel and Adventure in Far West*, p. 85.

4. Ibid, p. 91.

5. Anderson, *Delaware and Shawnee Indians*, pp. 231, 259

6. Ibid, p. 113.

7. Ibid, pp. 117, 118, 119.

47

Bleeding Kansas

William Quantrill and John Brown held sharply different viewpoints regarding slavery and the importance of the union of *all* of the United States, but they both resorted to violence so gross that it cannot be described in detail.

Delaware Indians were involved at the beginning and at the end of the murderous attack on the lovely town of Lawrence, Kansas on August 21, 1863, the worst event of the awful era that was branded forever with the name "Bleeding Kansas."

Only a few people–including a Delaware man—heard or saw the hundreds of armed men on horseback before dawn that morning of the attack, and tried in vain to warn the townspeople of Lawrence.

The Indian, Logan Ziegler, whose mother, Betsy Taylor, was a full-blood Delaware and whose father, Phillip, was German, actually tried to stop the stampede of killers into Lawrence. Logan had been born in 1825 in St.

William Quantrill

Joseph, Missouri, but his family had moved to Leavenworth County, not far from Stranger Creek.

"When the war [Civil War] came, they had settled down here in the Fall Leaf bottoms," their great-grandson told the *Leavenworth Times*. "Logan Ziegler was a young man then, and the story goes that he exchanged fire with Quantrill's Raiders when they were on their way to Lawrence."

The U.S. Congress had passed the controversial Kansas-Nebraska Act May 30, 1854, permitting residents in the Kansas and Nebraska territories to vote whether or not they allow slavery. The act repealed the Missouri Compromise, which had prohibited slavery in territories north of Missouri's southern border. After passage of the Act, both pro-slavery and anti-slavery supporters poured like running water into the Kansas Territory—each hoping to grab land and the reins of government in order to vote according to their own persuasion.

"When the day to vote came, Atchison (Senator David of Missouri) and nearly 5,000 armed pro-slavery men from Missouri—'border ruffians,' their enemies called them—flooded across the Kansas border, seized polling places, cast four times as many ballots as there were voters in the territory, and installed a legislature that made it a crime even to criticize slavery," author Geoffrey C. Ward declared.

"Free-Soilers countered with their own election. They drew up a constitution that outlawed slavery, and applied for admission to the Union as a free state. Kansas now had two governments. Its people were about to go to war with one another." [1]

The territory was labeled "bleeding Kansas" after multiple acts of violence, the worst in Lawrence, erupted in towns near the border of Kansas and Missouri. Fighting was furious between abolitionist settlers who came to Kansas from Massachusetts (they named their main street Massachusetts in Lawrence) and pro-slavery gangs from Missouri.

John Brown, abolitionist

At the age of twelve, John Brown had witnessed the brutal beating of a slave boy, a violent incident that he never forgot. When Brown was grown, he became a fervent abolitionist. In a prelude to the Civil War, he arrived in Kansas, where five of his sons had settled in 1855. On Dec. 7, 1855, Brown and four of his sons defended Lawrence during the Wakarusa War, which wasn't really a war, but a confrontation between 1,500 pro-slavery men camped in the Wakarusa River Valley and abolitionists led by Brown and Kansas troublemaker General James Lane.

Missourians sacked Lawrence on May 21, 1856, and in retaliation three days later, Brown and his sons raided Pottawatomie, hacking five pro-slavery settlers to death. Then on June 2, 1856, Brown led his militia against a pro-slavery force at the Battle of Black Jack, considered by some to be the first battle of the American Civil War. The battlefield has been preserved as the Black Jack Nature Park approximately twenty miles southeast of Lawrence.

Brown's later raid of a federal armory in 1859 at Harper's Ferry, Virginia resulted in seven deaths and ten men injured–and brought a noose around Brown's neck. Brown and his men were captured by none other than Colonel Robert E. Lee, who at that time was a commander of Federal forces. The father of twenty children, Brown lost five sons in the Harper's Ferry raid. He had hoped to arm slaves with the armory's weapons and lead a slave rebellion, but local slaves refused to cooperate. Brown was tried for treason and hung December 2, 1859 at the age of fifty-nine in Charles Town, Virginia.

Abraham Lincoln did not defend Brown's actions, but considered him an anti-slavery fanatic. While on his way to visit Leavenworth, Kansas, President Lincoln spoke in the small town courthouse of Troy, Kansas on December 1, 1859--the day before Brown was to be hung. Brown's attack on Harpers Ferry had been wrong for two reasons, Lincoln said.

"The act was a violation of the law, and it was futile," Lincoln, a man of few words, observed tersely.

"We have a means provided for our belief in regard to slavery," he added. "It is through the ballot box, the peaceful method provided by the Constitution." [2]

Lincoln spoke for an hour an a half two days later at Stockton Hall in Leavenworth, Kansas. John Wilkes Booth, Lincoln's future killer, would appear on the same stage four years later on Dec. 20, 1863. Booth would assassinate Lincoln at the Ford Theater in Washington, D.C. two years later on April 15, 1865.

Two other prominent men of the day thought differently than Lincoln about John Brown.

Ralph Waldo Emerson wrote: "[John Brown,] if he shall suffer, will make the gallows glorious like the cross."

And Henry Wadsworth Longfellow on the day of Brown's death penned these words: "Even now as I write, they are leading old John Brown to execution in Virginia for attempting to rescue slaves! This is sowing the wind to reap the whirlwind, which will come soon."

The grim reapers predicted by Longfellow came to Kansas soon enough and were responsible for one of the worst bloodletting attacks on civilians during the Civil War. They were pro-slavery guerillas, who called Lincoln "a gorilla," who murdered, looted and burned the Union town of

Lawrence, Kansas on August 21, 1863. Founded by abolitionists of the New England Emigrant Aid Company, Lawrence was home to the Redlegs militia and the Jayhawkers vigilantes, who often crossed into pro-slavery western counties in Missouri to retaliate against fighters who had attacked Kansas.

"Bandits took advantage of the lack of men in Kansas," wrote Bliss Isely and W. M. Richards in their book *Four Centuries in Kansas*.

"The most notorious of them was William Clarke Quantrill, 26, a one time Kansan, who had lived in various Kansas communities, but had fled to escape punishment for robbery…. At the outbreak of the Civil War Quantrill organized a guerilla gang. Among his raiders were Cole Younger and Frank James, brother of Jesse, all of whom later became notorious bank robbers.

"Most savage and cowardly of Quantrill's acts was his raid on the unprotected town of Lawrence … at a time when most of the able-bodied men of that place were serving in the Union Army…. Quantrill's men were not soldiers of the Confederacy. They were mere bandits, using the war as an excuse for robbery." [3]

Quantrill, a bandit *and* a pro-slavery fanatic, had lived and worked as a school teacher in Lawrence for a period of six months in 1859 under the assumed name of Charley Hart.

"He was under indictment for crimes of burglary, horse-thievery, and Negro-kidnapping (he'd fled town to avoid arrest)…. Lawrence was the special object of his vengeful wrath," author Kenneth S. Davis reported. [4]

Cole Younger and Frank James had their own reasons to hate and attack the abolitionist town of Lawrence.

"Kansas raiders murdered the Youngers' father and burned their home," explained Geoffrey Ward, author of *The West*. "Federal militia jailed the James boys' mother for spying." [5]

After several of Quantrill's raids in Kansas in 1862, "the Union Army issued a proclamation declaring that the guerrillas were outlaws, not part of the Confederate Army, and should be shot on sight." [6]

In defiance of the proclamation, Quantrill from then on shot all of his prisoners to death. He killed six people in Olathe, Kansas, and "killed eight men (Creeks); one of them [Quantrill's followers[shot a little boy and killed him." [7]

Quantrill's deepest hatred, however, was for Lawrence, which had been burned, but not destroyed, by Sheriff Samuel J. Jones of Douglas County, Missouri in 1856. Quantrill especially wanted to murder General James Lane, who escaped in his night shirt into a wheat field and hid during Quantrill's attack. Lane had raised a Kansas army to fight against slavery and commanded the Third, Fourth, and Fifth regiments against Confederate troops in Missouri. Quantrill also planned to destroy the town's newspapers that regularly published anti-slavery articles.

A Mrs. Jennings sent her eighteen-year-old African American servant, Henry Thompson, running to the town of Eudora to spread the news of the hundreds of horsemen headed toward Lawrence. The city marshal of Eudora, David Kraus, and two volunteers, Casper Marfelius and Jerry Reel, raced on horseback for Lawrence. The lawman was thrown from his horse, Reel's horse fell, crushing its rider, and Marfelius took Reel to a farmhouse, where he died the next day.

"A Shawnee Indian named Palathe came into Kansas City at midnight and heard a report that three hundred men were riding through the night," Wayne C. Lee related in his book *Deadly Days in Kansas.*

"A scout named Bartles concluded that it was Quantrill, and he was headed for Lawrence. Bartles had the best horses in the territory, and he took the Shawnee to his place and let him pick a horse." [8]

Palathe rode for hours, but his horse fell dead before he reached the town of Lawrence. Palathe ran the rest of the way, but just as he neared the besieged town, he heard the screams beginning.

1. Ward, *West, Illustrated History*, pp. 175, 176.

2. Dary, *True Tales of Old-Time Kansas*, pp. 246, 247.

3. Ibid, p. 354.

4. Isely and Richards, *Four Centuries in Kansas*, pp. 177, 178.

5. Davis, *Kansas*, p. 83.

6. Lee, *Deadly Days in Kansas*, p. 9.

7. Debo, *History of the Indians*, p. 179.

8. Lee, *Deadly Days in Kansas*, pp. 10, 12.

48

Dawn of Death

It was the morning of August 21, 1863, and as cocks began crowing at five a.m., some 400 raucous men led by Quantrill rode into the small town of Lawrence, population 2,000.

Quantrill's goal was to murder every man and "boys old enough to shoot a rifle" after rousing them from their beds in Lawrence. This goal he and his Raiders only achieved by half, but he was able to destroy the offices of *The Tribune*, the *Kansas Free State*, and *The Lawrence Republican* newspapers. Hated journalists also were targeted: Josiah Trask of the *State Journal* was murdered, but John Speer of the *Republican* escaped death.

The Raiders split up into small groups and went from door to door, shooting the men and their sons in their homes or as they emerged, looting the houses, and torching 200 residences. Unarmed males from boys as young as 14 to old men the age of ninety were shot, and all but two businesses burnt to the ground. (The town's weapons had been locked inside the public armory.) The Raiders robbed the town bank and looted businesses. Four hours after they arrived in Lawrence, at least 180 defenseless men were dead, eighty women were left widows, and 250 children were orphans. In one home, eight African Americans were murdered together, and eight men were shot at the same time in another place.

There were many heroines in and around Lawrence that day. One of them was Mary Brown, who, with her husband, William, owned a nearby dairy farm. The raiders set their house afire twice—and Mary saved it twice by throwing dirt on the fires.

"Two men came from a neighbor's barn which they had set on fire," author Lee explained. "They were dragging a Negro man. Their discussion was about how they were going to kill him. He claimed to be a free man.

"Mary Brown had an old pistol that she had never fired. She wasn't even sure it worked. But she pointed it at the head of the man holding the Negro and shouted that she would kill him if he didn't let the Negro go. Mary's audacity bewildered the men, and they let the Negro go." [1]

The Rev. Richard Cordley, pastor of Lawrence's Congregational Church, was an eye witness to Quantrill's Raid and submitted his version of what happened to the U.S. Congressional Record a few days later. Cordley described the horror of the morning, and also told of the ingenious means of escape of some men.

The Rev. S. S. Snyder was the first victim of the unruly gang, which shot him to death while he was milking his cow.

"Mr. Snyder was a prominent minister among the United Brethren," Cordley explained. "He held a commission as lieutenant in the Second Colored Regiment, which probably accounts for their malignity....

"Another and larger squad struck for the west part of the town, while the main body, by two or three converging streets, made for the [Eldridge] hotel [which was burned to the ground for the second time in 10 years by Missourians]. They first came upon a group of recruits for the Kansas Fourteenth [mostly teenage boys]. On these they fired as they passed, killing seventeen out of twenty-two.... At the Johnson House they shot at all that showed themselves, and the prisoners that were finally taken and marched off were shot a few rods of the house, some of them among the fires of the burning buildings. Such was the common fate of those who surrendered themselves as prisoners.

"Mr. R. C. Dix was one of these. His house was next door to the Johnson House, and being fired at in his own house, he escaped to the Johnson House. All the men were ordered to surrender.

"'All we want,' said a rebel, 'is for the men to give themselves up, and we will spare them and burn the house.' Mr. Dix and others gave themselves up. They marched them towards town, and when they had gone about two hundred feet, the guards shot them all, one after another.... Dr. Griswold was one of the principal druggists, Mr. Thorp was State Senator, Mr. Trask editor of the *State Journal*, and Mr. Baker one of the leading grocers of the place. Mr. Thorp lingered in great pain till the next day, when he died. Mr. Baker, after long suspense, recovered. He was shot through the lungs.

"Honorable S. A. Riggs, District Attorney, was set upon by the vilest ruffian of the lot. His wife rushed to his side at once. After a short parley the man drew his revolver and took aim. Mr. Riggs pushed the revolver aside and ran. The man started after him, but Mrs. Riggs, seized hold of the bridle rein and clung to it till she was dragged round a house, over a wood pile, and through the yard back on to the street again…. All this time the man was swearing and striking at her with his revolver, and threatening to shoot her.

"Several saved themselves by their ready wit. An officer in the camp of recruits, when the attack was made, ran away at full speed. He was followed by several horsemen, who were firing at him continually. Finding escape impossible, he dashed into the house of a colored family, and in the twinkling of an eye, slipped on a dress and shaker bonnet, passed out the back door and walked deliberately away. The rebels surrounded the house, and then some of them entered and searched, but found no prey," Rev. Cordley said

"Mr. Winchell, being hard pressed, ran into the house of Rev. Charles Reynolds, Rector of the Episcopal Church. Mrs. Reynolds at once arrayed him in female attire, shaved off his moustache with a knife, and set him in a rocking chair with a baby in his arms, and christened him 'Aunt Betsie.' The rebels searched the house but did not disturb 'Aunt Betsie.'

"Massachusetts Street was one bed of embers. On this one street, seventy-five buildings, containing at least twice that number of places of business and offices, was [sic] destroyed. The dead lay all along the sidewalk, many of them so burned that they could not be recognized, and scarcely be taken up. Here and there among the embers could be seen the bones of those who had perished in the buildings and been consumed.

"The work of burial was sad and wearying. Coffins could not be procured. Many carpenters were killed, and most living had lost their tools. But they rallied nobly, and worked night and day, making pine and walnut boxes, fastening them together with the burnt nails gathered from the ruins of the stores…. Thus the work went on for three days, till one hundred and twenty-two were deposited in the Cemetery, and many others in their own yards. Fifty-three were buried in one long grave.

"Early on the morning after the massacre, our attention was attracted by loud wailings. We went in the direction of the sound, and among the ashes of a large building, sat a woman, holding in her hands the blackened skull of her husband, who was shot and burned in that place. Her cries could be heard over the whole desolated town, and added much to the feeling of sadness and horror which filled every heart." [2]

Quantrill and his men left the burning town of Lawrence at 9 a.m., splitting up and fleeing. Quantrill's butchers suffered only one casualty: Larkin Skaggs, "an itinerant minister and farmer from Cass County, Missouri." Skaggs had attempted to snatch a ring from the finger of Lydia Stone, the daughter of Quantrill's old friend, Nathan Stone, owner of the City Hotel. But Skaggs was rebuked by Quantrill.

"It seems that one of the party had forcibly taken possession of a gold ring from Miss Stone, and she informed Quantrill of the fact, who told the fellow if he did not hand it over he would shoot him."

Ordered away by Quantrill, Skaggs threatened to return, which he and three companions did. "[Larkin Skaggs] said he wanted to kill Miss Lydia Stone, the landlord's daughter. But Miss Stone escaped…," Charles Harris related in his book *Alias Charley Hart, William C. Quantrill in Lawrence, Kansas in 1860*. [3]

When her father Nahan Stone objected, the burly, drunken Skaggs put a bullet into the innkeeper, silencing him forever. Skaggs got his bullet from a young boy and an arrow from a Delaware Indian a few minutes later.

"Skaggs then realized that he had been left behind and attempted to mount his horse," author Harris added.

"He was shot in the shoulder by a boy with a rifle. He was then killed by a Delaware Indian named Moon by an arrow shot through his heart. His body was dragged up and down the streets of Lawrence. Skaggs was the only guerrilla casualty in Lawrence." [4]

The Union was horrified by the attack on Lawrence. "*The New York Times* wrote: 'Quantrill's massacre…is almost enough to curdle the blood with horror. In the history of the war thus far…there has been no such diabolical work as this indiscriminate slaughter of peaceful villagers…'

"*The Chicago Tribune* wrote: 'What pen can depict the horrors…fiends incarnate…shooting down unarmed citizens…butchering them with wives and mothers clinging to them and begging for mercy.'

"The Leavenworth Conservative printed: 'Shot down like dogs...No fighting, no resistance-cold blooded murder.'" [5]

Retribution was swift, affecting hundreds of innocent and many not-so-innocent families who had cooperated with Quantrill near the Missouri border. Four days following the Lawrence attack, Brigadier General Thomas Ewing, Jr., commander of the District of the Border of Kansas and Missouri, issued General Order Number 11, requiring all residents of three Missouri border counties and part of a fourth to remove–or be removed--from their homes.

Quantrill launched another Kansas attack October 6, 1863, little more than a month after the Lawrence Massacre, murdering 101 of General James Blunt's soldiers at Baxter Springs. Quantrill

Quantrill tombstone

later was shot in the chest during a Union ambush May 10, 1865 near Taylorsville, Kentucky, and died from his wound on June 6 at the age of twenty-seven.

On the northwest corner of 8th and Indiana Street, stands one of the five homes west of Massachusetts that escaped the destruction of more than 100 homes. The magnificent two-story brick home was spared because the landlady, Emily Hoyt, screamed at the wild men banging at her door that this was a rooming house and her only means of support.

At the top of nearby Mount Oread, actually a hill, rest many of the first victims of the vicious guerillas. Others are interred at Oak Hill Cemetery, where a monument honors Quantrill's victims

"The Lawrence Massacre was the most atrocious act of the Civil War," wrote Albert Castel in his book *Civil War Kansas.* "Nothing else quite matched it in stark horror and melodramatic circumstances.... And it was the outstanding single event of the Civil War in Kansas, the bloody climax of the border strife with Missouri." [6]

Lawrence today is a charming city of 80,000 and home of the University of Kansas and the Haskill College for American Indians. The only commercial building still standing 150 years later that was not destroyed by Quantrill's raid of rage is the House Building at 729-731 Massachusetts Street.

The Delaware

Support Lincoln's Union

How different was Abraham Lincoln from William Quantrill, who hated blacks and slaves and murdered unarmed men and boys. Lincoln lost his own life because of his defense of the Union and slaves, but the state of Kansas and the Delaware Nation were his strong supporters during the Civil War and to the end of his life.

Photo by Charlene Scott-Myers

The House Building in Lawrence, Kansas is the only building left standing 150 years after the Quantrill attack.

As a child growing up in Kentucky, Lincoln learned a lasting positive lesson about life and slavery from his parents, Thomas and Nancy Lincoln, who were abolitionists and members of a Baptist church opposed to slavery. So strong were their beliefs that the Lincoln family left Kentucky to move to the Free State of Indiana, where

Photos by Charlene Scott-Myers

runaway slaves were welcome.   Lincoln was elected president by northern and western voters as a Republican moderate against slavery.

"Kansas also gave Abraham Lincoln the strongest support proportionately (17,000 to 4,000 [votes] in that election," historian Kenneth S. Davis reported. [7]

Carl Sandburg recorded the words of Lincoln to his Kentucky friend, Joshua F. Speed, to whom Lincoln had written years in 1855:

"Our progress in degeneracy appears to me to be pretty rapid. As a Nation we began by declaring that 'all men are created equal, except Negroes.' When the know-nothings get control, it will read 'all men are created equal except Negroes and foreigners and Catholics.' When it comes to this, I shall prefer emigration to some country where they make no pretense of loving liberty." [8]

The Delaware sent a high percentage of its male population into the Civil War on behalf of the Union. A total of 170 of the 200 Delaware men in Kansas between the ages of eighteen and forty-five fought in the Civil War. More than seventy percent of the Delaware Nation's men, including John and Benjamin Journeycake, served for three years with the Union Army, the largest number of any community–white or Indian--in the country.

But it was not until 121 years later on November 11, 1986 that the first national memorial honoring American Indian veterans was dedicated at Arlington National Cemetery in Virginia. In all, some 618,000 men out of a total male population of approximately 6,000,000 lost their lives in the disastrous U.S. Civil War. The South paid a fearful price for its rebellion, Avery Craven noted in his book *Reconstruction: the Ending of the Civil War*:

"In all, the best estimates that historians have been able to make show that the Union deaths were over 360,000; Confederate deaths uncertain, but something over 258,000 – or a fourth of Confederacy men in arms.

"Losses of the South were proportionately much heavier than those of the North, both in killed and wounded in battle. Had the North lost as many in proportion as the South, it would have suffered more than a million casualties instead of 360,000." [9]

The state of Kansas did not abandon its strong anti-slavery position following the Civil War, but became the first state to ratify the 15th Amendment to the U.S. Constitution, granting African-Americans the long-awaited right to vote. Neither did the Delaware Nation ostracize African Americans, but rather, as Moravian missionary David Zeisberger reported:

"A few negroes are found among the Indians, having been either bought from the whites or secured as prisoners. These are looked upon as of their own kind and allowed full liberty. Indians and Negroes intermarry and their mulatto children are as much loved as children of pure Indian blood." [10]

President Washington emancipated his slaves, but President Jefferson set free only two of his hundreds of slaves during his lifetime: Robert Hemings in 1794 and his cook James Hemings in 1796. While Jefferson served as minister to France from 1785 to 1789, he and his daughter were accompanied by two slaves, a brother and sister from the Hemings family at Monticello. James accompanied Jefferson to France in 1784 for training as a French chef, and in 1787, Jefferson's ten-year-old daughter Polly traveled to France via London in the care of Jefferson's 14-year-old fair-skinned slave Sally Hemings. Sally was the daughter of a white slave-owner, John Wayles, and the black slave Betty Hemings. Sally thus was a half-sister of Jefferson's late wife Martha, the white daughter of Wayles.

In Paris, Jefferson paid for Sally and her brother James to have a French tutor, and purchased expensive clothing for Sally to accompany Martha to Parisian soirées. Sally remained in France for 26 months, and some historians believe that Jefferson began a long-term relationship with her while in Paris. In 1787, Jefferson was re-elected to a second three-year term as minister to France, but he left the country in October, 1789 following the storming of the Bastille on June 14. And although they could have achieved their freedom by remaining in France, James and Sally Hemings chose to return with Jefferson to the United States.

Jefferson freed five additional enslaved men upon his death, including Madison and Eston Hemings, whom many historians believe were the two youngest of his four children with Sally Hemings. Madison and Eston were not set free until they were twenty-one. Another slave freed was Joe Fossett, but his wife and their eight children were sold to different slave owners in an auction after Jefferson's death. Six months after Jefferson died, 130 Monticello slaves--men, women, and children--were auctioned off to help pay Jefferson's debts.

When we visited Jefferson's stately house Monticello near Charlottesville, Virginia, a guide explained that Jefferson's grand home had no working kitchen. Slaves prepared the food for their master in a smaller, sweltering cook's house under the watchful eye of a guard. Then in order that no slave would be able to snatch a "nibble" of food guards accompanied the slaves as they carried huge steaming platters and bowls of food to the "big house."

But how were Jefferson's slaves treated? Jefferson's slaves, for the most part, fared better than most slaves in Southern states. But they were treated as slaves. They were not free.

1. Lee, *Deadly Days in Kansas*, p.15.

2. Cordley, *Lawrence Massacre*, pp. 3, 13.

3. Harris, *Alias Charley Hart*, pp. 77, 78.

4. Ibid, pp. 78, 79.

5. Griekspoor and Tanner, *Kansas, Prairie Spirit,* p. 63.

6. Castel, *Civil War Kansas*, p. 136.

7. Davis, *Kansas, History*, p. 86.

8. Sandburg, *Abraham Lincoln*, pp. 13, 14.

9. Craven, *Reconstruction*, pp. 43, 44.

10. Zeisberger, *History of Northern American Indians*, p. 27.

49

Delaware Removal from Kansas

After living less than four decades in what was promised by treaty to be their "forever home" of Kansas, the Delaware Nation and other tribes would be removed to yet another location, Indian Territory (Oklahoma), which finally would become their true "forever home."

"Beginning in 1854, the emigrant tribes started giving up portions of their lands in Kansas," Thomas Isern and Raymond Wilson wrote in their book *Kansas Land*.

"Among the first tribes to sign treaties were the Otoe and Missouri, Delaware, Iowa, Sac and Fox, and Kickapoo. The timberlands of the Delaware Indians attracted the attention of lumbermen. Railroad builders were interested in the lands held by the Delaware, Potawatomi, Osage, and Cherokee Indians." [1]

The first encroachment noticed by the Indians was "the threat to the unspoiled hunting ground on the Kansas tributaries," historian Angie Debo pointed out.

"When the Southern Cheyennes and Arapahos returned from the North in the fall of 1865, they found a new stage line in operation on the Smoky Hill route to Denver – a precursor, if they had known it, of the coming of the railroad. Still the whole area remained at peace through 1866." [2]

General William Sherman

The Civil War ended in 1865. General William Sherman—with no battles left to win, no land to scorch, and no cities to burn--conducted a personal inspection of Kansas during the summer of 1866, concluding:

"God knows when, and I do not see how, we can make a decent excuse for an Indian war." [3]

It was the railroads that came up with what they thought was a good excuse for removing the Indians. They needed land and timber – two precious commodities owned by the Delaware, who at first were not adverse to the idea of trains running through their lands.

"It was their belief that a railroad passing through the reservation would enhance the value of their land," Ruby Cranor wrote, "but they were duped, for the railroad could not pay off when they were supposed to, and the Indians had to take their pay in bonds or trust funds which were invested back in the railroad companies, with the result that the Indians made massive financial contributions to the very corporations that were contributing to their destruction." [4]

Commissioner George Manypenny, who actually tried to protect Kansas tribal interests in Washington, D.C., returned instead to Indian country with instructions to negotiate treaties that would shrink the size of nine reservations. The Delaware treaty that Manypenny negotiated in 1854 was disastrous for not only the Delaware, but for all the other Indian tribes in Kansas.

Commissioner Manypenny termed the treaty "the rape of the Delaware trust lands," and Delaware agent Benjamin F. Robinson asked the Indian Office: "Are treaties merely made for fun, and hence to be looked on as maneuvers played off for the benefit of a hungry crowd of land speculators?"

Authors Miner and Unrau called the hungry crowd "a combination of town speculators from Missouri and military officers from nearby Fort Leavenworth who planned the Leavenworth town site while the Delaware treaty awaited ratification…. On July 14, three days before the Delaware treaty was proclaimed, the promoters brazenly informed the local land office that they were 'laying out a town.'" [5]

Government officials eventually would inform the Delaware that it was "in their best interests to be removed," so that a large portion of their property (which happened to be trespassed by the Union Pacific Railroad and the Delaware Lumber Company) would be available for more tracks and trains.

"The superintendent of the agency at Fort Leavenworth wrote about this time (July, 1866): 'The passing of the Union Pacific Railroad through the Delawares' diminished reserve has been a source of grievous annoyance and damage to the Delawares, as has also an organization styled the Delaware Lumber Company,'" Baptist minister S. H. Mitchell reported.

"This seems to have been a company formed to help themselves to the Delawares' timber and sell it to the railway company," Mitchell wryly observed. [6]

Also writing about the superb Delaware land in the Kansas area, Weslager pointed out that "Not only was the soil watered by the rivers rich and black, but there were hundreds of acres of virgin trees, the reservation containing some of the best timbered land in Kansas." [7]

A powerful railroad lobby was making its influence known in Washington, DC, since the railroads needed timber, which was plentiful on the Delaware reserve.

By 1854, there were only 1,132 Delaware living among the eastern Kansas tribes, according to an Office of Indian Affairs "statement of number of Indians in Kanzas [sic] and Nebraska." The Osage boasted a population in Kansas of 5,000, five times that of the Delaware. The Pottawatomie had more than 4,000 members, the Sac & Fox of the Mississippi, 2,000, the Kansa more than 1,000, the Shawnee nearly 1,000, the Wyandot only 550, and the Kickapoo not quite 500. The Iowa, Miami, Ottawa, Peoria and Kaskaskia, Sac & Fox of Missouri, Wea and Piankeshaw were all lesser in number than the Kickapoo. The Chippewa (Swan Creek and Black River) were down to the pitiful number of thirty.

The majority of four of those tribes--the Pottawatomie, the Sac and Fox, the Iowa, and the Kickapoo--would remain in Kansas, refusing to move to Indian Territory. A few Delaware chose U.S. citizenship to continue to live in Kansas, relinquishing their tribal membership.

The Delaware and Shawnee met at a Council of Indian Tribes from late March until April 4 of 1854, and reluctantly decided to participate in land cession treaties. They did not want another war that they surely would lose. A series of treaties followed between 1854 and 1866, requiring the Delaware to sell portions of their Kansas reservation piece by piece. On April 11, 1854, two Indian delegations that included nine Delaware and eight to ten Shawnee left Kansas City, Missouri aboard the *Polar Star* on their way to Washington, D.C. They had been empowered to make land cession treaties.

On May 6, 1854, the Delaware men signed a treaty at Washington, ceding to the United States all of their lands lying north of the Kansas River, except for a tract of about 300,000 acres and two of thirty-nine sections previously sold to the Wyandotte.

The Delaware who signed the treaty to relinquish the majority of their lands were: Sarcoxey, Ne-con-he-cond, Kock-ka-to-wha, Qua-cor-now-ha (James Segondyne), Que-sha-to-wha (John Ketchum), Pondoxy (George Bullet), Kock-kock-quas (James Ketchum), Ne-sha-pa-na-cumin (Charles Journeycake) and Ah-lah-a-chick (James Conner). Among the witnesses were Thomas Johnson, Indian agent Benjamin F. Robinson, and interpreter Henry Tiblow.

The United States "twisted the arms" of the Delaware to offer the majority of the Kansas

Delaware reserve--which eventually amounted to more than 550,000 acres--for public sale on May 6. The United States sold the lands privately, rather than at public auction, resulting in a fraud for the Delaware of some $1.3 million dollars. The tribe also was swindled out of a strip of one million acres used for hunting; the strip sold for only $10,000. A century later in 1854, the Indian Claims Commission would announce that the same land actually had been worth sixty times that amount.

Charles Journeycake, Delaware chief

"There can be no question that many of the Delawares were perplexed about why they had to move, and probably even the tribal leaders did not fully understand the true reasons," Weslager wrote in *The Delaware Indian Westward Migration.*

"In retrospect, the picture is very clear why the Department of the Interior was so insistent upon relocating the Indians. Political pressures from the Midwest were heavy on Congress to rid Kansas of the Indians, and make the territory, which had become a state in 1861, available for settlement by pioneer white families.

"Railroad interests … were applying additional pressure to take over the Indian lands so that rail lines could be constructed to serve the Midwest and be extended to the west coast, where the population of California was burgeoning." [8]

The Delaware lost their Kansas lands, homes, crops, and livelihoods, and for many of them their lives. Some 200 tribal members perished during their march into the Indian Territory that would become Oklahoma, a small number compared to the Cherokee deaths of more than 4,000 on the Trail of Tears. But the Delaware Tribe was much smaller than the Cherokee, and a loss of 200 people was a great tragedy to them.

The Shawnee, "little brothers" or "cousins" of the Delaware, would fare no better. In their treaty concluded May 10, 1854 in Washington, the tribe ceded to the United States all of their estimated 1.5 million-acre reserve in the land that would be designated "Kansas Territory" later in May. (A 200,000-acre tract was receded to the Shawnee, including grants of land made to the missions of Methodists, Friends, and the American Baptist Missionary Union.) Among the eight Shawnee who signed the treaty were George Blue Jacket and Henry Blue Jacket, and among the witnesses was Charles Blue Jacket, interpreter (all descendants of Buckongahelas' old friend, Chief Blue Jacket).

Controversial Kansas-Nebraska Act

On May 25, 1854, the U.S. Senate met to consider the controversial Kansas-Nebraska Act that created the territories of Kansas and Nebraska and opened those areas to land settlement by whites, who would be able to decide for themselves whether or not they would allow slavery. At 1:15 a.m. on May 26, the bill passed and a salute of 100 guns burst from Capitol Hill. A heady night of intoxication followed for pro-slavery senators--and fierce anger from their opponents, who coalesced nationally into the anti-slavery Republican Party. The bill was blamed by many for hastening the onset of the Civil War, a war that would claim more than 600,000 lives between 1861 and 1865.

Stephen A. Douglas, seeking re-election to the Senate, defended his bill, as well as his position on the slavery-expansion issue. His opponent was the Republican Abraham Lincoln, who would defeat Douglas in the 1860 presidential election. Douglas also wooed Mary Todd before she became Mrs. Abraham Lincoln.

The sorrow of having to once again pull up his people's roots from Kansas must have broken the spirit of Delaware Chief Solomon Joneycake, who was "old" at the young age of sixty-five. Like Moses, he would not live to cross over into still another "Promised Land." Many Ohio and Kansas streams carried Solomon's name by the time of his death in 1855.

Stephen A. Douglas

In 1857, the territorial governor of Kansas, Robert J. Walker, spoke out in favor of the Indians' removal, claiming: "The Indian treaties will constitute no obstacle, any more than precisely similar treaties did in Kansas." William H. Seward echoed Walker's sentiments in the presidential campaign of 1860, in which he publicly insisted that "Indian Territory south of Kansas must be vacated by the Indians."

In 1858, the list of Delaware Indian pupils attending a Baptist Mission School in Kansas Territory included the names of Alex, Matilda, Polly, and Lucy Jane Journeycake. Another later list would display the names of Joseph, Isaac N., Adeline and Emeline (twins), Anna, Cora, and Emma

Journeycake—all descendants of the family of Chiefs Solomon and Buckongahelas Journeycake.

Statehood for Kansas was official January 29, 1861 (the same year that Abraham Lincoln was inaugurated as the first bearded president of the United States. The Homestead Act of 1862 opened more than 600 million acres of land for settlement, spurring the largest migration of Americans across the land. The Civil War would postpone the inevitable pain of relocating from Kansas to Oklahoma for the Delaware, who took the side of the Union in 1862. Government reports in 1866 stated that the Delaware harvested on their Kansas lands 72,000 bushels of grain and 13,000 bushels of potatoes. The Delaware also owned 5,000 head of cattle.

In July of 1866--only thirty-six years after the first Delaware arrived in Kansas and one year after the Civil War's end--Sally Journeycake, her son Charles, his wife, Jane, and family, and other Indians were notified they would be ousted from their "permanent" Delaware Reservation in Kansas. The government would require them to sell the remainder of their Kansas lands for $2.50 an acre. The Delaware property then would become a new source for real estate taxes, as three-fourths of Wyandotte County was composed of Indian lands not subject to taxation.

The Census of the Delaware tribe was compiled in August, 1866 with 985 Delawares agreeing to move to the Cherokee nation. Each head of family was paid for improvements on his Kansas land, and some men recovered losses for stolen livestock and timber. In June of 1868 these Delawares began drawing payments for their Kansas lands, writer Ruby Cranor reported.

Jane Journeycake, wife of Charles

"The Delawares made ready for another move, this time to the northwestern part of the Cherokee Nation in what is now Washington and Nowata counties," Cranor said.

Chief Sarcoxie of the Turtle Clan and twenty-five to thirty Delaware families began their journey in June. "Old Sarcoxie, now eighty-three years old, drove the lead team. He had a wife and his grandson in his wagon," Cranor added

Several people died along the way, including a nineteen-year-old boy whom the Osage robbed, scalped and stripped of his clothes. The murder "put a terrible fear in our little band for the safety of our lives," Katy Whiteturkey Day, a granddaughter of Chief Sarcoxie, wrote many years after the trip.

"This boy was buried near the camp where we were stationed at the forks of the Caney River," Cranor reported. "He was the first person buried in this cemetery, and it is the oldest cemetery in Washington County. It is located north-west of Bartlesville." [9]

Fewer than half a dozen of Oklahoma's tribes are indigenous, according to Rennard Strickland, author of *Indians in Oklahoma*. In 1867 and 1868, the Delaware and 10,000 Kickapoo, Shawnee, Sacs and Fox, Potawatomi, Ottawa, Wyandotte, Miami, and even the two naïve tribes, the Kansa and Osage, were removed from Kansas to Indian Territory. Many had died defending their property from intruders in Kansas.

"In retrospect it seems clear that the end of Indian Kansas and the obliteration of diverse Indian cultures were virtually assured the moment a group of fumbling, short-sighted politicians opened the door to white settlement in 1854…." writers Miner and Unrau observed. [10]

Michael Wallis, author of *Oil Man*, the story of Oklahoma Delaware oil tycoons, explained it succinctly: "It all boiled down to a single question—land. The Indians had it and the whites wanted it." [11]

1. Isern and Wilson, *Kansas Land*, p. 56.

2. Debo, *History of the Indians*, p. 215.

3. Ibid.

4. Cranor, *Kik Tha We Nund*, p. 119.

5. Miner and Unrau, *End of Indian Kansas*, pp. 12-14.

6. Mitchell, *Indian Chief Journeycake*, p. 50.

7. Weslager, *Delaware Indians*, p. 374.

8. Weslager, *Delaware Westward Migration*, p. 228.

9. Cranor, *Kik Tha We Nund*, p. 120.

10. Miner and Unrau, *End of Indian Kansas*, p. 3.

11. Wallis, *Oil Man*, p. 51.

50

Journeycakes in Kansas and Oklahoma

Resentment against the Journeycake family, Charles and Isaac Journeycake in particular, probably began among some traditional Delaware tribal members when Charles and his brother Isaac were children.

Charles was born in 1817 on the Upper Sandusky in Ohio (his cousin, Watomika, who would become a Roman Catholic priest, was born six years later.) The year that Charles was born, the Greenville treaty of 1795 signed by Charles' grandfather, Buckongahelas, ceded to the United States a great amount of land that the Delaware Indians claimed in Ohio and portions of Indiana, Michigan, and Illinois.

"Forced on the tribes by General ["Mad"] Anthony, the treaty extinguished the Indians' title to almost two-thirds of the land of present-day Ohio, part of Indiana, and the sites of what became Detroit, Chicago, and other important Midwestern cities," Alvin M. Josephy, Jr. explained in his book *500 Nations*. [1]

A year later, on October 3, 1818, the Delaware living on the White River in Indiana, led by Buckongahelas, were forced to sign a treaty ceding *all the lands* the Indians occupied in Indiana for a new home in the west.

At the age of sixteen, Charles became the first American Indian baptized a Protestant in Kansas in 1833. It had been the deep religious beliefs of his mother, Sally Journeycake, that brought about the resumption of Christian missions among the Delaware on their Kansas reservation in 1829, forty-seven years after the slaughter at Gnadenhutten separated the Delaware from all white clergy. Sally had converted to Christianity in 1827, and was the only Christian believer among the Delaware in Kansas until her son's baptism. She and her husband, Solomon, were baptized in 1841.

Charles was ordained a Baptist minister in Indian Territory in 1872. He baptized more than 100 Delaware in a creek near his church the first year in Indian Territory, and at the end of three years, the church had 188 members. Charles translated and compiled a hymn-book in Delaware for his people.

Charles also was resented because he had adopted the white men's ways, as well as their religion. Not only did he talk like a white man, Charles also dressed like a white man, wearing suits and ties and a beard like his priest cousin Watomika (Father James Bouchard). Once settled into Indian Territory, Charles drove a horse and buggy, lived in a white frame house, and owned herds of horses and cattle. He was a well-to-do man compared to many Delaware men, and like most well off men, he was envied by others.

"Charles Journey-cake ... took the white man's road, but not always willingly and always

Copyright 1895 by Judson Press, used by permission of Judson Press
The home of Charles Journeycake in Oklahoma.

with a searing knowledge of what had been inflicted upon his people," writers Bruce Johansen and Donald Grinde Jr. observed.

"He learned English at a young age, and moved between the two worlds." [2]

Some Delaware disliked the fact that Charles and Isaac studied English as children from their mixed-blood mother Sally (French and Indian), whose

mother was the famous Indian captive Mary Castleman of Virginia and whose grandmother on her dad's side was of the Delaware Wolf Clan. The Journeycake boys could write English correctly, read it easily, and speak it eloquently. This would cause suspicion as to the content and meaning of treaties that Charles and Isaac later would read and interpret, which other Delaware could not do.

Charles also was disdained

This marker was placed near the home of Charles Journeycake by his granddaughter, Roberta Campbell Lawson, and her brother, Herbert Lockhart Campbell in 1935. The marker states that Charles was the last chief of the Delaware, which is not true. *Photo by Carla Korthase*

because he didn't believe in gambling, was a staunch opponent of liquor, and wouldn't lend his fine horses for horse racing to men who drank.

"This young man [Charles] was a great lover of horse racing and hunting….," author Roark reported. "It was not an unusual thing for him to own several fast horses and to enter them in races both with the whites and Indians, but he always refused to gamble on the race or to ride in a race on which he knew wagers had been placed. He also refused to lend his horses to others who would gamble on them." [3]

It was not only the Delaware who were crazy about racing horses. Horse racing and gambling had been the most popular sports in the Five Civilized Tribes and other tribes for centuries. Despite the rancor against him, Charles was considered a moderate Delaware. In his book, *The Delaware Indians, a History*," Weslager talked about the difference between moderates and traditionalists in the Delaware Tribe.

"Over the years, two schools of thought had been developing: first, there were the traditionalists, who could not accept many of the white institutions, and who fought to preserve certain elements of the Indian way of life. These adherents refused to send their children to school or to the Christian missions, and they continued to observe their ancient religion." [4]

Then there were the moderates "who sent their children to mission schools and attended Christian churches with their families. Many of them were bilingual, speaking both English and Delaware, and some had succeeded to read and write. They looked on the Big House Ceremony and other feasts and dances as unchristian, and some Christian converts overtly opposed these ceremonies as pagan expressions from a past that was best forgotten.

"The most outspoken family among the modernists was the Journeycakes, whose most influential members were Charles Journeycake, his daughters, his brother Isaac, and Robert I. E. Journeycake, who was elected clerk of the Council," Weslager wrote. [5]

Charles and eight other Delaware didn't make many friends when on May 6, 1854 they signed the grievous treaty that ceded back to the United States their lands lying north of the Kansas River, lands that would be opened to white settlement. This was Charles' first trip to Washington. He was thirty-seven years old. Later treaties caused even more controversy for Charles.

The resentment against Charles further escalated among traditional Delaware when he organized the first Baptist church in Northeast Indian Territory (one of his daughters was chorister and organist). He translated the four gospels of scripture into Delaware and completed a hymnal in the Delaware tongue. He baptized 266 people--nearly all members of the Delaware tribe--during the first ten years of his ministry.

Frank M. Overlees, who married one of Charles' daughters, Carrie V. Armstrong, recalled a visit with the old chief: "Chief Journeycake was not an educated man, but he had a very brilliant mind and had a large library in his home near Coody's Bluff. One time I was enroute to Alluwe and stopped to talk with granddad.

"He was building an addition on his house and barn, and I asked him why he was making these additions at his age. He was very slow spoken and after considering my remark, he looked straight at me and said, 'Son, a man should work like he is going to live forever, and pray like he is going to die tomorrow.'" [6]

Charles was living up to one of his favorite sayings, but he was making enemies along the way. Even some Delaware criticized him (and still do) because he owned horses and cattle on a small scale, but years after his death some Indians owned huge herds.

"A number of adopted trial citizens and some full-bloods fully recovered from the effects of wholesale theft of Indian cattle by soldiers and traders during the Civil War and built large herds managed by Indian cowboys," wrote Jimmy M. Skaggs in his book *Ranch and Range in Oklahoma.*

"By 1885 C. W. Turner had some 5,000 head near Muskogee, Quanah Parker of the Comanches maintained a herd of 500, and herds of 1,000 roaming at will on the tribal common lands were familiar enough that elaborate Indian bank books were necessary to keep track of ownership. The Union agent reported in 1878 that 55,000 members of the Five Tribes had some stock, even if it was only a few cattle for household use." [7]

Charles was prosperous, but also generous with his money. As Harry M. Roark notes in his biography of Charles, "Since the Delawares had no missionary among them to administer the ordinances, it became necessary for Mr. Journeycake to submit to being ordained in order to carry on the full work of the church.

"This little church, during its first year, built a good frame church building, which cost about fifteen hundred dollars. Mr. Journeycake furnished practically all the money for the new building." [8]

Perhaps the greatest resentment against Charles resulted from his close relationship with the Rev. John G. Pratt, a Baptist missionary who was appointed as Indian agent for the Delaware tribe. Many traditional Delaware believed--and still believe--that Chief Charles Journeycake was unduly influenced by his friend of thirty years.

According to historian Weslager, the American Baptist Missionary Union had sponsored "an extremely successful mission which owed its origin to the prestige of the Reverend Isaac McCoy, who was held in high regard by the Delaware chiefs.

Rev. John G. Pratt

"As far back as 1818, when McCoy traveled from one Indian town to another along the White River in Indiana, several chiefs, despite the prevailing anti-Christian sentiment, promised him that when the tribe was permanently settled west of the Mississippi, they would allow him to build a school to teach their youth." [9]

Pratt, who first came to the Shawnee Mission in Kansas as a printer, was the man assigned to lead the Delaware mission, assisted by his wife Olivia. The Delaware Indian Agent Fielding Johnson also hired Pratt as a "practical physician" for $1,000 dollars a year, despite the fact that Pratt had no formal medical training. Later, Pratt would assume leadership of the Stockbridge Baptist Mission near Wadsworth, Kansas.

The Pratt-Journeycake relationship was further strengthened by the fact that Pratt's son, Lucius Bolles Pratt, married one of Charles Journeycake's daughters, Nannie, on March 2, 1860 at the Delaware Baptist Mission. Only five years later, Nannie was widowed at the age of twenty-four on September 7, 1865. She took as her second husband a Civil War Veteran who grew up in Kansas, Colonel Jacob A. Bartles, son of Joseph Bartles, who established New York City's first telegraph wire. Jacob moved to Silver Lake in Indian Territory in 1873, and in 1875 settled on the banks of the Caney River, where he bought a corn gristmill. The town of Bartlesville, Oklahoma was named for him.

By 1868, American Indians of all tribes in North America had signed nearly 400 treaties that were broken by the United States. The Kiowa, Comanche, Arapaho, Apache, and Cheyenne ceded their Kansas lands to the federal government at the Medicine Lodge Treaty in 1867 and "retired" to Oklahoma Territory. The Osage who lived in the Pratt County area of Kansas ceded their lands in 1871, also taking their "retirement" in rough, unwanted terrain in Oklahoma Territory.

"I remember hearing about a family related to us that was murdered, except for one child who was spending the night at a friend's house," said Tallchief, who gained worldwide fame by dancing Stravinsky's "Firebird." "Insurance scams were generally the way it happened, and the man who was behind those murders had come around trying to sell insurance to my grandmother, Eliza Tallchief. She sent him away because she didn't get involved with people like that." [10]

Years later, the Osage had their revenge. They became oil wealthy when thick black oil oozed from their rocky, inhospitable land. Unscrupulous white men married into the rich Osage families in the 1920s to gain access to their wives' head rights or oil royalties paid to each member of the Osage family. Several white husbands poisoned or shot to death their wives. A cousin of famed Oklahoma ballerina Maria Tallchief lost several relatives when their home was firebombed, killing all of the family members inside.

1. Weslager, *Delaware Indians*, p. 419

2. Ibid, 420.

3. Roark, *Charles Journeycake*, 77.

4. Weslager, *Delaware Indians*, pp. 384, 385.

5. Josephy, Jr. 500 Nations, p. 302

6. Johansen and Grinde, Jr. *Encyclopedia of Native American Biography*, p. 191.

7. Skaggs, *Jimmy M., Ranch and Range in Oklahoma*, p. 18.

8. Roark, *Charles Journeycake*, pp. 70, 71.

9. Ibid, pp. 26, 27.

10. Livingston, *American Indian Ballerinas*, p. 29, 30.

**Oklahoma's world famous
Maria Tallchief**

51

Broken Promises, Broken Dreams

The State of Kansas was being filled by "an energetic population who appreciate good land; and as the Indian reservations were selected as being the best in the State, but one result can be expected to follow," S. H. Mitchell reported the excuse used in an 1866 Commission of Indian Affairs report as to why the Delaware had to vacate their property. [1]

The Delaware Nation had cultivated and cherished, and yes, also had appreciated their Kansas lands, but now they would be pressured to give them up and remove once again to a strange land.

"In 1806, it is said, the government reports that the Delawares, still on their Kansas lands, in spite of depletion by army service and other causes of weakening and discouragement, 'raised seventy-two thousand bushels of grain, thirteen thousand bushels of potatoes, and owned five thousand head of cattle,'" Mitchell noted. [2]

Instead of receiving their own reservation as promised in 1866, a new agreement in 1867 between the Delaware and Cherokee, approved by the U.S. government, would force the Delaware Nation onto the Cherokee Reservation in Indian Territory (later the state of Oklahoma). The service, injuries, and deaths of Delaware soldiers during the Civil War were forgotten in the rush by railroad promoters and settlers to claim Delaware Kansas lands. Each Delaware man, woman, and child would purchase 160 acres of Cherokee land, and the United States promised the Delaware twenty-three sections of land to compensate for prior treaty violations.

The new treaty reaffirmed the Delaware tribe's independent status. The Delaware refused to give up their tribal sovereignty or identity to become Cherokee –or to allow Delaware children born in the future to be considered Cherokee at birth. The Delaware would purchase lands from within the Cherokee Nation only if they could maintain their own Delaware organization.

The Cherokee had been instructed to reach a favorable agreement with the Delaware, who had been loyal to the federal government during the Civil War (the Cherokee fought with the Confederates). The Delaware rejected the earlier Cherokee proposal to swallow the Delaware into their nation.

Delaware who signed the 1867 agreement that forced the tribe onto the Cherokee Reservation in Indian Territory included Isaac and Charles Journeycake, seated second and third from right.

Photo courtesy of the Bartlesville Area History Museum.

The Delaware believed that the new treaty recognized the continued existence of the Delaware tribe as a sovereign entity residing on lands owned in common with the Cherokee Nation, a nearly identical arrangement as one negotiated by the United States in 1855 for the Chickasaw residing on Choctaw lands. But later, the Cherokee would claim that the treaty only applied to the *original* Delaware who moved into Cherokee lands, not to their descendants.

With both the Delaware and Cherokee Treaties finally completed, the Delaware began to remove from their homes in Kansas Territory to their new property in the Cherokee Nation. The Cherokee had lived in the lush Georgia and North Carolina lands prior to the 1838 Trail of Tears that cost the lives of 4,000 Cherokee, on the trail and 2,000 more after they arrived, but they ended up with only fourteen counties in northeast Oklahoma, centered at the town of Tahlequah.

Throughout northern Indian Territory, "[Colonel Jacob] Bartles' village served as a mecca for early settlers who came to trade with the Osage, Delawares, and Cherokees," explained Michael Wallis in his book *Oil Man, the Story of Frank Phillips and the Birth of Phillips Petroleum.*

"One of Bartles' clerks, George Keeler—the young trader whose horse didn't like the taste of oil—watched his employer become a prosperous businessman…. He [Keeler] befriended William Johnstone, a young transplanted Canadian, who also worked for Bartles. Johnstone happened to be

The Nellie Johnstone No. 1 well was named for the Delaware Indian woman who owned the land on which oil was discovered. *Photo courtesy of the Bartlesville Area History Museum.*

married to Bartles' niece, the granddaughter of Chief [Charles] Journeycake.

"Aware that more people were settling on the south bank of the Caney, and much to Bartles' chagrin, Johnstone and Keeler quit their jobs in 1884, and the pair opened a competing store of their own directly across the river from Bartles. Each store tried to outdo the other, and a vigorous rivalry developed." [3]

Keeler's horse may have disliked oil, but its discovery in the area excited both Johnstone and Keeler. They joined Frank Overlees, who married Carrie V. Armstrong, granddaughter of Charles Journeycake, in obtaining a lease for drilling on fifteen square miles of Cherokee territory. On April 15, 1897 they struck oil, Oklahoma's first commercial oil well. They named it the Nellie Johnstone No. 1 for Johnstone's young daughter, on whose land allotment the drilling was successful.

My Delaware friend Jane Johnstone of Houston is a descendant of Charles Journeycake through his oldest daughter, Mary Elizabeth Armstrong, whose daughter Lillie Ann Armstrong on Jan. 12, 1982 married William Johnstone, Jane's great-grandfather.

William Johnstone also established the Bartlesville National Bank, serving as its president until May, 1908. He, Bartles, and Keeler installed

Jane Johnstone

the first phone lines in all of Northern Oklahoma. Johnstone spent portions of two winters in Washington, DC, working for the admission of Oklahoma as a state. The city of Bartlesville was named for Bartles, although he moved four miles north and founded the town of Dewey. Bartles, Johnstone and Keeler were considered the founders of Bartlesville, which became the headquarters for the Delaware Tribe of Indians in northeastern Oklahoma.

The oil business would benefit future generations of Johnstones. His grandson, Leo Johnstone Jr., worked forty-two years for Phillips Petroleum Company in Bartlesville (where my Uncle Walter Korthase and his son Bob were employed throughout their lifetimes). Leo also was instrumental in developing the annual OK Mozart International Festival, serving as its first chairman of the board from 1987 to 1994. OK Mozart dedicated the 1995 Festival season in his honor.

Charles Journeycake certainly ranked among these fine men, but he encountered grumbling among the Delaware when he became chief of the Turtle Clan after the death of Chief Kockatowha in April of 1861 (but not principal chief of all three clans, as has been erroneously reported). The fact that Charles was chosen to replace the Turkey Clan Chief when his mother was related to the Wolf Clan was galling to some Delaware. Charles eventually would become the principal chief (not the *last* principal chief, also mistakenly stated in some books) of the Delaware Tribe of Indians in Oklahoma.

After Pratt was appointed a federal agent assigned to the Delaware Agency in 1864, he was able to approve and appoint new chiefs to the Delaware Council--but Pratt did not favor Delaware traditionalists in his appointments.

"The last three Delaware agents – Thomas Sykes, Fielding Johnson, and John Pratt--tended to favor the men who were leaders in the local Christian communities," author Brice Obermeyer noted in his book *Delaware Tribe in a Cherokee Nation*.[4]

Such favoritism, at times, did not follow the Delaware custom of tri-clan representation, Obermeyer pointed out.[5]

The U.S. government would recognize Charles as principal chief of the Lenape after the death of Chief Conner in 1872, although no election was held among the tribesmen. Many Delaware resented that deviation from centuries of tradition. They also were angry to learn that John Pratt was a stockholder of the Missouri River Railroad Company. The 1866 Delaware Treaty stipulated that the Delaware would sell the remaining portions of their Kansas reservation to that company.

Agent Pratt had vested interests in Delaware removal, Obermeyer concluded, standing to gain financially from the sale of Delaware lands to the Missouri River Railroad Company.

Assistant Chief Charles Journeycake of the Wolf Clan (representing the Turkey Clan) signed the controversial 1866 Treaty, as did Principal Chief John Conner, Assistant Chief Anderson, and Sarcoxie of the Turtle Clan. The treaty with the federal government promised the Delaware tribe *a reservation of its own* in Indian Territory in exchange for the sale of Kansas Delaware lands to the Missouri Pacific Railroad Company.

But the Senate refused to ratify the 1864 treaty, just months before the new Delaware Treaty of 1866 was drafted and ratified. Somewhere along the line, the promise of *"a reservation of its own"* was waylaid, and the U.S. government decided to remove the Delaware into Indian Territory and onto the Cherokee reservation, which would cause strife between the two tribes for generations to come.

1. Mitchell, *Indian Chief Journeycake*, p. 42.

2. Ibid, p. 50.

3. Wallis, *Oil Man*, p. 408.

4. Obermeyer, *Delaware Tribe in Cherokee Nation*, p. 80.

5. Ibid, p. 84.

52

Tributes to The Buck and Charles

Rev. Charles Journeycake

The Moravians wrote spitefully following the death of Buckongahelas that he was "an enemy of the word of God." But although Christianity was anathema to The Buck, he spoke in defense of those who were believers.

The Moravian criticism was untrue, considering the fact that Buckongahelas had risked his own life to prevent the deaths of the nearly 100 Moravian Christian Indians at their missions at Gnadenhutten and Salem.

Despite the horrors of Gnadenhutten, Buckongahelas had encouraged the Moravians to establish a mission near the Delaware on the White River in 1801 (which he later regretted). It was true that until he languished on his deathbed, The Buck repeatedly reiterated the need for his people "to keep the customs and ceremonies his ancestors had received from God,'" as author Richard White reported in his book *The Middle Ground.* [1]

Perhaps the Moravians would not have been so critical of the chief if they had read his words about them as recorded by historian Benjamin Thatcher: "'Whilst at Gnadenhutten …God had instructed all Christian people to *love* their enemies – and even to pray for them!' – These words, he [The Buck] said, 'were written in the large book that contained the words and commandments of God!

"'Now, how would it appear, were we to compel our friends, who love and pray for their enemies, to fight against them! – compel them to act contrary to what they believe to be right! – force them to do that which would incur the displeasure of the Great Spirit, and bring his wrath upon them!'" Buckongahelas said.

"'That it would be as wrong in him to compel the Christian Indians to quit praying and turn out to fight and kill people, as it would be in them to compel him to lay fighting aside, and turn to praying only!'"

Thatcher reported that Buckongahelas often heard that Christian Indians were slaves to their teachers, and what the teachers commanded them to do, they must do, however disagreeable.

"'Now, (said he) how can this be true, when every Indian is a free man, and can go where he pleases! – Can the teacher stop him from going away? – No! he cannot! – well! How can he then be made a slave by the teacher! – When we come here among our friends, we see how much they love their teachers. – This looks well!"

To the Christian Delaware, Buckongahelas advised: "Continue, my friends … in loving your teachers, and in doing all good things; and when your friends and relations come to see you, satisfy their hunger as you have done to us this day!" [2]

The hunger for freedom of religion – and every other kind of freedom – was in the hearts of the thirty tribes that moved within the borders of Indian Territory by 1890. But by 1900, "the Nations" no longer in reality was "Indian Territory." The population had grown to nearly 400,000, including six times as many whites as American Indians. The grandson of Buckongahelas, the Rev. Charles Journeycake, did not live to see the tribes, including his Delaware people, granted U.S. citizenship in 1901.

Ruby Cranor wrote in 1985 about Rev. Journeycake in her book *Caney Valley Ghost Towns*, saying "He was the founder of [the] Christian religion among the Delawares who moved here from Kansas in 1866. The [Journeycake Memorial Baptist] Dewey Church was named in honor of Chief Journeycake and a famed stained glass window of the Chief is still an integral part of this famous Church." [3] (The church no longer stands, and a Delaware man purchased the stained glass window.)

Following his death on January 3, 1894, Charles received accolades, especially for his strong faith and mostly from ministers with whom he had worked. Jane, his wife of fifty-six years, had died two years earlier at Al-lu-we, Indian Territory on January 13, 1892, one month before she would be seventy-two. Both were buried in the Armstrong Cemetery at Lightning Creek south of Nowata, Oklahoma (later moved to the Nowata Cemetery when the Oologah Dam was built).

The tributes to Charles were many. The inscription above his grave reads: "A kind and loving father and a friend to the needy; he died as he lived, a pure and upright man, after many years of faithful service in the ministry and as chief adviser for his people, the Delawares." The inscription on Jane's headstone reads, "None knew her but to love her."

The Rev. David Crosby, a former professor at Bacone College in Muskogee, Oklahoma, had these kind words to say about him: "In the home social circle, in the church, and in business, he was the same true man and friend. One cannot conceive, after knowing him, of his doing a mean, scarcely in any sense, a selfish act …. He was exceptionally kind to the poor. Never did the needy go from his door empty-handed.

"I shall never forget the warm receptions he gave me… .that straight, slim, nervous form…. that kind face and gentle voice. Father Journeycake was a great man, in real Christian manhood; great in his uplifting influence among his people. It is indeed sad to lose such--a loss to earth, and a gain to heaven." [4]

Another tribute came from the Rev. S. H. Mitchell, the Baptist minister who succeeded Rev. Journeycake in the fall of 1890 as pastor of the Baptist Church in Indian Territory and wrote his biography.

In 1895, Mitchell noted: "Mr. Journeycake was a man of uncommon deliberations, especially in conversation. You would ask him a question, and he would be so long before replying that you would be led to think he had given it no attention. This peculiarity was quickly learned, and also that it paid to wait." [5]

Harry M. Roark, another Charles biographer, pointed out that Charles "served his people during the most difficult years that the Indians have faced in America. He failed on many occasions to accomplish that which both he and his people desired. Yet the marvel is not that he failed at times, but rather that he succeeded as often as he did." [6]

Isaac Journeycake

Courtesy of the Bartlesville
Historical Society

Charles Baptizes His Brother's Murderer

Charles visited Washington, D.C. at least twenty-four times on behalf of his people, despite an assassination attempt on his life, an attack on his home, and the senseless killing of his brother, Isaac, who was murdered by the resentful Cherokee Calvin Coker. (A forgiving Charles would baptize Coker into the Christian faith years later.)

Charles would lead his family and others to Indian Territory (Oklahoma) in 1868, just as his father, Chief Solomon, brought followers into the Kansas area nearly forty years earlier, and Solomon's father, Chief Buckongahelas, led his persecuted band of Delaware to areas that would become Pennsylvania, Virginia, Ohio and Indiana for nearly a century.

Charles' wife, Jane, who gave birth to fourteen children, is believed to haunt the halls of Journeycake Hall, a building named for her at Bacone College in Muskogee, Oklahoma. My daughter and I visited the lovely campus where the Rev. Charles Journeycake had preached to students long ago. He was a staunch supporter of Bacone, contributing his money and time and sharing his great faith.

The stained glass windows of Bacone's Rose Chapel were the work of the distinguished artist Woody Crumbo, a Potawatomi who served as art director at Bacone. The college for Indian students was founded in 1880 and is still in operation today as an American Baptist College.

"What most of the Christians who sit in this Baptist church do not recognize is that Crumbo has executed a window in symbols and colors … as if the chapel belonged to the Native American Church," Rennard Strickland wrote in his book *Indians in Oklahoma*. [7]

Roberta Campbell Lawson, a granddaughter of Charles Journeycake, commissioned a large round stained glass window in his memory. When she met with Crumbo, who would design and create the window, she asked that it symbolize her grandfather's life, "emphasizing the importance of religion." She also desired the window to reflect another important feature of her grandfather's life: hunting.

"She wanted bows, guns, and quivers of arrows, and stressed that he always attached small wooden crosses to his hunting weapons in recognition of the providence of his Heavenly Father," Crumbo's biographer Robert Perry wrote. [8]

"He [Crumbo] started at the center of the circular window with a four-point Delaware Cross design, taken from the medicine pouch the Delawares gave to William Penn, which at the time was owned by Mrs. Lawson. The rose window glass was thirteen feet in diameter and radiated with circles of eagle feathers around the four cardinal points like a rainbow of gleaming jewels from which a huge bird, placed in the center, appears to resemble the cross. This leaded glass window depicts the American Indian expression of the Christian religion." [9]

Unfortunately, the Bacone College chapel burned to the ground in December, 1990, "one year almost to the minute after Woody Crumbo's death," Perry reported. [10]

My daughter and I visited Bacone College to see the chapel windows, unaware that the chapel had been destroyed years earlier. A color photo of the rose window that no longer exists may be seen on page 39 in Gilcrease Museum's book *Woody Crumbo.*

Crumbo, the sacred flute-maker of the Kiowa tribe, played the original Kiowa flute at Will Rogers' funeral in 1935. We sat across from Crumbo's son, Woody Max, at an Edwards County Historical Society dinner in 2006 in Kinsley, Kansas. With tears in his eyes, Woody Max told the audience how his famous dad, the last of eleven children, survived in a cave by eating rabbits and squirrels after his mother died and his father deserted him while Crumbo was a young boy. Despite the hardships and sorrow of his early life, Crumbo initiated a century of fine Indian art upon the American landscape.

Twenty years after the Delaware were ousted from their reserved lands promised to them forever, Charles reflected on the sorry experience of the Delaware in Kansas. In her book *Both Banks of the River*, author Argye M. Briggs quoted from his speech to the Indian Defense Association in April, 1886.

"My people ... have suffered much from white men," he said.

"We [the Delaware] have been broken up and moved six times. We have been despoiled of our property. We thought when we moved across the Missouri River and paid for our homes in Kansas we were safe, but in a few years, the white man wanted our country.

"We had good farms, built comfortable houses and big barns. We had schools for our children and churches where we listened to the same gospel the white man listens to. The white man came into our country from Missouri, and drove our cattle and horses away, and if our people followed them, they were killed--."

Despite the bitter wrongs the Delaware and other American Indians of all tribes had endured, Charles found consolation in one aspect of his relationship with whites.

"But we try to forget these things. But we would not forget that the white man brought us the blessed gospel of Christ, the Christian's hope. This more than pays for all that we have suffered." [11]

Rev. Mitchell, the Baptist minister and close friend of Rev. Charles Journeycake, gave him a compliment of all for his years of toil in the ministry, saying: "His whole heart was in his work." [12]

And Rev. J. S. Morrow of the American Baptist Mission Society, who had labored for more than thirty-seven years in Indian Territory, said of Charles, "Brother Journeycake's faith in God's providential care was very strong, yet childlike. A ... lady asked Brother Journeycake to relate some incidents of his life.

"Being a very modest man, he replied that there was nothing in his life worth relating, except God's goodness and grace." [13]

1. White, *Middle Ground*, p. 506.

2. Thatcher, *Indian Biography*, p. 176.

3. Cranor, *Caney Valley Ghost Towns*, p. 191.

4. Mitchell, *Indian Chief Journeycake*, p. 74.

5. Ibid, p. 67.

6. Roark, *Charles Journeycake,* p. 65.

7. Strickland, *Indians in Oklahoma*, p. xiii.

8. Perry, *Uprising! Woody Crumbo's Indian Art*, pp. 104, 105.

9. Ibid, p. 294.

10. Ibid, p. 259.

11. Briggs, *Both Banks of the River*, p. 331.

12. Mitchell, *Indian Chief Journeycake*, p.74.

13. Ibid, pp. 68, 69.

53

Delaware Move Back to Kansas

My great-grandfather Tom Greenstreet and his family were not part of the Cherokee Strip Land Run that opened seven million acres to 100,000 settlers on Sept. 16, 1893, but they journeyed into Indian Territory after that raucous event. (Three other land runs into Indian Territory were held previously in 1889, 1891, and 1892.) Thus the Greenstreets were not among the "Sooners" who snuck into the territory before the run and gave Oklahoma the name "Sooner State."

"I'd sooner be damned than be a damned Sooner," people said of the Okies, a chant later repeated at many University of Oklahoma football games.

"My father, Tom Greenstreet, refused to add his name to the government's Indian rolls because he thought the rolls were like welfare," my great-aunt Mary Ollive told me.

The Dawes Rolls were created by the Dawes Commission in 1893 and closed in 1907. They were to be the final rolls of members of the Five Civilized Tribes (Cherokee, Choctaw, Creek, Chickasaw, and Seminole). Delaware Indians adopted by the Cherokee tribe were enrolled as a separate group within the Cherokee.

Tom Greenstreet's mother, Mary T. Elliott (born May 20, 1817 in Perquimans, North Carolina), also did not apply for the rolls, although she lived until 1887 and died at age seventy in Henry County, Indiana. (Max Greenstreet, Tom's grandson, wrote "Indian" on Mary Elliott's photo more than fifty years ago.) Mary Elliott was the great-great-granddaughter of Buckongahelas.

Rosella Hightower was one of Oklahoma's five famed Indian ballerinas, the "Five Moons," who also included Maria and Marjorie Tallchief, Yvonne Chouteau, and Moscelyn, "Mouissa," Larkin, founder of the Tulsa Civic Ballet (with whom my daughter, Anne, studied ballet). Rosella told the story of her Choctaw great-grandmother, who in her old age called a family reunion attended by 400 relatives.

Rosella Hightower

317

The great-grandmother firmly announced to her family that she would not register for the Mississippi Choctaw rolls with the Office of Indian Affairs. No Hightower ever would be able to claim payments for land purchase agreements with the federal government, but such was the great respect for their Indian elders that none of her descendants or relatives objected to her decision.

Many Indians were threatened with imprisonment and coerced to join the Dawes Rolls, which were a means of further cheating Native-Americans by changing their communal land system to individual ownership. The large amount of land left over after the parceling of plots to Natives was made available for homesteading by whites.

American natives for thousands of years shared in common their sacred land, the vegetables they grew, the meat their hunters brought back from the forests, and fish retrieved from the sea. To parcel off and fence the land into plots was a concept foreign to Natives.

The Delaware were forced out of Kansas into Oklahoma, where they purchased 157,000 acres of land from the Cherokee. The Delaware would retain their tribe and nationality, and be enrolled as a separate group within the Cherokee Nation. The 41,785 people enrolled as Cherokees included only 197 Delaware.

Land was precious to American Indians. The indigenous peoples of America, the first Americans, they did not buy or sell land hundreds of years ago. As Chief Seattle in the Pacific Northwest said to Americans who sought to purchase his land, "How can you buy or sell the sky and the warmth of the land?... if we do not own the freshness of the breeze and the reflections of the water, how can you buy them?" [1]

Unfortunately, after the white man's arrival, if the American Indians wouldn't sell the land on which they and their ancestors had dwelled for centuries, it was either taken from them, or the Indians were forced to sell their lands.

But now, the Delaware Tribe of Indians has bought back a piece of the land lost on their Kansas reservation nearly 150 years ago. Some Delaware are returning to live in Kansas to a portion of the land between Leavenworth and Lawrence that was their reservation from 1829 to 1866.

After the Civil War, the federal government forced the Delaware tribe to sell more than two million acres in Kansas and move to Indian Territory (later the state of Oklahoma). U.S. officials had promised the Delaware "a reservation of your own" in 1866, but later had a change of heart. The Delaware were coerced into signing an agreement with the Cherokee to purchase a portion of Cherokee land in Indian Territory which the Delaware occupied in 1867.

One hundred and forty-six years later on July 10, 2013, the Delaware began its controversial move back to Kansas, having purchased some ninety-two acres from the Pine family in north Lawrence.

"This land was the allotment of Chief Anderson Sarcoxie," explained Annette Ketchum of Bartlesville, Oklahoma, a second term elected Delaware Tribal Council member. "Sarcoxie [the town] is close to the site where the last Big House Church in Kansas stood."

The Kansas land had been in the Pine family since it was purchased from the first Kansas governor in 1868, and the Pines

Annette Ketchum

were the only owners before the recent Delaware tribal purchase. Since July 2013, the land has been leased to a sod farm, which provides some revenue to the tribe.

"The soil is Class I, the best in the world, therefore using it for agriculture and horticulture is likely the best use," said Annette, wife of former Delaware Chief Dee Ketchum.

The tribe received a Heritage Grant in May, 2014 to study land use for the property. The Heritage Group, from Douglas County, provides funding to projects that might be of benefit to the City of Lawrence and Douglas County.

The move has been opposed by several members of the Delaware Tribe in Oklahoma, and also by several tribes in Kansas, including the Prairie Band Potawatomi Nation, the Kickapoo Tribe in Kansas, the Sac and Fox Nation of Missouri in Kansas and Nebraska, and the Iowa Tribe of Kansas and Nebraska. These tribes opposed the Delaware move because of the possibility of the Delaware opening a casino in the Lawrence area.

Delaware Chief Paula Pechonick, Annette Ketchum's sister, gave notice that "No tribe would ever take gaming off the table as a viable option as long as it is legally available. Gambling is nothing more than a means to an end, which provides our tribe the resources to strengthen our

**Delaware Chief Paula
Pechonick**

community and bring up the lives of our people."

"We hope a plan will materialize to everyone's liking," Annette said. "Approximately 30 acres of the land contains a 4,300 square foot house that is the tribal headquarters. The tribe has not officially moved to the location, but it has been used for meetings. The tribe hopes the City of Lawrence will annex the 30 acres so that the Delaware can perform the governmental functions in our former reservation, which the tribe was given in exchange for its reservation in Indiana.

"The tribe is returning to Kansas because it has never had a good relationship with the Cherokee Nation historically. After thirty years in and out of courts and losing our federal recognition and regaining it twice, we are finally in a position with the Cherokee administration whereby it is supportive of the move to Kansas, although this is an action that has no chartered course.

"Tribes simply have not returned to former reservations," the chief added. "There are many matters of jurisdiction, service area, funding, and grants that are in the process of being worked out. The Delaware Tribe will continue to have its presence in Bartlesville and Chelsea and provide for its membership. Because of the agreements with the Cherokee that are clearly and legally established, all services that a blood Cherokee enjoys, the Delaware also receive."

The Delaware Tribe has offices in Caney and Emporia, Kansas, and at the time of this book's publication was in the process of placing the land in Caney in trust with the U.S. government as off-reservation property. The Delaware Tribal Court and tribal businesses are located in Caney.

In 2000, the tribe considered building a casino complex in the same area, but those plans floundered after strong opposition from local residents.

1. Gallman, *I Dreamed of Africa*, pgs. 257, 258.

54

Never Again Any Partings

The constitution of "Sequoyah," the name the Indians wanted for their own proposed state, was approved in 1905, but the attempt to create an all-Indian state failed.

In 1906, Congress passed an act enabling Oklahoma and Indian Territory to become a single state. Oklahoma became the forty-sixth state admitted into the Union on Nov. 16, 1907, with a population of little more than five percent Indians. Indian Territory had ceased to exist. On June 2, 1924, American Indians became U.S. citizens by an Act of Congress.

"Fifty years ago [1900], it was said that there were not more than three full-blood Delaware living in the Cherokee Nation," Muriel H. Wright wrote in 1950 in *A Guide to the Indian Tribes of Oklahoma.*

"Today, tribal descendants are largely an admixture of Anglo-American and various Indian stocks with which they have been associated during the three hundred years since leaving the Atlantic Seaboard." [1]

By the time of the last Indian slaughter of 300 Lakota Sioux at Wounded Knee in 1890, many North American tribes were either extinct or rapidly vanishing, their population down from a high of several million in the pre-Columbian period to only 228,000. There are 562 federally recognized Indian tribes and Alaskan Natives in the United States today, but many tribes have only a few surviving members.

Oklahoma was named for the Choctaw words *okla* and *humma*, meaning "red people." Tulsa, the city in which I was born and reared, has a sixty-five-mile radius that constitutes the highest non-reservation concentration of Indians anywhere in the world. Oklahoma was the only state that did not oust its large Indian population, but state policies drove many of them to near famine and starvation.

"The Great Depression brought to the rest of the nation economic conditions that many Oklahoma Indians had known since statehood," author Rennard Strickland pointed out in his book *The Indians in Oklahoma.*

"In 1930 and 1931 the United States Senate held a series of hearings on reported famines among Oklahoma Indians. Ross Daniels testified that 'They are in bad condition. A lot of them do not have bread and grease. They are in the worst sort of condition. I believe they have died from the effects of improper nourishment.'"

Some Indians were starving because they had been stripped of their lands in Oklahoma, where they thought they would prosper.

"The process by which the Indian became landless is part of a dark chapter in white Oklahoma's relations with its Indian citizens," Strickland stated. "More than twenty murders were never solved….Millions of acres and other accumulated resources were wrested from the Indians. Of the 30 million allotted acres, more than 27 million passed from Indians to whites." [2]

American Indians live on 326 Indian reservations in this country, and many are among the poorest of the poor. According to the 2000 census, Indians still remain the *poorest* minority group in the United States, with one-third of Indian children living *below* the poverty line. Some children never have seen a doctor, and infant mortality rates are nearly three times the national average. Suicide rates on reservations today are three times the national average of thirteen per 100,000, and the rate is ten times the national average on South Dakota reservations.

ABC's *World News Tonight* former anchor Diane Sawyer visited the Oglala Lakota Sioux Indian Reservation in South Ridge for her Oct. 14, 2011 televised program *Hidden America's Children of the Plains*. She revealed that "Pine Ridge residents live amid poverty that rivals that of the Third World. Forty-seven percent of the population lives below the federal poverty level, sixty-five to eighty percent of the adults are unemployed, and rampant alcoholism and an obesity epidemic combine with under-funded schools to make it a rough place to grow up."

More than 200 years after the ghastly massacre of nearly 100 Delaware (including some sixty women and children) at Gnadenhutten, Ohio, I would be seated at a Wild Onion dinner in Dewey, Oklahoma with my daughter, 600 Delaware and several representatives of other tribes. (A beautiful painting of an Indian mother and daughter, *Picking Wild Onions on the Cimarron River*, by Oklahoma Pawnee artist Brummet Echohawk hangs in the St. John Siegfried Health Club in Tulsa, Oklahoma. Echohawk won three Bronze Stars and three Purple Hearts for his bravery in World War II.)

We all rose from our seats at the onion dinner, and with right hands upon our hearts respectfully recited the Pledge of Allegiance to the flag of the United States of America. Then came a swell of song as the Indians celebrated our national anthem, *The Star Spangled Banner*, written by Francis Scott Key in 1814 after the British bombardment of Fort McHenry. As I heard the stirring words of that patriotic piece, I remembered the terrible grief of the Delaware after the slaughter at Gnadenhutten, the deep sorrow of the Cherokees who lost 4,000 on the Trail of Tears, and the tragedies of other Indian nations. I thought what powers of forgiveness and forbearance these Natives possess and what a deep love they still have of our country!

Senator Ben Nighthorse Campbell of Colorado, whose relatives were murdered at Sand Creek, Colorado by white soldiers, and his spiritual advisor Austin Two Moons rode in the parade honoring the inauguration of Bill Clinton as president of the United States in January 1993. Austin Two Moons was the grandson of Cheyenne Chief Two Moons, who had fought alongside Campbell's great-grandfather Black Horse against Custer in the Battle of the Little Bighorn.

"You know, we have a right to this [American] flag," Austin Two Moons said during the parade. "When Custer came to drive us from our land, he carried it. My grandfather told me that at the Little Bighorn, Custer dropped the flag, and the Cheyenne picked it up. We have kept it ever since. Now the flag unites all of us in this great country...." [3]

In the end, Thomas Jefferson's words to the Delaware came to pass:

"You will unite yourselves with us, join in our great councils, and form one people with us, and we shall all be Americans. You will mix with us by marriage. Your blood will run in our veins and will spread with us over this great island." [4]

Approximately 600,000 Oklahomans are of American Indian descent. My siblings and I, our children and grandchildren, owe the gift of life to our American Indian ancestors. So do countless other Americans. My brothers and I also owe the gift of Catholicism to the example of our relatives with Indian blood in their veins.

Writing in his book *American & Catholic*, Clyde F. Crews noted:

"The official 1990 census calculated the number of Native Americans at 1.9 million. Of these, church sources report some 285,000 Catholic Indians in the United States." [5]

Today there are approximately 3.2 million American Indians and 2.3 million of them are Roman Catholics, representing about 3.5 percent of the nation's Catholics.

In a lecture to the Springfield Library Association in 1860, Abraham Lincoln described writing as "the great invention of the world…. enabling us to converse with the dead, the absent, and the unborn, at all distances of time and space."

It has been a great joy to "to converse with the dead, the absent, and the unborn, at all distances of time and space." American Indians often are hidden in the shadows of American life and history books and forgotten in the nation's daily life and conversations.

"There are reminders that exist yet of the times when New York City itself was completely Indian land," asserted the editors of *Native Universe, Voices of Indian America*, the inaugural book of the National Museum of the American Indian in Washington, D.C. on the Mall, which opened September 21, 2004.

"Native people have lived there for as many as 12,000 years," wrote Gerald McMaster and Clifford E. Trafzer. "George Gustav Heye, founder of New York's Museum of the American Indian which is now the Smithsonian's National Museum of the American Indian, collected samples of this ancient legacy.

"Some of the most striking examples are the carved stone faces found within the city limits. Known as the Living Solid Face, these sculptures are the embodiment of a forest guardian spirit pertaining to the Lenni Lenape or Delaware people. Some of these have been found in caves throughout the city, such as those in Staten Island.

"As millions of people bustle through their lives in the city, unconscious of the Lenape legacy, Living Solid Face still watches them." [6]

Millions of buffalo no longer roam North America; wigwams are wasted away; campfires extinguished. My Lenni Lenape ancestors sleep in their graves, but they are not forgotten. The Delaware Tribe of Indians today has approximately 10,500 members who still hold dear the memory of those who came before them.

Russell H. Booth, Jr. said it best. In the epilogue of his book, *The Tuscarawas Valley in Indian Days, 1750-1797*, he wrote: "By 1797, most of the Delawares had long since left the valley and were living in northwestern Ohio or Indiana. Eventually they would be pushed farther west and finally end up on reservations in Kansas and Oklahoma. Some went to Canada....

"They're all gone now, but the story of what they did in the valley is preserved in these journals. Through their writings we have been able to see the valley as they saw it, and hear the people speak as they heard them speak. We have come to know them." [7]

My family has come to know and respect our Delaware ancestors. After my son, Chris, read our lengthy family tree, he wrote to me: "That would make quite a family reunion if you could get all those folks together at once!"

May we all meet again some day as one people, one family in the home of *Kishelamukonk*, the Great Spirit, the God of all, where there will be no more tears, no more pain or suffering, and never again any partings.

1. White, *Middle Ground*, p. 506.

2. Thatcher, *Indian Biography*, p. 176.

3. Mitchell, *Indian Chief Journeycake*, p. 74.

4. Ibid, p. 67.

5. Roark, *Charles Journeycake,* Appendix 8, p. 95.

6. Ibid, p. 65.

7. Wright, *Guide to Indian Tribes of Oklahoma*, p. 154.

8. Strickland, *Indians in Oklahoma*, pp. 72, 73.

9. Allen and Smith, *As Long as Rivers Flow*, pp. 232, 233.

10. White, *Middle Ground*, p. 474.

11. Crews, *American & Catholic*, p. 12.

12. McMaster and Trafzer, *Native Universe*, p. 75.

13. Booth, *Tuscarawas Valley in Indian Days*, p. 222.

BIBLIOGRAPHY

Abels, Jules. *Man on Fire, John Brown and the Cause of Liberty.* New York: Macmillan
    Company, 1971.

Adcock, Clifton. *Delaware Tribe on the Brink of Federal Recognition.*
    Tulsa, Oklahoma: *Tulsa World Newspaper*, June 9, 2009.

Allen, Paula Gunn and Patricia Clark Smith. *As Long as the Rivers Flow, Stories of
Nine Native Americans.* New York: Scholastic Inc., 1996.

Anderson, H. Allen. *Delaware and Shawnee Indians and the Republic of Texas, 1820-
    1845, Southwestern Historical Quarterly, vol. 94, no. 2.* Austin: Texas State
    Historical Association, October, 1990.

Angelou, Maya. *Even the Stars Look Lonesome.* New York: Random House, 1997.

Athearn, Robert G. *New World.* New York: Fawcett Publications Inc., 1971.

Athon, Bobbie. *Reflections.* Topeka: Kansas Historical Society, Spring, 2009, vol.
    3, no.1.

Audubon, John James. *Birds of America from Original Drawings.* New York:
MacMillan Co., 1946; orig. ed., London, England: 1827-1838.

Axtell, James. Ed, College of William and Mary. *Indian Peoples of Eastern America, a
    Documentary History of the Sexes.* New York, Oxford: Oxford University Press,
    Inc., 1981.

Bakeless, Katherine and John Bakeless. *Spies of the Revolution.* New York: Scholastic
Book Services, 1962, seventh printing, 1973.

Barry, Louise. *The Beginning of the West.* Topeka: Kansas State Historical
Society, printed by Robert R. Sanders, state printer, 1972.

Berger, Thomas. *Little Big Man.* Greenwich, Connecticut: Fawcett Publications, Inc.,
    1964.

Berthrong, Donald J. *Southern Cheyennes.* Norman: University of Oklahoma Press,
    1963.

Black, Glenn A., Eli Libby, Georg K. Neumann, Joe E. Pierce, C. F. and Erminie Voegelin, and Paul Weer, contributors. *Walam Olum, the Migration Legend of the Lenni Lenape or Delaware Indians*. Indianapolis: Indiana Historical Society, 1954.

Booth, Jr., Russell H. *Tuscarawas Valley in Indian Days, 1750-1797*. Cambridge, Ohio: Gomber House Press, fourth printing, May 2000.

Bouchard, Rev. James Chrysostom, *Biographical Sketch of Watomika*, Florissant, Missouri: St. Stanislaus House of Probation (Jesuit Novitiate), 1855.

Brandon, William. *Indians*. Boston: Houghton Mifflin Co., 1987, a reprint of *The America Heritage Book of Indians*, published in 1961.

Briggs, Argye. *Both Banks of the River*. Grand Rapids, Michigan: Wm. B. Eerdmans Publishing Co., 1954.

Brown, Dee. *Bury My Heart at Wounded Knee*. New York: Henry Holt and Co., 1970.

Brown, John W. and Rita T. Kohn. *Long Journey Home, Oral Histories of Contemporary Delaware Indians*. Bloomington: Indiana University Press, 2008.

Buehrle, Marie Cecilia. *Kateri of the Mohawks*. Milwaukee, Bruce Publishing Co., 1954.

Burnet, Jacob. *Notes on the Early Settlement of North-Western Territory*. New York: D. Appleton & Co., Cincinnati: Derby, Bradley & Co., 1847; *Legacy Reprint Series,* Kessinger Publishing.

Caffrey, Margaret M. *Complementary Power: Men and Women of the Lenni Lenape*. American Indian Quarterly, Jan. 1, 2000.

Carvalho, Solomon Nunes. *Incidents of Travel and Adventure in the Far West*. New York: Derby & Jackson, 1857; Philadelphia: The Jewish Publication Society of America, 1954.

Carrigan, Gina J., J.D. and Clayton Chambers, B.S. *Lesson in Administrative Termination, an Analysis of the Legal Status of the Delaware Tribe of Indians,* second edition. Bartlesville, Oklahoma: 1998-2002.

Carter, Dr. Cynthia Jacobs. *Africana Woman, Her Story through Time*. Washington,

D.C.: National Geographic Society, 2003.

Castel, Albert. *Civil War Kansas, Reaping the Whirlwind.* Lawrence, Kansas: University Press of Kansas, 1997; originally published in 1958 by Cornell University Press as *A Frontier State at War: Kansas, 1861-1865.*

Catholic Biblical Association of America (translators). *St. Joseph Edition of the New American Bible.* New York: Catholic Book Publishing Co., 1970.

Chudacoff, Howard P.; Paul D. Escott; David M. Katzman; Mary Beth Norton;

Thomas G. Paterson; William M. Tuttle, Jr. *People and a Nation, a History of the United States,* 1877. Boston: Houghton Mifflin Company, second edition, vol. I, 1986.

Conlon, Czarina C. *Chronicles of Oklahoma,* Oklahoma: self-published March, 1926.

Connell, Evan S. *Son of the Morning Star.* San Francisco: North Point Press, 1984.

Cooper, James Fenimore. *Last of the Mohicans.* New York: Barnes & Noble Classics, 2004, first published in 1826.

Cordley, Richard. *Lawrence Massacre.* Lawrence, Kansas: J. S. Broughton, from the Kansas collection of Kenneth Spencer Research Library and the Department of History of University of Kansas, 1865.

Cox, Mike. *Texas Disasters, True Stories of Tragedy and Survival.* Guilford, Connecticut: Morris Book Publishing, LLC, 2006.

Cranor, Ruby. *Kik Tha We Nund, Delaware Chief William Anderson and His Descendants.* Bartlesville, Oklahoma: Delaware Tribe of Indians, 2004.

_____*Talking Tombstones, Pioneers of Washington County.* Bartlesville, Oklahoma: 1974; Image Makers, revised edition, 1996.

_____ Caney Valley Ghost Towns & Settlements, Tulsa, Oklahoma: Kinkos, 1985, s second printing, 1997.

Craven, Avery. *Reconstruction: the Ending of the Civil War.* New York: Holt, Rinehart & Winston, Inc., 1969.

Crews, Clyde F. *American & Catholic, a Popular History of Catholicism in the United States*. Cincinnati, Ohio: St. Anthony Messenger Press, 2004.

Dary, David. *True Tales of Old-Time Kansas*. Lawrence, Kansas: University Press of Kansas, 1979, 1984.

Davis, Burke. *To Appomattox, Nine April Days, 1865*. New York: Popular Library Edition, August 1960; originally published by Rinehart & Co., Inc.

Davis, Kenneth S. *Kansas: A Bicentennial History*. New York: W. W. Norton & Company, Inc., 1976.

Debo, Angie. *History of the Indians of the United States*. Norman, Oklahoma: University of Oklahoma Press, 1970.

Debo, Angie. *Still the Waters Run–Betrayal of the Five Civilized Tribes*. New Jersey: Princeton University Press, 1940; paperback, 1991.

Deloria, Jr., Vine and Raymond J. De Mallie. *Documents of American Indian Diplomacy, Treaties, Agreements, and Conventions, 1775-1979 (Legal History of North America)*, vol. 1, 1999.

Drake, Samuel G. *Book of the Indians of North America: Comprising Details in the Lives of About Five Hundred Chiefs and Others*. Boston: Antiquarian Bookstore, first published 1833; DSI Digital Reproduction, 2001.

Eckert, Allan W. *A Sorrow in Our Heart, the Life of Tecumseh*, New York: Konecky & Konecky, 1992.

Edgerton, Robert B. *Hidden Heroism, Black Soldiers in America's Wars*, New York: Barnes & Noble with Westview Press, 2001.

Ehle, John. *Trail of Tears, Rise and Fall of the Cherokee Nation*. New York: Anchor Books/Doubleday, 1988.

Erdrich, Louise. *Grandmother's Pigeon*. New York: Hyperion Books for Children, 1996.

Flaherty, Thomas H., ed. *Mighty Chieftains*. Alexandria, Virginia: Time Life Books, 1993.

Flato, Charles. *Civil War*. New York: Golden Press, 1976.

Fletcher, Sydney E. *American Indians*. New York: Grosset & Dunlap, Inc., 1950.

Foreman, Grant. *Advancing the Frontier, 1830-1860*. Norman: University of Oklahoma Press, first edition, 1933, second printing, 1968.

Frost, Lawrence A. *Court-Martial of General George Armstrong Custer*. Norman: University of Oklahoma Press, first edition, 1969; second printing, 1979.

Gallmann, Kuki. *I Dreamed of Africa*, New York: Penguin Books, 1991.

Garraghan, Gilbert. *Jesuits of the Middle United States, vol. 1*. Chicago: Loyola University Press, 1983.

Graham, W.A. *The Custer Myth*. Lincoln: University of Nebraska Press, 1953, r renewal copyright by Helen B. Graham, 1981.

Graybill, Florence Curtis and Victor Boesen. *Edward Sheriff Curtis, Visions of a Vanishing Race*. Boston: Houghton Mifflin Co., 1976.

Griekspoor, Phyllis and Beccy Tanner. *Kansas, the Prairie Spirit –History People Stories*. Carson City, Nevada: The Grace Dangberg Foundation, Inc., 2000.

Grumet, Robert S. *Lenapes*. New York, Philadelphia: Chelsea House Publishers, 1989.

Hall, Jesse A. and Leroy T. Hand. *History of Leavenworth County, Kansas*. Topeka: Historical Publishing Company, 1921.

Hanson, Margaret Brock, ed. *Frank Grouard, Army Scout*. Cheyenne, Wyoming: Frontier Printing, Inc., 1983.

Harrington, M. R. *Indians of New Jersey,* New Jersey: Rutgers University Press, 1963; originally published by Holt, Rinehart and Winston, Inc., 1938.

Harris, Charles F. *Alias Charley Hart, William C. Quantrill in Lawrence, Kansas in 1860*. Wyandotte, Oklahoma: Gregath Publishing Company, 2008.

Hirschfelder, Arlene. *Native Americans*. New York: Dorling Kindersley Publishing, Inc., 2000.

Hodge, Frederick Webb. *Handbook of American Indians North of Mexico*. New York:

Greenwood Press, 1907, reprinted 1969.

Hoig, Stan. *Beyond the Frontier, Exploring Indian Country.* Norman: University of Oklahoma Press, 1998.

_____ *Sand Creek Massacre.* Norman: University of Oklahoma Press, 1961.

Isely, Bliss and W.M. Richards, *Four Centuries in Kansas.* Topeka: Published by the State of Kansas, 1944.

Isern, Thomas D. and Raymond Wilson, *Kansas Land.* Layton, Utah: Gibbs Smith, Publishers, 1993.

Jackson, Helen Hunt. *Century of Dishonor.* Mineola, New York: Dover Publications, Inc., 2003.

Johansen, Bruce E. and Donald A. Grinde, Jr. *Encyclopedia of Native American Biography.* New York: Da Capo Press, 1998.

Josephy, Jr., Alvin M., ed. *Indians,* New York: American Heritage Publishing Co., 1961.

_____ Ed. *500 Nations, Illustrated History of North American Indians.* New York: Gramercy Books, 1994.

Katz, William Loren, *Black Indians, Hidden Heritage,* New York: Simon Pulse, 1986.

Kelly, Sharon, *The Trouble With Fracking,* National Wildlife Magazine, October/November 2011, Reston, VA: National Wildlife Federation, p. 16.

Kennedy, John F., *Profiles in Courage,* New York: Harper & Row, 1955, 1956, 1961.

Killoren, John J., S.J., *Come Blackrobe,* Norman: University of Oklahoma Press, 1994.

Kopper, Philip. *Indians before Coming of the Europeans.* Washington, D.C.: Smithsonian Books, trade distribution by Harry N. Abrams, Inc., 1986.

Lafferty, Ray A. *Okla Hannali.* Norman: University of Oklahoma Press, 1991, reprint; originally published Garden City, New York: Doubleday, 1972.

Landau, Elaine. *The Sioux.* New York: Franklin Watts, 1989.

Lawson, Roberta Campbell. *My Oklahoma, Pathos and Romance Blended in the*

Story of the Latter Days of Delawares. Tulsa: Philbrook Museum of Art,

Chapman Library, Vol. 1, no. 5, August, 1927.

Lee, Wayne C. *Deadly Days in Kansas.* Caldwell, Idaho: Caxton Printers, Ltd., 1997.

Livingston, Lili Cockerille. *American Indian Ballerinas.* Norman: University of

Oklahoma Press, 1997.

Lucey, Donna M. *I Dwell in Possibility; Women Build a Nation, 1600-1920.*

Washington, D.C.: National Geographic Society, 2001.

Lutz, J.J. *Methodist Missions among Indian Tribes of Kansas.* Topeka: Transactions of

the Kansas State Historical Society, vol. 9, 1905-1906.

Mails, Thomas E. *Fools Crow, Wisdom and Power.* San Francisco and Tulsa:

Council Oaks Books, LLC, 1991, 2001.

Mankiller, Wilma and Michael Wallace. *Mankiller, Chief and Her People.* New

York: St. Martin's Press, 1993.

Matthaei, Gay and Jewel Grutman. *Sketchbook of Thomas Blue Eagle.* San

Francisco: Chronicle Books, 2001.

Maxson, H. A. and Claudia H. Young. *Lenapehoking: Land of Delawares.* Dover,

Delaware: Bay Oak Publishers LTD, first published, 2001, reprinted 2001.

Maxwell, James A., ed. *America's Fascinating Indian Heritage.* Pleasantville, New

York: Readers Digest Association, 1978.

McClure, Tony Mack. *Cherokee Proud.* Sommerville, Tennessee: Chunannee Books,

1999.

McCullough, David. *1776.* New York: Simon & Schuster, 2005.

McGloin, John Bernard, S.J. *Eloquent Indian, Life of James Bouchard, California

Jesuit.* Stanford, California: Stanford University Press, first printing, 1949;

second printing, April 1950.

McKnight, Charles. *Our Western Border, One Hundred Years Ago.* Philadelphia: J.C.

McCurdy & Co. 1876; reprinted by Johnson Reprint Corporation, New York,

1970.

McMaster, Gerald and Clifford E. Trafzer, eds. *Native Universe, Voices of Indian America.* Washington, D.C. National Geographic Society, 2004.

McMillan, Beverly C., ed. *Captive Passage, Transatlantic Slave Trade and Making of the Americas.* (Gene Alexander Peters Collection) Old Saybrook, CT: Smithsonian Institution, 2002.

McNaughton, Halford R. *Buckongahelas, Last of the Great Delaware War Chiefs and an Early History of His People.* Muncie, Indiana: Self-Published, 1978.

McWhorter, John C. *Scout of the Buckongehanon.* Parsons, West Virginia: McClain Printing Co., 1964; orig. ed. Boston: Christopher Publishing House, 1927.

McWhorter, Lucullus Virgil. *Border Settlers of Northwestern Virginia from 1868 to 1795.* Parsons, West Virginia: McClain Printing Co., 2004; orig. ed., Baltimore, Maryland: Baltimore Genealogical Publishing Co., 1935.

Meredith, Martin. *Elephant Destiny, Biography of an Endangered Species in Africa.* New York: Public Affairs™, Persus Books Group, 2001.

Miller, William Lee. *President Lincoln, Duty of a Statesman.* New York: Alfred A. Knopf, 2008.

Miner, H. Craig and William E. Unrau. *End of Indian Kansas, Study of Cultural Revolution, 1854-1871.* Lawrence: University Press of Kansas, 1990, Regent Press of Kansas, 1978.

Mitchell, Barbara. *Tomahawks and Trombones.* Minneapolis, Minnesota: Carolrhoda Books, 1982.

Mitchell, S. H. *Indian Chief Journeycake.* Philadelphia: American Baptist Publication Society, 1895.

Momaday, N. Scott. *House Made of Dawn.* New York: Harper & Row, 1968.

Montefiore, Sebag. *Prince of Princes, Life of Potemkin.* New York: St. Martin's Press, 2000.

Moscinski, Sharon. *Tracing Our Irish Roots.* Santa Fe, New Mexico: John Muir Publications, 1993.

Myers, Albert Cook, ed. *William Penn: His Own Account of Lenni Lenape or Delaware Indians.* Wallingford, PA: Middle Atlantic Press, 1970.

Myers, David Scott, ed. *People of Plains.* Castle Rock, Colorado: *Douglas County News-Press*, March 17, 1999.

_____*Sand Creek Purchase Possible.* Castle Rock, Colorado: Elbert County News, March 5, 1998.

Nardo, Don. *Irish Potato Famine.* San Diego, CA: Lucent Books, Inc., 1990.

Nerburn, Kent, ed. *Wisdom of the Native Americans.* New York: MJF Books, 1999.

Niethammer, Carolyn. *Daughters of the Earth, Lives and Legends of American Indian Women.* New York: Simon & Schuster, 1977.

Nouwen, Henri. *Love in Fearful Land, Guatemalan Story.* New York: Orbis Books, 2006.

Obermeyer, Brice. *Delaware Tribe in Cherokee Nation.* Lincoln, Nebraska: University of Nebraska Press, 2009.

Oestreicher, David M. *Unmasking Walam Olum: 19th-Century Hoax.* New Jersey: Bulletin of Archaeological Society of New Jersey, #49, 1994.

Osage Indian Agency, *Indian Herald.* Indian Territory, 1875.

Palladino, Lawrence B., S.J. *Indian and White in the Northwest, History of Catholicity in Montana, 1831 to 1891.* Lancaster, PA, Wickersham Publishing Co., 1922.

Perry, Robert. *Uprising! Woody Crumbo's Indian Art.* Ada, Oklahoma: Chickasaw Press, 2009.

Philbrick, Nathaniel. *Mayflower, Story of Courage, Community, and War.* New York: Viking, 2006.

Philbrick. *Last Stand, Custer, Sitting Bull, and Battle of the Little Bighorn.* New York: Viking, 2010.

Porter, C. Fayne. *Battle of the 1,000 Slain.* New York: Scholastic Book Services, 1964; second printing, 1968.

Potok, Chaim. *In the Beginning.* New York: Fawcett Crest, 1975.

Pritzker, Barry M. *Native American Encyclopedia, History, Culture, and Peoples.* New York: Oxford University Press, Inc., 2000.

Ramsey, Bruce. *Under All Is the Land.* Vancouver, Canada: Quest Travelbooks Ltd., 1969.

Readers Digest. *America's Fascinating Indian Heritage.* Pleasantville, New York: Readers Digest Assn, Inc., 1978.

Rieff, David. *God and Man in Rwanda.* New York: Vanity Fair, December, 1994.

Ringold, Francine. *Oklahoma Indian Markings.* Tulsa: Nimrod, Arts and Humanities Council of Tulsa, vol. 32, no. 2, Spring/Summer, 1989.

Roark, Harry M. *Charles Journeycake, Indian Statesman and Christian Leader.* Dallas, Texas: Taylor Publishing Co, 1948.

Rose, Helen York. *I Walked the Footsteps of My Fathers.* Seminole, Oklahoma Dogwood Printing, 1989; Manuscript, Denver Public Library, Denver, Colorado; FHL, US/CAN Film, 1697594 – Item 3, Family History Library, Church of Jesus Christ of Latter Day Saints.

Ruff, L. Candy. *Leavenworth Times*; *Indians Buried at Delaware Cemetery, Koerner Recalls Family Ties.* Kansas: October 25, 1988; reprinted with permission from Leavenworth County Historical Society and Museum and *Leavenworth Times.*

Sandburg, Carl. *Abraham Lincoln, Prairie Years and War Years.* New York: Dell Publishing Company, reprinted by arrangement with Harcourt, Brace & Co., 1964.

Silverburg, Robert and Grania Davis, eds. *The Avram Davidson Treasury.* New York: Tom Doherty Associates, Inc. (TOR), 1998.

Skaggs, Jimmy M. *Ranch and Range in Oklahoma*, Oklahoma City, OK: Oklahoma Historical Society, 1978.

Sperger, Ann M. and Eric Lax. *Bogart.* London: Phoenix, a division of Orion Books Ltd. 1998, paperback; first published in Great Britain by Weidenfeld & Nicolson, 1997.

Spurgeon, Mary. *Will O' the Wisp.* Meade, Kansas: Ohnick Enterprises, 2008.

Standard, Stella. *Our Daily Bread.* New York: Funk & Wagnalls, 1970.

Stein, R. Conrad. *The Trail of Tears.* Chicago: Cornerstones of Freedom, Children's Press, 1994.

Strecker, Archbishop I. J. *Church in Kansas, 1850-1905, Family Story.* Kansas City: Archdiocese of Kansas City, 1999.

Strickland, Rennard. *Indians in Oklahoma.* Norman: University of Oklahoma Press, 1980.

Sugden, John. *Blue Jacket, Warrior of the Shawnees.* Lincoln, Nebraska: University of Nebraska Press, 2000.

Thatcher, Benjamin B., Esq. *Indian Biography, or an Historical Account of Those Individuals Who Have Been Distinguished Among the North American Natives as Orators, Warriors, Statesmen and Other Remarkable Characters.* two vols. Glorieta, New Mexico: The Rio Grande Press, Inc., first published 1832; first printing 1973.

Tucker, Glenn. *Tecumseh, Vision of Glory.* Indianapolis: Bobbs-Merrill Co., Inc., 1956.

Twain, Mark. *Prince and the Pauper.* New York: Scolastic Book Services, 1958.

Unrau, William E. *The Kansa Indians, a History of the Wind People, 1673-1873.* Norman: University of Oklahoma Press, 1971.

Utley, Robert M. and Wilcomb E. Washburn. *Indian Wars.* Boston and New York: Houghton Mifflin Company, First Mariner Books edition, 2002.

Vanderwerth, W. C. *Indian Oratory, Famous Speeches by Noted Indian Chieftains.* New York: Ballantine Books, University of Oklahoma Press, 1971.

Viola, Herman J. *After Columbus, Smithsonian Chronicle of North American Indians.* Washington, D.C.: Orion Books, New York, 1990.

Waldman, Carl, ed. *Atlas of the North American Indians*, New York: Facts on File Publications, 1985.

Waldman, Carl. *Dictionary of Native American Terminology*. New York: Castle Books, 2009.

Wallis, Michael. *Oil Man, the Story of Frank Phillips and the Birth of Phillips Petroleum*. New York: Doubleday, 1988.

Ward, Geoffrey C. *The West, an Illustrated History*. Boston, New York, Toronto, London: Little Brown and Company, 1996.

Wells, Spencer. *Deep Ancestry –Inside the Genographic Project*. Washington, D.C.: National Geographic Society, 2007.

Wells, *Journey of Man, a Genetic Odyssey*. New York: Random House, 2003.

Wenzel, Timothy F., *Legacy of Faith, History of Diocese of Dodge City*. Dodge City, Kansas: Diocese of Dodge City, 2001.

Wertz, Jay. *Native American Experience*. Guilford, Connecticut: The Lyons Press, 2009.

Weslager, Clinton A. *Delaware's Buried Past*. New Brunswick, New Jersey: Rutgers University Press, 1968; University of Pennsylvania Press, 1944.

Weslager. *Brief Account of Indians of Delaware*. Delaware: University of Delaware Press, 1956.

Weslager. *Delaware Indians, a History*. New Brunswick, New Jersey: Rutgers University Press, 1972.

_____*Delaware Indian Westward Migration*. Wallingford, Pennsylvania: Middle Atlantic Press, 1978.

Wheeler, Keith (text). *The Old West, the Scouts*. Alexandria, Virginia: Time-Life Books, 1978.

White, Jo Ann, ed. *African Views of the West*. New York: Julian Messner Publisher, a division of Simon & Schuster, Inc., 1972.

White, Richard. *Middle Ground -- Indians, Empires, and Republics in Great Lakes Region, 1650-1815*, Cambridge, England: Cambridge University Press, 1991.

Winfrey, Dorman H., ed. *Texas Indian Papers, 1844-1845, Vol. II*. (Edited from original manuscript copies in Texas State Archives.) Austin: Texas Library and Historical Commission, Texas State Library, 1960.

Wood, Norman B. *Lives of Famous Indian Chiefs*, Aurora, Illinois: American Indian Historical Publishing Company, 1906.

Wright, Muriel H. *Guide to Indian Tribes of Oklahoma*, Norman: University of Oklahoma Press, first edition, November 1951, second edition, November 1957.

Zeisberger, David. *History of Northern American Indians*. Columbus, Ohio: F. J. Heer, first edition, 1910; second printing, Print on Demand, General Books, 2010.

_____ *Indian Dictionary*. Cambridge: John Wilson and Son, first edition, 1887; Charleston, South Carolina: printed from the original manuscript in Harvard College Library, copyright BiblioLife, 2010.